Coffee Is Not Forever

Ohio University Press Series in Ecology and History
James L. A. Webb, Jr., Series Editor

Coffee Is Not Forever

A Global History of the Coffee Leaf Rust

Stuart McCook

OHIO UNIVERSITY PRESS
ATHENS

Ohio University Press, Athens, Ohio 45701
ohioswallow.com
© 2019 by Ohio University Press
All rights reserved

Printed in the United States of America

Ohio University Press books are printed on acid-free paper ♾

29 28 27 26 25 24 23 22 21 20 19   5 4 3 2 1

Library of Congress Cataloging-in-Publication Data
Names: McCook, Stuart George, 1965- author.
Title: Coffee is not forever : a global history of the coffee leaf rust / Stuart McCook.
Other titles: Ohio University Press series in ecology and history.
Description: Athens, Ohio : Ohio University Press, 2019. | Series: Ohio University Press series in
    ecology and history | Includes bibliographical references and index.
Identifiers: LCCN 2019026882 | ISBN 9780821423868 (hardback) | ISBN 9780821423875
    (paperback) | ISBN 9780821446843 (pdf)
Subjects: LCSH: Hemileia vastatrix. | Coffee rust disease--History. | Coffee rust disease--
    Environmental aspects.
Classification: LCC SB608.C6 .M33 2019 | DDC 663/.93--dc23
LC record available at https://lccn.loc.gov/2019026882

For Lucía, my light.

Contents

Illustrations

Figures

Maps

Preface

DURING THE late 1990s, when I was doing research on the agricultural sciences in Latin America, I noticed a curious pattern in my primary sources. In the nineteenth century, most of the world's tropical crops were struck by a series of devastating crop diseases. Many of these diseases were global, crossing oceans and continents. I started to wonder what had caused these epidemics; biologically, neither the pathogens nor the host plants had much in common. The one thing they *did* have in common was that all the host plants were tropical commodities. It seemed likely that the plants' lives as global commodities had contributed to the outbreaks of these global epidemics. I set out to write a global and comparative history of the most important of these epidemics: the South American leaf blight of rubber, the Panama disease of the banana, the mosaic disease of sugarcane, the witches' broom of cacao, and the coffee leaf rust.

For several years I worked on pieces of this story, but I struggled to find an effective way of organizing the narrative. I had conversations with many other historians about this. One of the people I spoke to was Jim Webb, who, in addition to being an accomplished historian, is also a keen and thoughtful listener. Over pints at a pub in Kew, he suggested that I focus on just one of these diseases, which would allow me explore the issues that interested me in much greater detail. And he encouraged me to focus on the coffee leaf rust. I took his advice, and have never looked back.

This book is a biography of a global crop disease, and a global environmental history of coffee as seen through the lens of the disease. My approach to this global history reflects what Lynn Hunt has described as global history from the ground up. The essential methodology is simple—at least in theory. I followed the fungus on its long journey from the forests of Africa out across the global coffeelands, from the mid-nineteenth century to the present. From the fungus, I moved outward to consider the broader forces that moved it around the world and shaped the vulnerability of coffee ecosystems to the rust at particular moments in time. I explore how farmers and farming communities have responded to the rust and how, if at all, they learned to coexist with it. I have been particularly interested in the role of scientists and scientific institutions that have, with varying degrees of success, tried to help farmers adapt to the rust.

Writing a global environmental history involves inevitable compromises. The historian John McNeill has complained (only half-jokingly, I'm sure) about how he suffered from inadequate research anxiety syndrome (IRAS) as he worked on his magisterial environmental history of the twentieth-century world. Although my project is more modest than his, I confess to being a fellow sufferer of IRAS. The primary and secondary literature on coffee and the coffee rust is vast, which is both a blessing and a curse. Like coffee itself, the sources are distributed widely across the globe, and they are written in four main languages: English, French, Spanish, and Portuguese, with some additional important works in Dutch and German. With a project of this scale, it is simply impossible to be either definitive or encyclopedic. In many instances, I have had to be ruthlessly selective. Given the project's scope, I decided to work mostly with the secondary and published primary literature, although I did make a few forays into select archives. I have tried to give readers a sense of the world of coffee in each place that I describe, and also the evolving scientific ideas about the rust and coffee farming. But many richer, local histories of the rust remain to be told in fuller detail.

At the same time, a global approach offers insights that would not be as clear otherwise. In particular, writing the history of the rust has revealed a largely hidden "horizontal" history of coffee, which reveals the complex and constant global circulation of plants, pathogens, people, and technologies across the world's coffeelands. This disease-centered global history offers a new approach to thinking about coffee itself. Much of the academic and popular writing on coffee focuses on arabica coffee, especially the high-quality arabicas produced for the specialty market. The story of the rust also sheds light on the entwined histories of commodity arabica, of the oft-despised robusta coffee, and of ephemeral coffees such as Liberian coffee, and it gives us a glimpse of the dozens of wild coffee species found in forests across tropical Africa.

The story of the rust will also, I hope, offer some insights about climate change. It is, at its heart, a story of how farming communities across the Global South prepared for and responded to a sudden and sometimes catastrophic change in their environment. We can learn from some of their successes and failures. But the rust is more than just a precursor to climate change; its own history has recently been transformed by climate change. As I write these words in 2019, the rust's history looks markedly different from how it did when I began the project in 2004. Then, a number of people told me that the history of the rust was basically over. The rust remained a problem, but it had effectively been domesticated. It was just another disease that was no longer a major agent of change. Farmers knew how to cope with it. I imagined that my story would end there. But starting in 2007, a series of severe rust outbreaks swept first through Colombia and later through the Andes, Central America, and the Caribbean. This outbreak is literally a new chapter in the rust's history; it is now clear that this history is far from over. These new outbreaks, triggered by climate change and a series of political and economic crises, mark the beginning of a new phase in the story of the rust—and of the global coffee industry.

Acknowledgments

THIS BOOK has been a long time in the making, and over the years I have accrued many debts. Jim Webb first pointed me toward coffee rust as a subject, and I have never looked back. Steven Topik and Jonathan Coulis provided vital feedback on early chapter drafts, helping me clarify my thinking. Jacques Avelino has patiently helped me make sense of coffee rust science. Audra Wolfe gave invaluable editorial suggestions on the first full draft of the manuscript. I have been fortunate to have excellent research assistants, including Lara Andrews, Jonathan Coulis, Wainer Coto Cedeño, Jessica Dionne, Juan Ignacio Arboleda, Kuusta Laird, Miguel Marín, Gustavo Lemos, Lisa Maldonado, and Brody Richardson.

The work has been enriched by conversations and email exchanges with historians, scientists, and other people involved in the worlds of coffee and tropical commodities, including Katey Anderson, Francisco Anzueto, Peter Baker, William Clarence-Smith, Patrick Chassé, Claiton da Silva, Harry Evans, Fabio Faria Mendes, Leida Fernández Prieto, Andrés Guhl, Jonathan Harwood, Carlos Hernández Rodríguez, Jó Klanovicz, Jeff Koehler, John McNeill, Jonathan Morris, Miguel Mundstock de Carvalho, Hanna Neuschwander, Philip Pauly, Paul Peterson, Wilson Picado, Robert Rice, Fabio Rodríguez Prieto, Corey Ross, Mario Samper Kutschbach, Ellen Sancho Barrantes, Karen-Beth Scholthof, Shawn Steiman, Robert Thurston, Frank Uekötter, Vitor Várzea, John Vandermeer, and Jim Waller.

I am sincerely grateful for the friendship, the example, and the sharp critical eyes of my fellow environmental historians, including Eve Buckley, Chris Boyer, Micheline Cariño Olvera, Kate Christen, Greg Cushman, Nicolás Cuvi, Sandro Dutra e Silva, Sterling Evans, Reinaldo Funes, Stefania Gallini, Regina Horta Duarte, Claudia Leal, Casey Lurtz, Heather McCrea, José Pádua, Megan Raby, Myrna Santiago, Lise Sedrez, John Soluri (again), Paul Sutter, Tom Rogers, Shawn van Ausdal, Jeremy Vetter, Emily Wakild, Robert Wilcox, and Gustavo Zarrilli. My colleagues at the

University of Guelph offered valuable comments on early drafts of several chapters. Thanks especially to Tara Abraham, Catherine Carstairs, Alan Gordon, Matthew Hayday, Kris Inwood, Sofie Lachapelle, Doug McCalla, Susan Nance, Karen Racine, and Norman Smith.

McGill University's history department offered me an institutional home for two research semesters. During my time there, I had valuable conversations about coffee, commodities, and history with Brian Cowan, Catherine LeGrand, and Daviken Studnicki-Gizbert. Ben Forest, Juliet Johnson, and Eleanor Forest gave our family a pied-à-terre in Montreal, and so much more beyond that (including delightful company, excellent wine, and not-so-excellent dad jokes). Thanks to Ben and Juliet for your feedback and encouragement as I worked through the final stages of the manuscript.

I am also grateful for the suggestions offered to me by participants in seminars and workshop papers I presented at Cambridge University, the Consejo Superior de Investigaciones Científicas (Spain), the Fundação Oswaldo Cruz (Brazil), McGill University, the Miami University of Ohio, the Rachel Carson Center at the University of Munich, Rutgers University, the University of London's School of Oriental and African Studies, the Universidad Nacional de Costa Rica, the Universidad Nacional Mayor de San Marcos (Peru), the Universidade Estadual do Oeste do Paraná (Brazil), the Universidade Federal da Fronteira Sul (Brazil), the University of Edinburgh, the University of Guelph, the University of Kansas, the University of Minnesota, and the University of Pennsylvania.

I learned a tremendous amount about the rust and the world of coffee at several workshops that brought together academics and people in the coffee trade, including the Workshop on the Moral, Economic, and Social Life of Coffee at the Miami University of Ohio in 2008; East Coast Coffee Madness in Montreal in 2016; and especially Sustainable Harvest's Let's Talk Roya workshop in El Salvador in 2013. This workshop included a field trip to Café Pacas's Finca El Talapo, where we could see the impacts of the rust firsthand. I am also grateful to the history department at the Universidad Nacional de Costa Rica for organizing a field trip to the Cafetalera Herbazú and the Finca Vista al Valle in Naranjo in 2016.

This work would have been much poorer without the help I received from librarians and archivists at the following organizations: ANACAFÉ (Guatemala); the Biblioteca Carlos Monge, Universidad de Costa Rica; the Biblioteca Conmemorativa Orton, CATIE (Costa Rica); the Biblioteca Nacional de Costa Rica; the Bibliothèque et Archives nationales du

Québec; the British Library; CABI Bioscience (UK); CIFC (Portugal); ICAFÉ (Costa Rica); the International Coffee Organization; the Library and Archives, Royal Botanic Gardens, Kew; the Linnean Society, London; the McGill University Library; the National Archives (UK); the Natural History Museum (UK); the North Carolina State University Libraries; and the Royal Commonwealth Society Library, Cambridge University. I am particularly grateful to the Interlibrary Loan staff at the University of Guelph, who for more than a decade have scoured the world's libraries for obscure sources on my behalf.

During this book's long gestation, important collections of primary sources from the nineteenth and early twentieth century have been digitized and placed online. These digital resources make the task of doing global history much easier and are a valuable complement to traditional libraries. For this project, I made extensive use of the Internet Archive's Text Archive, the Bibliothèque nationale de France's Gallica, the Biodiversity Heritage Library, the USDA Foreign Agricultural Service's Global Agricultural Information Network (GAIN), and the Colombian Federation of Coffee Growers' Biblioteca Cenicafé.

The cartographer Marie Puddister turned my amateurish scrawls into the elegant maps found throughout the book. The biologist Angel Luis Viloria Petit offered his considerable talents as a natural history illustrator to depict the life cycle of the coffee leaf rust. Doña Rosa Maria Fernández kindly gave me permission to reproduce the delightful illustrations by her late husband, the cartoonist Hugo Díaz Jiménez; the journalist Carlos Morales provided vital help in coordinating these permissions. I thank the editors of the *Annals of Botany*, the British Library; the Royal Botanic Garden, Kew; the Tropenmuseum; and World Coffee Research for permission to reproduce images in this book. I have previously explored some of the ideas that inform this book in articles published in the *Journal of Global History*, *Phytopathology*, the *Revista de historia* (Costa Rica), and *Varia historia* (Brazil), as well as a chapter in the edited collection *Knowing Global Environments*, edited by Jeremy Vetter and published by Rutgers University Press. They are reprinted with permission, where permission was necessary.

The staff at Ohio University Press have been consistently supportive and patient. Thanks to Nancy Basmajian, Gillian Berchowitz, Rick Huard, Samara Rafert, Sally Welch, and the whole team at the press who helped turn this project into a reality. Beth Pratt designed the striking cover, which I am sure will catch people's attention and invite them to take a look inside the book. Alice White carefully copyedited the manuscript, giving it a vital final polish. Robert Kern skillfully guided the complex process of transforming my raw manuscript into the book you have before you.

This research was supported by a generous Standard Research Grant from the Social Sciences and Humanities Research Council of Canada, which gave me the time and resources necessary to conduct the initial research.

Much of this book was, appropriately enough, composed in cafés. In Guelph, the Red Brick Café and Planet Bean provided congenial writing environments. Much of the book was drafted and revised at the Brûlerie St. Denis on Rue St. Denis in Montreal, which for the price of a coffee allowed me to occupy the same table every morning, day after day, month after month. I could look up from my computer and see chalkboards listing coffees from the countries that I was writing about at that moment. Thanks especially to Stacey Cote-Jacques for the delicious lattés that fueled my muses, and for the conversations about coffee and origins.

During the years I worked on this project, I lost a number of people close to me. Between 2006 and 2010, my parents Buff and Monica McCook and my brother Douglas McCook passed away. My parents were deeply committed to ensuring that their children had a good education, a commitment that is the foundation of my life as a historian. My grandmothers Edith McCook and Marion Sullivan also passed away during these years; they each leave me with fond memories of lively conversations, and so much more. My uncle Brian Blomme passed away in 2016; I miss his quiet sense of humor and his deep commitment to environmental issues. My father-in-law, Angel Antonio Viloria, who loved reading and had a boundless curiosity about the world around him, died just a few weeks before I submitted the final manuscript. I regret that they are not here to celebrate its completion.

I would like to give a warm thanks to my families by birth and marriage in Canada and Venezuela. My extended Guelph family—my sister Sue McCook and brother-in-law Robert Chin and their children Cameron, Becca, and Gabby—helped in many ways. In the final weeks of the project, we adopted a cat named Luna, who helped keep things in perspective by reminding me that (mysteriously) some creatures don't care at all about the history of coffee, or the coffee rust. Alicia Viloria-Petit has been both a literal and metaphorical companion on this project's long journey; her love and support have made it possible. Our daughter Lucía was born while this project was in progress, and happily has inherited her parents' love of travel. She now knows far more about the coffee commodity chain than the average Canadian eleven-year-old. Without Lucía, the book would have been finished much more quickly, but my life would have been infinitely poorer. Lucía brings me joy every single day; in return, I dedicate this book to her.

Abbreviations and Acronyms

AMECAFÉ   Asociación Mexicana de la Cadena Productiva del Café, A.C. (Mexican Association of the Coffee Production Chain)

ANACAFÉ   Asociación Nacional del Café (National Coffee Association; Guatemala)

CABI   Commonwealth Agricultural Bureaux International

CADA   Companhia Angolana de Agricultura (Angolan Agriculture Corporation)

CAFÉNICA   Asociación de Cooperativas de Pequeños Productores de Café de Nicaragua (Association of Cooperatives of Small Coffee Producers of Nicaragua)

CATIE   Centro Agronómico Tropical de Investigación y Enseñanza (Tropical Agricultural Research and Higher Education Center; Turrialba, Costa Rica)

CBD   coffee berry disease

CEFCA   Comissão Executiva da Erradicação da Ferrugem do Cafeeiro (Executive Committee for the Eradication of the Coffee Rust; Brazil)

CENICAFÉ   Centro Nacional de Investigaciones de Café (National Center for Coffee Research; Chinchiná, Colombia)

CIFC   Centro de Investigação das Ferrugens do Cafeeiro (Centre for Research into Coffee Rusts; Oeiras, Portugal)

CIRAD	Centre de Coopération Internationale en Recherche Agronomique pour le Développement (French Agricultural Research Centre for International Development)
CRS	Catholic Relief Services
EMPBRAPA	Empresa Brasileira de Pesquisa Agropecuária (Brazilian Agricultural Research Corporation)
ENA	Escola Nacional da Agricultura (National Agricultural School; Portugal)
FAO	Food and Agriculture Organization of the United Nations
FNC	Federación Nacional de Cafeteros (National Federation of Coffee Growers; Colombia)
GERCA	Grupo Executivo de Racionalização da Cafeicultura (Executive Group for the Rationalization of Coffee Farming; Brazil)
GTZ	Deutsche Gesellschaft für Technische Zusammenarbeit (German Technical Cooperation Agency; West Germany)
IAC	Instituto Agronômico de Campinas (Campinas Agronomic Institute; Brazil)
IBC	Instituto Brasileiro do Café (Brazilian Coffee Institute)
ICA	International Coffee Agreement
ICO	International Coffee Organization
IFCC	Institut Français du Café et du Cacao (French Coffee and Cacao Institute)
ICAFÉ	Instituto del Café de Costa Rica (Costa Rican Coffee Institute)
IHCAFÉ	Instituto Hondureño del Café (Honduran Coffee Institute)

IICA   Instituto Interamericano de Cooperación para la Agricultura (Interamerican Institute for Cooperation on Agriculture; Costa Rica)

INEAC   Institut National pour l'Etude Agronomique du Congo Belge (National Institute for the Agronomic Study of the Belgian Congo)

INMECAFÉ   Instituto Mexicano del Café (Mexican Coffee Institute)

JIU   Junta de Investigações do Ultramar (Board of Overseas Research; Portugal)

MAG   Ministerio de Agricultura y Ganadería (Ministry of Agriculture and Livestock; Costa Rica)

NISM   Netherlands India Steam Navigation Company

OIRSA   Organismo Internacional Regional de Sanidad Agropecuaria (Regional International Organization for Agricultural Health; Mexico and Central America)

ORSTOM   Office de la Recherche Scientifique et Technique Outre-Mer (Office of Overseas Scientific and Technical Research; France)

PIAC   Plan Integral de Atención al Café (Integrated Program for Coffee; Mexico)

PROMECAFÉ   Programa Cooperativo Regional Para el Desarollo Tecnológico y Modernización de la Caficultura (Regional Cooperative Program for Technological Development and Modernization of Coffee Production)

PSF   Permanencia Sostenibilidad y Futuro (Permanence, Sustainability, and Future; Colombia)

ROCAP   Regional Office for Central America and Panama, Office of USAID

SAGARPA   Secretaría de Agricultura, Ganadería, Desarrollo Rural,
           Pesca, y Alimentación (Secretariat of Agriculture, Livestock,
           Rural Development, Fisheries, and Food; Mexico)

SENASICA   Servicio Nacional de Sanidad, Inocuidad, y Calidad
           Agroalimentaria (National Health Service, Food Safety,
           and Food Quality; Mexico)

SICA   Sistema de Información Cafetera (Coffee Information
           System; Colombia)

STICA   Servicio Técnico Interamericano de Cooperación Agrícola
           (Interamerican Technical Service for Agricultural
           Cooperation)

UPASI   United Planters' Association of Southern India

USAID   United States Agency for International Development

WCR   World Coffee Research

Chapter 1

The Devourer of Dreams

IT CAME as a surprise: a familiar nuisance suddenly turned an unfamiliar catastrophe. Over several seasons, coffee farmers from Peru to Mexico saw more and more yellow spots appear on the leaves of their trees. In previous seasons, the rust might have caused the occasional spot, but nothing serious. Now, however, leaves engulfed with lesions fell to the ground, leaving skeletal trees alive but entirely defoliated. The disease moved into highland areas that had previously escaped the disease. In February 2013, Guatemala's *Prensa libre* interviewed smallholders whose farms had been devastated by the rust. "I never thought this would happen to me," said Mauricio Méndez, whose farm had escaped the first rust outbreak in the 1980s. A smallholder named Bartolo Chavajay "could not contain his tears in the face of his rust-infested plot." The rust had destroyed Chavajay's entire harvest—his only source of income. Without the income, he wondered how he would feed his family. Yet another farmer, Moisés Misa, worried that the disease would harm his coffee's quality, reducing the price he would receive from buyers and lowering his modest income. Over several seasons, similar scenarios played out in thousands of farms across the Americas. The rust, wrote the *Prensa libre*, devoured the hopes of farmers. Even five years later some farmers—and some countries—are still struggling to rebuild their coffee farms.[1]

This outbreak, now known as the Big Rust, was the latest episode in a much longer story. The coffee rust is caused by a fungus known scientifically as *Hemileia vastatrix*. It first entered the written record in 1869, when it was found on a remote coffee farm in Ceylon (now Sri Lanka)—then the world's third-largest coffee producer. A little more than a decade later, the rust had driven Ceylon's coffee growers to abandon coffee. Between 1870 and 1990, the rust slowly made its way around the world's coffeelands, first striking Asia and the Pacific, then Africa, and finally reaching Latin America's vast coffeelands in 1970. By 1990, it had reached virtually every major coffee-growing region in the world except Hawaii. In some places, as in Ceylon, it was a catastrophe. The rust helped drive the collapse of coffee farming in Java, an island whose name remains synonymous with coffee. As the rust made its way across the globe, however, farmers and scientists gradually learned how to adapt their farms and farming practices to the disease. Farmers were supported by a complex network of national and international organizations. By the 1990s, it seemed that the rust was just another disease. Coffee communities had adapted to the rust, much the same way that communities around the world had adapted to the influenza virus. Like the flu, the rust could be a nuisance. But properly managed, it was nothing more than that—at least in theory.

Disease, Landscape, and Society

To understand the coffee rust's tangled history, it is helpful to understand how crop epidemics work. The coffee leaf rust is much more than the fungus alone. The fungus is present in many coffee ecosystems; in some, the coffee plants have mild infections that never develop into full-blown, disruptive epidemics. So clearly the epidemic is much more than the pathogen. We need to look beyond the pathogen alone and ask, What makes the disease a disease? To answer that, we need to consider how the coffee rust fungus interacts with the rest of the coffee ecosystem. It is helpful to consider an epidemic as a *system* with three major elements: the pathogen (the fungus *H. vastatrix*), a susceptible host (in this case the coffee plant), and the appropriate environmental conditions (rainfall, temperature, sunshine, cropping patterns, etc.). These three elements—virulent pathogen, susceptible host, and environmental conditions—can be represented as a triangle (fig 1.1).[2]

Epidemics are only possible if all three elements are in place. Most obviously, if the pathogen is not present, there can be no outbreak. But while the fungus is necessary for an outbreak, it is not in itself sufficient to cause one. The fungus and the susceptible coffee plant may be present in an ecosystem, but environmental conditions—say, the temperature or the farm structure—may prevent the fungus from reproducing rapidly, so there is no outbreak. In still other cases, the fungus may be present and the environmental conditions may favor the disease, but the coffee cultivar is resistant to the rust, so there is no outbreak. Furthermore, none of the three elements is absolute; different strains of the fungus can be more or less virulent, and different coffee cultivars can be more or less resistant. The environmental conditions also favor the epidemic to a greater or lesser degree. We can use the disease triangle to understand how the host, pathogen, and environment interacted in each place to produce an outbreak.

Each of these three elements is not only biological, it is also historical. Each element changes over time, the product of interactions among human and natural forces. People have, by planting thousands or even millions of susceptible plants together, unintentionally created environments that favor rust outbreaks. They have unintentionally carried spores of the rust

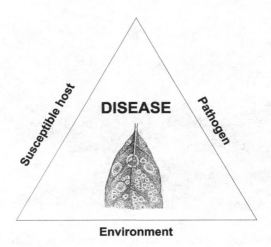

Figure 1.1. The disease triangle, showing how the pathogen, host, and environment interact to produce a disease outbreak.

farther and faster than the rust would have traveled on its own, infecting coffee zones that had previously been free of the disease. As farmers and scientists learned more about how the disease worked, they manipulated the host, pathogen, and environment to *limit* the rust. They tried to contain the pathogen through quarantines and to kill it with chemicals. They have strengthened the host by breeding rust-resistant coffee varieties. They have altered the coffee ecosystem, in places, by reducing or eliminating shade trees (fig 1.2), hoping that exposing the coffee farm to full sun would inhibit the rust.

The rust attacks the leaves of the coffee plant, but it harms the whole plant. A healthy coffee tree obtains most of its nutrition through its leaves, by photosynthesis. Nutrients allow the tree to produce new branches and buds, which in due course flower and develop into the fruit. In shaded forests, the coffee plants produce few flowers, and the leaves can provide more than enough nutrients to allow the fruit to develop properly. On the farm, farmers often manipulate the plant and the landscape to encourage the plant to produce more fruit. They reduce or eliminate shade, which encourages the plant to produce more flowers and, in turn, more fruit. They can also increase crop yields by pruning and manuring the trees. But they have to be careful not to ask too much of the tree, particularly the

PICKING COFFEE.

Figure 1.2. Coffee monoculture, nineteenth century. Dense stands of coffee like this were highly productive but also highly susceptible to diseases and pests. (In Thurber, *Coffee*, facing p. 7)

leaves. If the nutrition required by the fruit is greater than the tree can provide, the fruit may fail to develop properly; in some cases, the branches can become starved and die. So even in disease-free ecosystems, farmers have to ensure that they do not ask the tree for more nutrients than it can deliver. Sometimes they cut it close. Heavy fruit loads can cause coffee harvests to fluctuate widely from one season to the next. A heavy crop one season can draw so many nutrients that it inhibits the growth of branches and flowers the following season, leading to a lower fruit load—a pattern commonly described as biennial bearing.[3]

The rust disrupts this delicate balance. When a microscopic rust spore germinates, it sends shoots into the leaf and develops into a mycelium that colonizes the leaf and feeds off the leaf tissue. It creates a circular rust-colored lesion on the leaf, which gives the disease its name. If a leaf has just a few lesions, it can continue functioning more or less normally (see fig. 1.3). But if the conditions favor the fungus, the leaf can develop many lesions, making it difficult for it to deliver nutrients to the plant. Badly infected leaves can drop off altogether. During severe outbreaks, trees can be defoliated, depriving the tree of vital nutrients. Branches fail to develop normally and die back. The fruit, likewise, may not develop properly, or at all (see fig. 1.4). Severe rust outbreaks cause significant losses during the current season (primary losses).

The most serious effects of the rust, however, are typically felt in later seasons (secondary losses). After an outbreak, the trees may seem to recover; the next season they produce a new flush of leaves, and to a casual observer all seems well. But damaged or dead branches can no longer produce fruit. A recent study of coffee diseases and pests in Central America found that primary losses could be as high as 26 percent, while secondary losses reached 38 percent.[4] The rust exacerbated the patterns of biennial bearing; both the troughs and the peaks were lower. Once the fungus was present in the ecosystem, it was effectively impossible to eliminate. The coffee farm itself became a reservoir of infection. Farmers had to find ways of coexisting with the disease.

Picture a tropical mountainside, then divide it into three belts by altitude. The fungus is highly sensitive to temperature, and in the tropics, temperature is in turn heavily influenced by altitude. In the highest belt, temperatures are relatively cool. The rust fungus may be present but does not cause any significant damage to the plant. Coexistence is easy; farmers in this belt do not usually have to take any special measures to control the rust. Conversely, in the lowest and warmest belt coexistence is virtually

Figure 1.3. Coffee leaf with a few rust lesions, El Salvador. (Photo by author)

impossible. The fungus flourishes and causes such extensive damage that farmers cannot produce the crop profitably. Yields are too low, or the costs of managing the disease are too high. Those farmers typically abandon coffee cultivation. Much of our story will focus on the middle belt, the space where coexistence is possible but requires effort. Here, the rust can cause significant damage, but coffee may still be profitable if farmers can manage

Figure 1.4. Branch of rust-infected coffee tree, showing malformed coffee cherries and dieback, Costa Rica. (Photo by author)

it. The three belts lie on a continuum. The boundaries between them ebb and flow according to changing economic and ecological conditions. A sudden drop in the farm gate price of coffee, for example, may cause farmers to abandon expensive chemical control programs, which in turn would allow the disease to run its course. Conversely, a new rust-resistant coffee variety might make coffee production viable in a lowland region where the rust had previously made it impossible. Rising temperatures might trigger severe rust outbreaks in highland areas where they had previously been rare. The coffee ecosystems and the coffee economy—not to mention the rust fungus itself—are constantly changing, so coexistence with the rust is always provisional.

Themes

This story follows the global odyssey of the rust fungus from its home in the forests of southwestern Ethiopia, to its first spectacular outbreak in Ceylon, and then its spasmodic century-long journey across the global coffeelands. In each region, I move the focus outward from the fungus to consider how the coffee landscapes, societies, and economies shaped the rust outbreaks and the responses to them.[5] Histories of tropical commodities typically focus on vertical linkages, which follow the commodity from plantation to cup, from producers in the Global South to consumers in the Global North. Here, I offer a horizontal approach to the history of commodities: the rust reveals the evolving—and deepening—connections among people and landscapes across the Global South. Just as global coffee markets became more tightly connected and interdependent over the nineteenth and twentieth centuries, so too did global coffee producers.[6]

This horizontal history of coffee reveals the complex connections between coffee's life as a commodity and its life as a plant. The global coffee rust epidemic was triggered by a historically specific conjuncture of political, economic, social, technological, and environmental processes. It was, at first, a product of conquest, of empire, of liberalism, of steamships, and of migrations, both free and forced. These processes, among others, reconfigured the relations between *H. vastatrix*, the coffee plant, and the coffee landscapes in ways that favored a global epidemic. The coffee rust was not an isolated event; it was just one of a series of crop epidemics—commodity diseases—that started to break out at the same time, for many of the same reasons. The mosaic disease (a virus) wreaked havoc on global sugar production, while witches' broom and monilia decimated cacao production in places. Banana growers grappled with new global diseases like fusarium and sigatoka. These diseases could be devastating; in Central America even the powerful United Fruit Company struggled to maintain banana production in the face of fusarium and sigatoka.[7]

Commodity diseases have, in places, changed the global dynamics of commodity production. Producers in disease-free regions often had a significant advantage over producers in diseased regions, who had to contend with declining yields and the financial and logistical burdens of disease control. Even before the rust broke out, coffee growers in Asia and the Pacific struggled to compete against Brazil, whose coffeelands outproduced everyone else's. The rust outbreak simply helped consolidate Brazil's advantage. But the larger history of the rust also suggests that such regional advantages are temporary. Over time, the rust made its way around the world. Other significant diseases and pests, driven by the same forces as the rust, followed. The coffee berry borer (known as the *broca* in Spanish and Portuguese) traveled across the South Atlantic from Africa to Brazil in the 1920s and, since the 1970s, has spread through Central America. As coffee cultivation continues, farmers have to grapple with an accumulating array of local and global diseases and pests. Like the Red Queen in *Through the Looking Glass*, coffee farmers must run faster and faster just to stay in place.[8]

Coffee farmers—from smallholders to owners of estates—have never simply been passive victims of the disease. From the beginning, they innovated creatively and continuously in their quest to control the rust. They discovered and propagated rust-tolerant or rust-resistant coffees, some of which scientists would later use as stock for breeding programs. Well-heeled farmers bought exotic coffees at tropical nurseries in Europe's capital cities; some enterprising planters even organized collecting expeditions of their own. They experimented with virtually every chemical known or suspected to control crop diseases. They manured their farms and—depending on their situation and their particular understanding of the disease—they increased or reduced the amount of shade. They debated the causes of the rust; in Ceylon, the farmers who practiced what they called "high cultivation" blamed other farmers for the devastation caused by the rust. In Africa, European settlers sometimes blamed African farmers for infecting their farms with the rust. Debates about rust control have always been embedded in broader, intensely moralistic debates about good farming practices. Both individually and collectively, farmers searched for explanations for the outbreak and for strategies to coexist with it. Now, as then, farmers adopted whatever control methods best suited their particular situations, both economic and ecological.

Some places gradually developed administrative and scientific infrastructures to coordinate collective responses to the rust. Before World War II, these included imperial and colonial botanical gardens, ministries of agriculture, and national coffee institutes. After the war, this infrastructure grew to include multilateral research organizations—especially Portugal's Coffee Rust Research Centre (CIFC), bilateral and multilateral development organizations such as the US Agency for International Development (USAID), nongovernmental organizations, and private corporations. From the very beginning, these institutions have operated as an informal and decentralized yet powerful research network. Experts across the global coffeelands have constantly shared knowledge, technologies, and germplasm. This has been true ever since 1869, when the naturalist George Thwaites first sent samples of rust-infected leaves from Ceylon to the Royal Botanic Garden at Kew for analysis. Each contributed something to the growing global pool of knowledge about the rust, and in turn each benefited from the knowledge developed elsewhere. This openness may seem surprisingly altruistic—and it was—but it was also pragmatic. Most coffee research institutions were, and remain, small and inadequately funded. It was in their interest to share as much as they could and to learn how other communities were responding to the rust.[9]

Scientists have, from the very beginning, sought to understand the fungus and how it behaved in the field. In the 1880s, Harry Marshall Ward used the latest techniques in laboratory and field biology to demonstrate that the disease was caused by the fungus and to explain how cropping practices shaped rust outbreaks. Over the twentieth century, scientists have continued to refine and complicate our understanding of the rust's ecology in wild and cultivated ecosystems. They have also shed new light on the biology of the fungus and the genetics of rust resistance and virulence. They collected and circulated new varieties and species of coffee around the world; botanical gardens across the tropics built collections of coffee varieties, which formed the raw material for selection and breeding programs. Breeding was a long-term process that involved brute-force, large-scale systematic trial and error over years and sometimes decades. Researchers in the Dutch East Indies, for example, developed commercially viable selections of robusta. Starting in the 1960s, Portuguese researchers developed the Timor hybrid, a rust-resistant coffee that was the foundation for research. More recently, a network of researchers at the US-based World Coffee Research has been developing new F_1 hybrid coffees by blending classical breeding and selection with some of the latest biotechnologies. Scientific research is also vital to localizing tools and technologies developed elsewhere. For example, chemical fungicides have to be applied at just the right moment in the fungus's life cycle, which is shaped by local conditions. So the optimal time for spraying in Kenya, for example, is not necessarily the same as that in Costa Rica. In these ways and others, science has helped farmers around the world sustain production in the face of the rust.

Even so, science alone has seldom been a panacea, and relations between scientists and farmers have not always worked smoothly. Over the nineteenth century, scientists learned a lot about the rust but could not offer coffee farmers effective ways of controlling it. Some of the disease-control strategies they later developed did not meet the farmers' needs in other respects. In the 1970s and 1980s, scientists, backed by national coffee institutes and international research organizations, encouraged farmers to technify their farms by eliminating shade, planting high-yielding cultivars, and using fertilizers and fungicides. This technical package would, in principle, both control the rust and boost yields. But in most places only a minority of farmers adopted the full package. Others only adapted parts, or they continued farming coffee as they had done before. The package was simply not suitable for many of the region's smaller farmers, who did not have access to capital, expertise, and technology to transform their farms. Some were reluctant to give up the traditional arabica cultivars that produced the high-quality coffees for which the region was famous. Farmers were not opposed to scientific innovation in general; they readily adopted cultivars and technologies that fit well in their economic and ecological niches. Since the 1990s, scientists have paid more attention to developing rust-control strategies that are both economically and ecologically sustainable, for farmers large and small.

The rust's effects have rippled along the commodity chain—from coffee mills to roasters to consumers. According to one apocryphal story, the coffee rust outbreak in Ceylon explains why British consumers abandoned coffee for tea.[10] This is a compelling story about the power of commodity diseases. But there is no evidence to support it, and plenty to contradict it. The collapse of Ceylon's coffee industry caused barely a ripple in British consumption; any shortfalls from Ceylon could have easily been offset by imports from other sources. The most recent outbreaks in Central and South America may mark a change to this pattern, however, as this region produces most of the world's high-quality mild arabicas, which are difficult to replace with coffees produced elsewhere. This helps explain the coffee industry's growing interest in rust research and mitigation.

While the rust has not significantly reduced the global supply of coffee (to date), it has changed the global coffee trade in other ways. The Dutch developed the low-quality robusta coffee as a commercial species after 1900 because it was resistant to the rust. It has since transformed the global coffee trade, now typically accounting for between 30 and 40 percent of global coffee production. It is widely used in blended and instant coffees. And although it is typically associated with low-quality coffees, some Italian coffee aficionados argue that a little bit of robusta is an essential component of espresso blends since it helps the coffee develop its characteristic crema. The specialty coffee industry, which has long disdained robusta coffee, is now slowly starting to accept hybrid coffees that contain some robusta genes, like Colombia's Castillo coffee.[11]

The heaviest burdens of the coffee rust, like the burdens of most commodity diseases, have been borne by the producers. The rust has disrupted livelihoods and landscapes. In myriad ways, the global coffeelands bear the imprint of the rust. It has transformed coffee farming, forcing farmers to either find strategies to coexist with the disease or abandon coffee cultivation altogether. It has driven farmers and laborers out of the countryside, to seek their livelihoods elsewhere. The imprint of the rust is visible in places where farmers use chemical control or have switched to resistant varieties to keep the rust levels down. The rust has changed the economics of coffee farming; rust control has made coffee production more expensive. Farmers have to pay for the supplies, labor, and technology necessary to carry out effective programs of rust control. Still other farmers cope with the rust by cultivating coffee in complex agroforestry ecosystems, which are ecologically resilient but typically produce far less coffee and, therefore, less income. Farmers can bear these costs if the price of coffee is high enough to offset them. The rust alone does not devastate coffee farms; the combination of disease and low coffee prices does.

While this study is organized around the coffee rust, it is also about the environmental history of coffee writ large. The rust is acutely sensitive to the broader conditions in which coffee is cultivated. Small changes in the conditions can trigger larger changes in the disease. The rust epidemic allows us to do the environmental equivalent of atom smashing. Physicists explore the behavior of subatomic particles by smashing particles into atoms and seeing what happens. The results shed light on the structure and function of atoms. A rust epidemic does the same thing: it sheds light on how the coffee ecosystem functions by disrupting it. Viewed as a time lapse, global coffee frontiers have been in constant motion, expanding in some places while contracting in others. The rust opens a window into these forces, showing the complex reasons why some regions survived the epidemic while others did not. The story of the rust embodies the broader environmental challenges that coffee producers face, including climate change. As we try to make sense of climate change, which in many respects is without precedent, the history of the coffee rust can offer some insight into how farmers have adapted to other permanent, large-scale changes to their ecosystems.

The Story, in Brief

The story begins with a prehistory of the coffee rust, before it became legible in the mid-nineteenth century. There is no evidence of any significant outbreaks before about 1870. Nor, based on what we know of the disease, is there any reason to believe that there *were* any major outbreaks that went unrecorded. The fungus was present in the forests of southwestern

Ethiopia, the wild home of arabica coffee. But the structure of coffee production in Ethiopia likely kept any potential outbreaks in check.

The early global migrations of arabica coffee accidentally kept the rust contained to this small area. Arabica coffee was first cultivated on a large scale across the Red Sea in Yemen, on landscapes so hot and dry that the coffee plants had to be irrigated and cultivated under shade. These landscapes were singularly hostile to the development of the rust fungus, which requires water droplets on the leaves in order to germinate. Yemen's coffeelands were an ecological filter against the rust, which matters because the world's coffee farms were established by coffee seeds and plants acquired from Yemen, rather than Ethiopia. So as commercial coffee production spread globally in the seventeenth and eighteenth centuries, the rust fungus was contained in Ethiopia. There was no rust to impede the development of coffee cultivation in Africa, Asia, and the Americas—especially on intensive plantations. In the absence of the rust, coffee flourished in places where it would have otherwise been impossible.

The first wave of the rust, which lasted almost a century, was decisively shaped by European colonialism. The first outbreak was recorded in Ceylon, in 1869. Over the next century, it spread through Europe's tropical colonies in Asia, the Pacific, and Africa. These were fundamentally colonial epidemics; the rust spread through the networks of empire that linked previously isolated coffeelands ever more tightly. Spores of the fungus traveled on the wind and also stowed away on steamships, railroads, and airplanes. They were carried on the bodies of planters, laborers, and others who moved within and between the coffeelands. The fungus found purchase on the booming colonial coffee plantations, where it often found dense monocultures on which to feed and propagate. Within a decade of the first outbreak, the rust had caused the collapse of Ceylon's coffee industry and seriously harmed production across the Eastern Hemisphere. It destroyed most of East Africa's emergent coffee farms and limited global arabica production to a few highland enclaves where the fungus could be managed.

Colonial governments debated about how best to support coffee farmers, or even whether to do so. Each state emphasized some measures over others, depending on a range of considerations such as the intensity of the outbreak, the control measures available, the economic and political importance of the coffee industry, and broader ideas about the state's obligations to farmers. In Ceylon, the imperial government (grudgingly) sent Harry

Marshall Ward to study the problem. While Ward conducted brilliant and innovative experiments on the rust, he could not offer any effective means of controlling the outbreak. The government was unwilling to support any further research or to offer the planters any other support, so they were left to their own devices. In contrast, the colonial state in the Dutch East Indies was much more willing to support its coffee farmers. Researchers at the coffee experiment station in Dutch Java conducted pioneering studies on resistance and on breeding commercially viable strains of robusta coffee, which was widely adopted as a replacement for the devastated stands of arabica. But in spite of this research, effective controls remained elusive, and the rust contributed decisively to a broader decline in arabica coffee production in the Eastern Hemisphere.[12]

The second phase of the global rust epidemic, which lasted from the mid-1950s to the mid-1980s, was decisively shaped by the Cold War. Before the 1950s, coffee farmers in Latin America saw rust as a remote problem. But as the epidemic spread through West Africa, a handful of people, like the American Frederick Wellman, began to sound the alarm. In 1970, the rust was detected on a farm in Bahia, Brazil. Over the next fifteen years, farmers—along with a slew of national and transnational organizations—attempted to contain the rust as it spread inexorably across the Americas. The rust broke out in Nicaragua in 1976, and by the early 1980s, it had reached almost every corner of Latin America's coffeelands.

This epidemic and the responses to it were shaped by Cold War politics. This included international trade agreements, especially the International Coffee Agreement, which were, in part, designed to forestall rural unrest. The United States—particularly through the US Department of Agriculture (USDA) and the USAID—assumed a significant role in shaping coffee cultivation generally, and responses to the rust specifically. It helped finance the Coffee Rust Research Centre in Portugal and the Center for Tropical Agricultural Research (CATIE) in Costa Rica. During these decades, the national coffee industries across Latin America were arguably as strong as they had ever been. National coffee institutes conducted research and offered coffee farmers financial and technical support. Organizations like Brazil's Instituto Brasileiro do Café, Colombia's CENICAFÉ, and Costa Rica's ICAFÉ conducted innovative research on breeding, chemical control, and other facets of the disease. In many places, the rust epidemic triggered a Green Revolution–style modernization of coffee farming. Scientists and government bureaucrats encouraged farmers to switch to higher-yielding dwarf coffees. The higher productivity—along with heavy application of fertilizers and fungicides—more than offset any losses caused by the rust. Farmers were also encouraged to reduce or eliminate shade on the assumption that full sunlight was inimical to the rust. Still, many farmers across the Americas only partially technified their farms, for example choosing to use chemical control but continuing to plant traditional arabicas.

In Latin America, the rust caused panic before it arrived. But when it did arrive, it did not produce a wholesale collapse of coffee production as it had elsewhere. Some individual farmers suffered, at times catastrophically. But collectively, the coffeelands of Latin America did not see significant declines in production. The coordinated scientific and institutional responses played a part in controlling the fungus. But there was also a strong element of geographical luck: most of Latin America's coffeelands were in comparatively cool, high-altitude landscapes with distinct dry seasons, where the rust either was not a significant problem or could easily be managed. By the end of the 1980s, the rust had been domesticated virtually everywhere in the Americas. Farmers had adapted to it and treated it as just another disease. As long as farmers in susceptible areas kept spraying and fertilizing their farms, it seemed that the rust no longer presented a significant threat.

A third phase—the neoliberal phase—of the coffee rust began around 2008. A new series of devastating rust outbreaks, known as the Big Rust, began in Colombia, spread to Central America in 2012, and ultimately encompassed a vast area bounded by Puerto Rico, Mexico, and Peru. Unlike the previous rust epidemics, the Big Rust was not triggered by the migration of a pathogen to an area that had previously been free of the disease. Rather, it was fueled in part by a complex set of changing weather patterns that favored the fungus. It was also caused by fundamental changes in the economic and institutional context of global coffee production, which once again made the coffeelands vulnerable to outbreaks. The collapse of the International Coffee Agreement's price stabilization system in 1989 triggered a new, highly volatile cycle of booms and busts. During the busts, farmers economized by cutting back or delaying measures that had previously kept the rust in check. Farmers were, in many cases, more poorly equipped to respond than they had been a generation before. In the 1980s and 1990s, many of the public institutions that had previously provided essential research, credit, and extension to coffee farmers fell victim to austerity programs.

The Big Rust has been far more devastating than the initial outbreak of the 1970s and 1980s, and recovery has been much slower. In many respects, Colombia's coffee industry responded quickly and effectively; its national research institute, CENICAFÉ, rolled out new resistant varieties and advised farmers on other disease-control measures. The National Federation of Coffee Growers effectively lobbied the government for financial support for afflicted farmers. But even in this best-case scenario, it took five years for Colombian coffee production to recover to pre-rust levels. Elsewhere in Latin America, few states could emulate the Colombian model. In places like Mexico, the epidemic encouraged farmers to mobilize and demand more resources from the state. Out of necessity, the private sector—especially the specialty coffee industry—started to offer technical and financial support to some farmers. They are now financing new research organizations, such as World Coffee Research. Or, like Starbucks, they are conducting their own research. While these private-sector initiatives are important, their reach remains limited; they can help only a small portion of afflicted farmers. New technologies, such as systemic fungicides and F_1 coffees, also help in the fight against rust. But fundamentally, the main obstacles to managing the rust remain organizational and financial as much as technical.

The Big Rust is a bellwether event, foreshadowing the kinds of adaptations that coffee farmers will need to make in the face of climate change. While it remains unclear whether or not the Big Rust was caused by long-term climate change, unusual weather patterns certainly played a critical role. As researchers and farmers adapt to the rust and to the other environmental challenges facing coffee production, their paradigms are gradually shifting. Before the 1990s, most rust-control efforts focused on increasing productivity. The assumption was that increased production would offset the costs incurred by disease control. Now, even in conventional coffee production, control programs focus more on ecological and economic sustainability. Both the ecological and economic challenges must be addressed if coffee is to have a long-term future.

CHAPTER 2

Coffee Rust Contained

HISTORIES OF epidemic disease often begin with a dramatic story of the first outbreak and the chaos it produced. While this approach makes for a compelling beginning, it also privileges the pathogen's role in the disease. It diminishes, and sometimes erases, the critical role played by the other two elements of the disease triangle. Shifting focus to these other elements—in this case, the coffee plant and the ecosystems—reminds us that epidemics do not appear out of nowhere. Rather, epidemics are fundamentally historical; they are the product of long-term processes that produce vulnerable ecosystems. Here, we will follow arabica coffee's journey around the world, in a series of transfers that took it from a small corner of southwestern Ethiopia across the global tropics, while leaving the rust fungus behind. We will track how political and economic forces—especially but not only European colonialism—shaped coffee's growing popularity as a crop and as a drink. As coffee became more popular, farmers continued to expand coffee frontiers, which consisted almost exclusively of rust-susceptible arabica cultivars. They also intensified coffee production. By the mid-nineteenth century, the world's coffeelands produced more coffee than ever, but they were also more vulnerable to diseases and pests. Productivity and vulnerability were, at that moment, two sides of the same coin.

The coffee that most of us drink is known botanically as *Coffea arabica*. The plant belongs to the genus *Coffea*, which includes more than one hundred species. Species of *Coffea* grow in a wide range of ecosystems across equatorial Africa, from dry lowlands to wet highlands, and from Liberia in the west to Madagascar in the east (see map 2.1). Arabica coffee, however, is native to one small corner of this range: the montane forests of southwestern Ethiopia, west of the Great Rift valley, between 1,300 and 2,000 meters above sea level in the regions of Kaffa and Illubabor. It enjoys the temperate highland climates, growing best in the shaded, diverse understory of the forest canopy with temperatures between 15°C and 28°C and moderate amounts of rain.[1] It is a small woody tree, like a shrub, that usually has one main stem with lateral branches growing almost horizontally. The branches are densely covered with dark green leaves, which the plant retains year-round. It produces fruit: the coffee "cherries." The coffee we drink is made out of the dried and roasted seeds of this fruit (see fig. 2.1). "When man does not interfere," wrote the coffee expert Pierre Sylvain, "the forest is quite dark and the coffee trees are spindly; they reach considerable height but produce only enough fruit to ensure the survival of the species."[2]

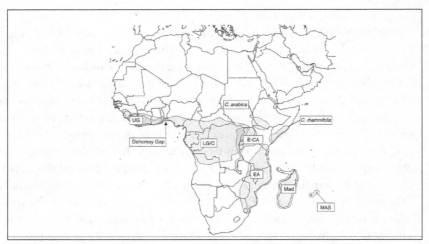

Map 2.1. Distribution of coffee species in the wild. (From Maurin et al., "Towards a Phylogeny for *Coffea*," 1571)

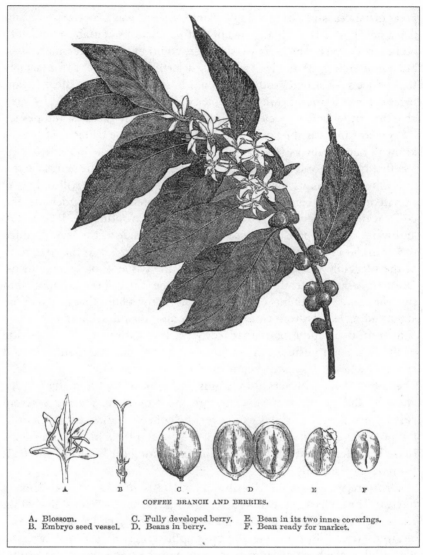

COFFEE BRANCH AND BERRIES.

A. Blossom. C. Fully developed berry. E. Bean in its two inner coverings.
B. Embryo seed vessel. D. Beans in berry. F. Bean ready for market.

Figure 2.1. Coffee branch and berries. (In Thurber, *Coffee*, frontispiece)

Genetically, the arabica coffee plant differs from other *Coffea* species in one significant way. It is self-fertile (autogamous), meaning that only one parent plant is necessary to flower and produce seeds. All other species of *Coffea* are allogamous, requiring two parents to flower and produce seeds. Arabica's distinctive genetic makeup made it suitable for transplant over great distances, since only a single plant (or seed) was necessary to establish a new population.[3] It also meant that populations of arabica tended to be homogeneous, which, as we shall see, could be environmentally risky but commercially desirable. Arabica's self-fertility made it easy for farmers to produce a consistent product from one harvest to the next. These advantages came at a price, however. Arabica coffee is also less genetically variable than other coffee species, leaving it susceptible to diseases and pests.[4]

One of these is the coffee leaf rust, caused by the coffee rust fungus known scientifically as *Hemileia vastatrix*. It is an obligate parasite of coffee; that is, it can only complete its life cycle on plants of the genus *Coffea*. The fungus begins its life cycle as a tiny spore. The spore will only germinate in specific conditions: it must be deposited on the underside of a coffee leaf, the air temperature must be 15°C–28°C (optimally 21°C–25°C), and water droplets must be present on the underside of the leaf. A coffee writer in the 1920s aptly described fungi like *H. vastatrix* as the "vampires of the vegetable world" since they feed on the tissue of other organisms. Once *H. vastatrix* germinates, it penetrates the leaf and sends shoots into the leaf tissue. The fungus creates a branching mycelium that feeds on the surrounding leaf tissue, forming circular orange pustules. Ultimately, these shoots produce spore buds that pierce back out through the underside of the leaf. Each pustule can contain as many as one hundred thousand spores, each of which can begin the infection cycle anew (see fig. 2.2). The spores can be dispersed by winds and rain, or by the many insects, animals, and people that pass through the ecosystem. During a severe rust outbreak, rust pustules can cover the coffee leaves, causing them to fall prematurely. Defoliation deprives the coffee plants of vital nutrients. Repeated infections debilitate the plant, preventing the branches and fruit from developing fully.[5]

The precise geographic distribution of *H. vastatrix* in the wild remains unclear. The coffee expert Albertus Eskes argues that "it is most likely that *H. vastatrix* has coevolved simultaneously on many coffee species from all over Africa."[6] In principle, the geographic range of *H. vastatrix* in the wild could have been as large as the range of the *Coffea* genus. But some fragmentary historical evidence, discussed in later chapters, suggests that *H. vastatrix*'s wild range spanned the Great Lakes region and Ethiopia in East Africa, as well as the eastern half of the Congo River basin. The genetics of the coffee plant and the fungus also offer clues about the fungus's historical distribution. The fungus has evolved into strains (physiological "races") that specialize in attacking particular species of coffee. Most *Coffea*

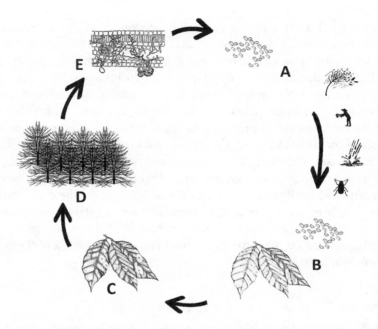

Figure 2.2. Coffee rust infection process, simplified. A. Rust spores are disseminated by wind, humans, rain splash, insects, and animals. B. Spores are deposited on healthy coffee leaf. C. Spores germinate and infect leaf tissue, producing characteristic orange-colored lesions on the leaf. D. Infection causes premature leaf fall. E. Cross-section of infected leaf, showing how fungus colonizes leaf tissue and then sporulates, beginning the infection process anew. (Illustration by Angel Luis Viloria Petit)

species, in turn, have developed some degree of resistance to the fungus. The most highly rust-resistant species, such as *C. canephora*, grew in warm and humid areas favorable to the fungus. The least rust-resistant species, including *C. arabica*, grew in cooler and drier areas that were less hospitable to the fungus.[7] The presence of resistant genes in each coffee species therefore offers clues to the presence of the rust in its habitat.

Although *H. vastatrix* was widely distributed across Africa, serious outbreaks were unknown. "The available information," writes Eskes, "suggests that most African coffee species have developed a balanced relationship with *H. vastatrix*, showing generally little disease under natural conditions."[8] Both the historical and genetic records suggest that the rust fungus was widespread in the wild home of arabica coffee, yet it is unlikely that there was ever a major outbreak there. Wild arabica, like other coffee species, developed ways of coexisting with the rust. All arabica varieties have some degree of resistance, but genetic resistance alone does not explain the absence of major outbreaks in Ethiopia. Under the right conditions, as coffee farmers would later discover to their dismay, arabica could be highly susceptible to the rust. But the rust was also kept in check by the environment of Ethiopia's highland forests. The average temperatures of the highlands are, in places, cooler than ideal for the rust spores to germinate. The dense forest intercepted rainfall, which made it more difficult for the spores to germinate and spread. The forest also blocked the wind, which limited the circulation of rust spores. The comparatively low density of coffee plants in the forest also limited the opportunities for spores to find a host to reproduce upon. And, in Ethiopia, *H. vastatrix* was itself parasitized by hyperparasitic fungi found in the forest, of the genera *Darluca* and *Verticillium*.[9]

"Arabian" Coffee in the Islamic World, 1450–1700

The first people to regularly consume coffee likely left the forest cover intact, at first. The people of southwestern Ethiopia may have first consumed the leaves of the coffee—as a tisane—rather than the fruit. But at some point, they also began consuming the fruit. According to one often-repeated legend, a goatherd named Kaldi discovered coffee's stimulant properties when his goats started dancing after eating coffee fruit. Although this charming story is likely not true in its specifics, it does suggest one way that people may have discovered the bean's stimulant properties. There is some debate as to whether Ethiopians consumed coffee beans as a food— mixed with butter, honey, and spices—or as a drink.[10] At first, the people of Kaffa likely foraged for coffee, harvesting the fruit from wild trees. At some point they realized, speculated the botanist Pierre Sylvain, that plants exposed to the sun yielded more coffee. So they began to manage the forest canopy, reducing the shade to increase the yields of wild plants. Some people transplanted wild coffee seeds and seedlings from the forest to gardens near their houses, where they cultivated coffee alongside other crops. As coffee became more popular in Ethiopia, people started moving coffee plants beyond their native range.[11] These changes presented the rust with new opportunities to spread, though if it did, the levels of infection likely remained low. "Diseases and pests do not seem to be a problem in the coffee forest," wrote Sylvain in 1956, "where man has not changed the biological equilibrium."[12] The rust was likely not a major problem on the semiforest or garden coffees either. The coffee plants were protected by a measure of genetic resistance, cropping practices, and temperatures that were favorable to the plant but inimical to the rust.

Coffee's life as a global commodity began early in the fifteenth century CE, carried along trade routes that linked southern Ethiopia to the Red Sea through the port of Zeila. At first, the growth of coffee consumption in precolonial Africa did little to alter the relationship between the plant and the pathogen in Ethiopia because most coffee was harvested from wild plants.[13] Sufi Muslims were instrumental in diffusing coffee consumption beyond Ethiopia. The monks in Sufi orders used caffeine to stay awake through their long rituals.[14] They first carried the coffee habit to cities of the Arabian Peninsula in the early fifteenth century, including Aden and Mocha—which later became globally important as a center for coffee *exports*. By the 1490s, coffee had been introduced to Cairo; by the 1520s it was being consumed by the Ottoman court in Istanbul. The new drink also gave birth to a new institution: the coffeehouse. Coffee and coffeehouses spread in tandem to the major cities of the Ottoman Empire, including Mecca, Medina, and Aleppo. Until the mid-sixteenth century, most of this demand was supplied by Ethiopia. After the 1570s, Yemen supplanted Ethiopia as the world's dominant center of coffee production.[15]

Yemen enjoyed a virtual monopoly on global coffee production and trade until the early eighteenth century. This was driven in part by imperial politics: the Ottomans conquered Yemen in the late 1530s, and in the 1550s they also attempted to gain control of parts of Ethiopia. The Ottomans began to promote coffee cultivation in the 1570s, and taxes on coffee offered local and imperial governments a significant source of revenue. Coffee gradually made its way into the Red Sea trading networks that linked Yemen to the Ottoman Empire and the worlds of the Mediterranean and the Indian Ocean. In 1635, the Qasimi ousted the Ottomans from Yemen, though the Qasimi state continued to sell coffee to consumers in the Ottoman Empire. In the early eighteenth century, Cairo merchants purchased about half of Yemen's total coffee production.[16] The historian Nancy Um characterizes the Qasimi as the "coffee imamate." The imam received a quarter of the sale price, and coffee generated more revenue for the state than any other crop.[17] Yemeni coffee reached growing populations of coffee drinkers in places as far afield as Surat in Mughal India in the east, and London, Amsterdam, and Paris in the west. European traders first appeared at Mocha around 1610; a century later, European trading companies were a regular presence. In the eighteenth century, Yemen exported between 12,000 and 15,000 tons of coffee per year.[18]

Coffee cultivation in Yemen likely began sometime in the fifteenth or sixteenth century as coffee drinking became more popular in the Middle East. The anthropologist Daniel Varisco suggests that coffee was one of a trio of major crops (along with mango and qat) that were introduced to Yemen in the fifteenth century CE. Both coffee and qat (another stimulant plant) were introduced to Yemen from Ethiopia.[19] This movement was part of a much larger history of global botanical exchanges; Yemen had often served as a relay point between African and Asian biota.[20] These transfers had greatly enriched Yemen's agriculture—farmers there cultivated wheat, millet, sorghum, watermelons, citrus, sugar cane, and dozens of other exotic crops. The coffee plant was, at first, integrated into existing agricultural ecosystems, particularly in the interior highlands, often in terraces on the side of steep hills.[21]

Yemen's climate was marginal for arabica cultivation; it lacked the rainfall and forest cover of arabica's home in Ethiopia. Farmers in the Yemeni highlands used artificial shade trees to protect the delicate arabica plants in areas otherwise exposed to the full sun during the long dry season.[22] The French traveler Jean de la Roque, who visited Yemen's coffee farms in the early eighteenth century, wrote that were it not for the shade trees, "the [coffee] blossoms would soon be burnt up, and never produce any fruit, as it happens to those trees that have not the advantage of such a neighborhood; and in effect these [shade trees] stretch out their branches to a prodigious length, which are so disposed in an exact circle, as to cover everything underneath."[23] Through the dry season, farmers sustained the coffee plants by irrigating them using water collected in reservoirs during the rainy season. During the warm and moist rainy season, which lasts approximately from April to September, the countryside receives between 800 and 2,000 millimeters of rain.

While the coffee plant prospered on the Arabian Peninsula, *H. vastatrix* did not. It is possible that the fungus has never been introduced to Yemen. The fungus feeds on the leaves of the coffee plant, and arabica was most likely brought to Yemen as seeds, which are much easier to transport. But even if the fungus had crossed the Red Sea on live plants or in some other way, it would have struggled to survive in Yemen. The rust spores would have struggled to survive and reproduce during the long dry season and cool nights of Yemen's coffee zones. When the botanist Pierre Sylvain surveyed coffee cultivation in Ethiopia and Yemen in the 1950s, he was struck by the sharp differences between the health of coffee farms on either side of the Red Sea. He found that in Yemen, coffee could be cultivated at elevations as low as 1,000 meters; at a similar altitude on the Ethiopian side of the Red Sea, "diseases and insects would make coffee cultivation hazardous."[24] In the mid-1950s, Sylvain found no *H. vastatrix* anywhere in Yemen, which is telling because the rust was, by then, present in every other coffee-growing region in the Indian Ocean basin. Yemeni farming practices may also have helped limit the disease. Yemeni farmers managed disease in coffee (and other crops) by cultivating healthy seedlings and by using shade trees to limit the amount of dew on the leaves.[25] None of these disease-control practices were unique to the coffee plant, nor were they specifically directed at controlling the rust. But this broader history reminds us that the health of Yemen's coffee farms was not only an accident of geography.

The rust's absence from Yemen matters since Yemen—not Ethiopia—was the center of diffusion for the world's cultivated arabicas. Yemen was much more tightly connected to global networks of exchange than south-western Ethiopia was. This is why the coffee we drink is called arabica coffee instead of, say, Abyssinian coffee. India's coffee farms were founded from coffee seeds taken from the Arabian Peninsula. The Dutch, French, and British also visited the Arabian Peninsula repeatedly to obtain coffee seeds or plants for their expanding tropical empires in Africa and Asia. The progeny of Yemen's arabica plants also formed the genetic basis for the New World's coffee industry. Before the mid-nineteenth century, none of the arabica coffee cultivated outside eastern Africa was descended from seeds or plants obtained directly from its wild range in Ethiopia. All of the world's cultivated coffee descended—directly or indirectly—from a coffee zone singularly free of rust. The health of the world's cultivated arabica coffee had been preserved by an accident of ecology and history.[26]

The Ecological Pax Arabica

In the seventeenth and eighteenth centuries, coffee production and coffee consumption expanded in tandem. In the mid-seventeenth century, coffee drinking spread to Europe. Some Europeans developed a taste for coffee through contacts with the Ottoman Empire. The Viennese, for example, supposedly developed their taste for coffee after an Ottoman siege of the city was broken and the fleeing Ottomans left behind many sacks of coffee. In other parts of Europe, coffee appears first to have been introduced by individual "Turks" (i.e., people from the Islamic world) who set up coffeehouses in major commercial and cultural centers.[27] Europeans were attracted by the drink and also by the coffeehouse as a social institution. In the 1650s and 1660s, coffeehouses sprang up across London, where they attracted the attention of the cosmopolitan English virtuosi, who valued the exotic.[28] Some people expressed concern about the possible influence of the "heathen," "infidel" drink on English society—as in the famed British pamphlet titled *The Women's Petition against Coffee*. As in the Ottoman Empire, ruling elites sometimes voiced concern about the coffeehouse as a place for sedition. But official efforts to close or control coffeehouses were ultimately futile.

Coffee consumption soon spread across the social spectrum. In some of London's coffeehouses, people of all social classes rubbed shoulders, although other coffeehouses served a more exclusive clientele. Coffee became part of popular culture; the composer Johann Sebastian Bach wrote a coffee cantata in which a young woman sings "how sweet coffee tastes, more delicious than a thousand kisses. . . . Coffee, I have to have coffee."[29] By the eighteenth century, coffee prices had fallen so much that, as the Dutch trader François Valentijn noted, "coffee had broken through so generally in our land that maids and seamstresses now had to have their coffee in the morning or they could not put their thread through the eye of their needle."[30] European demand for coffee grew steadily across the eighteenth and nineteenth centuries as coffee prices continued to fall. Americans embraced coffee drinking in the nineteenth century, although coffeehouses were less popular. Americans usually bought green coffee at general stores and roasted it at home. After the Civil War, large coffee companies began to roast and market coffee on a large scale.[31]

Coffee cultivation spread across the global tropics in tandem with the coffee boom in Europe. Initially, Europe's coffee boom was fueled by coffee from Yemen. European trading companies—the British East India Company and the Dutch East India Company (VOC)—started to export coffee from Yemen to London and Amsterdam, and then to consumers across Europe. As European demand grew, Yemen gradually lost its monopoly on coffee cultivation. Beginning in the late seventeenth century, people disseminated coffee plants throughout the Indian Ocean basin. European trading companies, especially the Dutch VOC, played some role in this dissemination. But the plant also circulated through parallel non-European (largely Muslim) trade and pilgrimage networks in the Indian Ocean basin. By the late seventeenth century, arabica coffee was cultivated in western India, where most of the coffee was consumed locally. The Dutch introduced coffee to Java from India rather than from Yemen. By the late seventeenth century, arabica coffee was widely, if not yet densely, cultivated along an arc reaching from Yemen in the east to Java in the west.[32]

Arabica coffee was introduced to the New World in the early eighteenth century. In 1696, the Dutch transported a single coffee tree from Java to Amsterdam, where it was cultivated in the city's botanical garden. From Amsterdam, some of the plant's offspring were sent to Paris and cultivated in the Jardin du Roi. Based on this plant, the French naturalist Antoine de Jussieu published one of the earliest botanical descriptions of coffee, which he classified as *Jasminum Arabicum*.[33] Between about 1710 and 1720, both the Dutch and the French took progeny of this plant to the New World. According to popular French legend, it was taken to Martinique by one Chevalier de Clieu, who sustained the fragile plant by giving it some of his water rations. Even if this story is true, de Clieu was not alone; around the same time, and with much less fanfare, the Dutch took arabica coffee to Suriname. By the mid-eighteenth century, the arabica coffee plant—based on the progeny of these early introductions—had been disseminated across the Americas, from Mexico to Brazil.[34] The founding populations of arabica coffee in the New World were built on a limited genetic base.

It is safe to assume that *H. vastatrix* was not present in the Americas before the twentieth century. In the unlikely event that the rust had been present in Java, it would have faced a series of significant bottlenecks on its journey to the Americas. It is virtually impossible that the delicate fungus could have survived the extreme temperatures of the voyage around Cape Horn from Java to Amsterdam. Before the nineteenth century, live plants were usually transported in pots on the ship decks; more delicate plants may have been placed in wood or glass cases to protect them from the elements, but even those were left open so that air could circulate. Had the fungus somehow survived, watchful gardeners at the botanical gardens in Paris or Amsterdam would certainly have seen it; there is no evidence they did. The fungus (and the plant) would have again been exposed to extreme conditions during the Atlantic crossing.

Coffee-farming practices would, at first, have kept rust levels so low that the rust would not have significantly affected production. In the Dutch East Indies, Javanese farmers usually cultivated coffee in densely planted hedgerows (*kopi pagar*) close to their households. Farmers in India cultivated coffee both as a garden crop and as a forest crop. In Mysore, coffee was cultivated in fenced gardens called *hittlus*, and coffee was intercropped with "lime, plantain, ginger, and mango." Kandyan farmers on Ceylon also cultivated coffee as a garden crop, mixed with other cash and subsistence crops. This strategy allowed them to minimize economic and ecological risks. Coffee required little care or attention beyond some basic weeding, and it provided a good source of income. Few native planters produced coffee exclusively, nor did they depend on it as their major source of cash income. It was simply part of a diversified ecological and economic repertoire.[35]

Power and Vulnerability in the Nineteenth Century

By the mid-nineteenth century, the world's coffeelands had become critically vulnerable to commodity diseases like coffee rust. A series of political, economic, and technological revolutions had sharply increased production and consumption of coffee around the globe. Many of these changes had their roots in the Industrial Revolution. Among other things, the Industrial Revolution helped spur mass consumption in the metropolises and factory towns of Europe and North America. Europe's industrial powers competed aggressively to control trade and territories in Asia and Africa and to consolidate control of tropical territories they already held. Colonial states often obliged their subjects to produce tropical commodities, both to meet metropolitan demand and to provide revenue for the colonial states. Settlers also flocked to the tropical colonies, many of them encouraged by the hope that plantations would offer them a quick path to prosperity. In some cases, colonized peoples took advantage of the new colonial networks and started producing tropical commodities on their own. In Latin America, the leaders of the newly independent nations pursued economic development by exporting commodities to the industrializing Global North. In industrializing Europe and the United States, coffee gradually became a cheap stimulant, accessible to rich and poor alike. Coffee consumption in the United States exploded during these years, fueled by growing production from Brazil. By the century's end, Americans drank more coffee than all European countries combined. New railroad and steamship networks reduced transportation costs, helping drive prices downward. The production of tropical commodities expanded as farmers across the global tropics produced ever more sugar, tea, cocoa, rubber, bananas, and—of course—coffee.[36]

In these years, global demand for coffee typically increased faster than supply, which encouraged farmers to continually expand production.

Initially, producers in Asia—especially in the Dutch East Indies, Ceylon, and India—dominated global production, accounting for about a third of global coffee production until the 1880s.[37] But over the nineteenth century the Americas, especially Brazil, decisively surpassed Asia. Coffee cultivation in Brazil quickly expanded into the forest regions around Rio de Janeiro and then vast forest regions beyond. By midcentury, Brazil produced half of the world's coffee; by the end of the century, it produced more than 80 percent.[38]

The boom was initially led by small and medium producers. In the early decades of Ceylon's coffee boom, for example, most of the island's coffee was produced by Kandyan smallholders. Most of this coffee was grown under shade, as part of a complex production system. Similarly, smallholders in Java "preferred to clear only undergrowth and small trees, planting coffee at stake under tall jungle trees. The coffee trees took longer to bear, and yields were lower, but they lived longer, and soil damage was checked."[39] These cultivation systems embodied a different view of agriculture, economy, and environment. Farmers were not simply seeking to maximize productivity and profit. Profit was certainly *one* goal, but they also took a longer view about what we would now call ecological and economic sustainability. Perhaps it also reflected the fact that they did not have the same access to "virgin" forests as better-funded farmers.

More specialized estate coffee cultivation began in the eighteenth century. Europeans, especially the French, first cultivated coffee as a plantation monoculture in the Indian Ocean's Île Bourbon (now Réunion) and in the West Indies: Martinique, Guadeloupe, and—above all—St. Domingue.[40] By the second half of the eighteenth century, coffee production in the West Indies had far surpassed production in the Indian Ocean. Arabica coffee had been introduced to St. Domingue in the 1720s; just fifty years later, in 1775, the island exported almost 22,500 metric tons of coffee. By 1789, it was the world's single largest coffee producer, exporting about 40,000 metric tons.[41] These levels of productivity depended, however, on slave labor. St. Domingue's coffee exports collapsed in the wake of the slave uprising that began in 1789, which also toppled the colonial government. Between roughly 1790 and 1830, estate coffee production across the West Indies collapsed as a result of political strife, abolition movements, and competition with the booming sugar industry for scarce labor. Cuba was the only place in the West Indies where estate production survived, although even there coffee producers had to compete with more-prosperous sugar producers for increasingly scarce slave labor.

While estate coffee declined in the West Indies, it boomed in Asia and mainland Latin America. In those places, coffee monocultures became much more common as planters, often using coerced labor, sought to maximize the productivity and profitability of their farms. Planters cleared "virgin" forests in Brazil, Ceylon, and many other places. Following the so-called West Indian model (developed in colonial St. Domingue), they planted coffee trees in dense rows, eliminating all other plants from the farm. In Ceylon, this could mean a density of between 1,200 and 2,700 plants per acre, depending on the spacing between the trees. The goal, in the words of one planter, was to plant "the great[est] number of trees in a given space so that none shall incommode or interfere with the growth or sustenance of its neighbor."[42] The first generation of European coffee planters generally preferred to plant their coffee in open sun, eliminating all shade trees. The British coffee planter Edmund Hull argued that they did so because the native coffee farmers always did use shade, and "the tendency of the European farmer [was] to regard with the utmost contempt all idea of instruction coming from that quarter."[43] While this kind of prejudice may have been a factor, settlers likely rejected shade trees because they believed that shade reduced yields and, therefore, profits.

In some places, coffee grew as far as the eye could see. At high altitudes in Ceylon, one could see "fields of dark, ever-green, luxuriant coffee-trees, so well clothed with foliage that not a square yard of bare ground is visible for acres."[44] Later in the century the Brazilian novelist Monteiro Lobato described São Paulo's coffee farms as a "green wave of coffee."[45] On such farms, the coffee trees were planted at carefully measured distances in neat rows. This arrangement reflected European ideas about rationality; it also helped maximize production and manage labor. The goal of this layout, wrote Hull, was to "admit large gangs of laborers working together on an estate without confusion, to enable the employer more easily to check the amount of work done by each person, as well as to economize surface to the utmost, by having the largest number of plants on a given area, each with its due share of ground."[46]

But this superficial order masks just how improvised these landscapes were.[47] Most European planters had little experience with tropical agriculture; in fact, many had little experience with agriculture of any kind. They learned how to farm coffee by trial and error. In the eighteenth century, French coffee planters seem to have transmitted their knowledge orally. The settlers "had no books or schools to guide them," wrote the French botanist Auguste Chevalier, "but like the peasants of France they transmitted the improvements they had made from one generation to the next." Because there were "frequent connections from one colony to the other," continued Chevalier, "the [farming] methods and techniques were quickly unified" across colonies. From the mid-eighteenth century, then, "the coffee tree was cultivated identically, and coffee was cultivated on [the Île] Bourbon as it was in the Antilles and the diverse countries of the Americas."[48] In Ceylon, some British planters developed an apprenticeship system called "creeping" in which a recently arrived planter would assist an experienced planter for a year or so before setting up a farm of his own.

Over the nineteenth century, some of this practical knowledge was codified in texts. The first significant publication in this genre was P. J. Laborie's *The Coffee Planter of Saint Domingo*, published in 1798. Laborie had owned a coffee plantation in Saint Domingue, but he lost it during the revolution. In 198 pages, Laborie meticulously described how to clear forests, build the farm, and cultivate and process the coffee, as well as how to manage slave labor. Laborie's book became a model for coffee plantations around the world; it was a model for the West Indian system of cultivation adopted by British planters in Ceylon. It offered some useful guidance, although some of his suggestions did not always work well in other environments.[49] Publications on coffee planting proliferated after the mid-nineteenth century, many of these reflecting the experience of farmers in different coffee zones. Planters also shared their practical knowledge through newspapers and periodicals. And gradually, at least in the British colonies, planters published coffee manuals of their own, usually integrating their practical experience with whatever scientific innovations they felt to be relevant.[50]

At this point, no particular scientific knowledge was necessary for running a coffee farm; farmers increased production by clearing forests and using more labor.[51] And for their part, scientists had not devoted much attention to studying the coffee plant or the practical problems of coffee agriculture. The botanists at Ceylon's botanical garden were more concerned with acclimating exotic crops than working with the coffee planters. In Brazil, the first coffee research station was not founded until 1887. In the Dutch East Indies, the first dedicated coffee research station was founded in 1896, although coffee researchers at the Cultuurtuin (botanical garden) in Java had started doing some coffee research as early as the 1870s.[52] Coffee planters only showed much interest in science when they began experiencing production problems that they could not solve on their own. For that reason, they showed particular interest in Justus von Liebig's pioneering work on chemical fertilizers. But so long as "land remained cheap and plentiful," wrote the always-insightful Hull, "the simple but wasteful method of opening up new estates as soon as the old ones begin to be exhausted, seemed always preferable to an intricate and laborious study of the best means of preserving land already under cultivation."[53]

This production boom made the world's coffee farms more vulnerable to diseases and pests than ever before. Viewed from an epidemiologic perspective, it greatly increased the global population and distribution of susceptible arabicas. The limited genetic diversity of these cultivated arabicas made them even more vulnerable. The world's globally traded arabicas depended on just two cultivars, Bourbon and Typica, both of which originated from the narrow arabica populations of Yemen. The expanding shipping and railroad networks offered diseases and pests new opportunities to move beyond their native range. The most significant change, however, was the spread of coffee monocultures; many of the new coffee farms were radically simpler than earlier ones. These monocultures involved a trade-off between economic productivity and ecological vulnerability, which may not have been immediately apparent. By sharply reducing the biological diversity of farms—by devoting the farm space to a single crop—farmers also removed the physical and genetic obstacles that kept diseases and pests in check. Looking back on this period, the French coffee expert Auguste Chevalier wrote that "the coffee plant was cultivated on still-virgin lands, in regions not wholly deforested; all the cultivated coffee trees descended from a handful of plants free of disease; and they were cultivated in lands where insects [and] natural enemies of the coffee tree had not yet been imported."[54]

Harbingers of the Rust

A closer look suggests that Chevalier's idyllic picture of coffee farming was not entirely accurate. As early as 1773, a French coffee planter on Île Bourbon complained of "little black scarabs that eat the leaves of the coffee tree," of a "louse that attaches itself to the branches, leaves, and even the roots of the coffee trees, and makes them languish," and of a "singular malady" in which the "leaves, branches, and often even the fruits of the coffee tree were largely covered with a black matter that 'freezes' the plant and dries it."[55] These localized outbreaks foreshadowed the global commodity diseases that were to plague coffee farms in the next century.

Even as the world's coffee farms became more vulnerable to disease before 1870, they suffered only localized outbreaks of diseases and pests.

A "coffee leaf disease," likely an insect rather than a fungus, disrupted production on coffee estates in Ceylon for a few years in the 1840s. Indeed, during the pioneering phases of coffee production, insect pests tended to cause more problems than did diseases. Various species of mealybugs (genus *Planococcus*) fed on the sap of new tissues in the coffee plants. One of these, the "black bug"—which first appeared in Ceylon in 1843—ate the fresh shoots of young coffee plants and destroyed the cherries. Another, the "white bug," lived in the axils of leaves and cut them off "either during the blossom stage or just after the young berries have been formed."[56] The most serious insect pest of coffee was the borer (probably the coffee white stem borer, *Xylotrechus quadripes* Chevrolat), first detected in Coorg in the mid-1860s.[57] This insect bored into the trunk of the coffee tree. The leaves of infested plants wilted and fell, and over time the tree died back to the entry point.[58] Grubs sometimes attacked the coffee plant's taproots, ultimately killing the trees. The planters also faced problems from grasshoppers, "which [were] addicted to cutting down young trees close to the ground, and to sawing off the branches of older trees."[59]

While some of these pests were undoubtedly native to Ceylon, others were probably introduced, particularly from other parts of South Asia. The "coffee bug" that appeared in Ceylon in the early 1840s was previously unknown in Ceylon; apparently these insects were first detected on "plants near coolie lines" of laborers from southern India. Some planters argued that the insect emerged spontaneously in poorly cultivated plantations. Others, however, attributed the introduction of the bug to "Mocha" coffee plants imported from Bombay. George Gardner, the botanist of the Peradeniya Botanic Garden, noted that the insect had not been present on the island five years before. The planters also noticed that the outbreaks of the bug were associated with outbreaks of a fungus. The naturalist Miles Berkeley concurred, noting that "there is a great reason to believe that many of these plagues are in the first instance imported, and we know that some vegetable productions of foreign extraction and some insects also become peculiarly luxuriant and abundant in their new quarters."[60]

The entomologist John Nietner disputed this idea. "With reference to this comparatively recent appearance of the bug in the island," he wrote, "it has been suggested that it was not indigenous, but had been introduced with seed-coffee, from some other country." But he argued that the bugs were indigenous, noting that he had seen the white coffee bug "upon orange, guava, and other trees," while the brown bug "attacks almost every plant and tree that grows on a coffee estate, more particularly though those that are grown on gardens."[61] Nietner did not explain why the outbreaks occurred at that particular time, but he was clearly aware that they were connected to prevailing farming practices.

Significantly, Nietner was also aware of the broader global context of these outbreaks, noting that "at about the same time [as the bug outbreaks in Ceylon] the potato, vine, and olive disease[s] became very alarming in Europe."[62] This was a historical moment in which microorganisms were becoming increasingly mobile. It was in these years, for example, that the potato blight made its way from South America to Europe and cholera spread from India to Europe and later the Americas.[63] Microbes like these traveled on the same modern transportation infrastructure that swiftly moved goods and people around the globe.

Yet for the first half of the nineteenth century, at least, the coffee plant (and by extension the coffee rust) did not circulate. There was little incentive for coffee planters, large or small, to move the coffee plant. It had been so widely distributed in the eighteenth century that further long-distance transfers were unnecessary. Coffee planters almost everywhere could easily obtain planting material locally and saw little advantage to acquiring it from afar. In Ceylon and Southern India, for example, coffee planters obtained planting material from plants that had escaped into the forest, or they purchased planting material from local farmers. Long-distance transfers of coffee began anew in the 1870s, when Europeans found a new species of coffee—Liberian coffee—in West Africa.[64]

By the late 1860s, the pioneering phase of coffee cultivation was ending in India, Ceylon, and Java—the region's three largest producers. In Ceylon, most of the viable coffeelands were occupied by the mid-1870s. In India, the coffee zones in Mysore and Coorg were similarly almost fully occupied. "Comparatively little land suitable for planting purposes now remains in the hands of the government in either the Neilgherries, Coorg, or Wynaad," wrote Edmund Hull in 1877, "while there is great difficulty in securing what there is at any price, except under the most stringent conditions."[65] George Watt wrote that the coffee tracts of Southern India "extend in nearly an unbroken line along the summits and slopes of the Western Ghauts, from the northern limits of Mysore down to Cape Comorin."[66] Java was ringed with a coffee belt extending from 600 to 1,200–1,400 meters above sea level.[67] The ecological limits of coffee cultivation—as defined by a combination of temperature, rainfall, and climate—had been reached. Nonetheless, coffee planters in these places continued to open new farms in marginal lands or migrate to new frontiers. Some astute planters began to question the long-term viability of the pioneering estate model, which treated forest landscapes and their soils as nonrenewable resources. Hull questioned the "great and serious difficulties in the way of keeping up that constant, unremitting care and culture which appear necessary to maintain in a state of perfect health a plant, which, however hardy in some respects, is after all an exotic in our Indian settlements, and is moreover being grown under a forced and artificial system."[68] Hull found an alternative model in the native farms, some of which contained "trees of an age far beyond the power of the oldest inhabitant to define, and which have very probably been flourishing for generations."[69] Unfortunately, it seems that Hull's voice was in the minority.

BY THE mid-nineteenth century, the intensification of production had left the world's coffee farms highly vulnerable to diseases and pests. This vulnerability was itself a product of coffee's history as a commodity. In the wild, arabica coffee and the *H. vastatrix* fungus lived concomitantly, yet the fungus did not cause serious harm to the plant. The disease was kept in check by the structure of Ethiopia's forest ecosystem and likely also by fungi that parasitized *H. vastatrix*. By accident or design, the coffee plant was transferred to Yemen without the rust. From Yemen, rust-free arabica coffee was then dispersed across the global tropics. The coffee plant prospered as it was cultivated in diverse ecosystems that were largely free of significant diseases and pests, at least initially. This ecological Pax arabica eroded as the scope and scale of coffee cultivation intensified over the nineteenth century. As production increased, monocultures became much more important, especially in the world's largest producers—Brazil, Java, and Ceylon. These monocultures were highly productive over the short term. In the absence of any pests or pathogens that could take advantage of this vulnerability, the coffee plants prospered. But these landscapes were also highly susceptible, as Ceylon's coffee planters would discover after 1869.

Chapter 3

The Epicenter
Ceylon

THE GLOBAL rust epidemic began, without fanfare, on a coffee farm in a small corner of Ceylon. Early in 1869, a farmer in the Madulsima district noticed some orange spots on the leaves of a few of his coffee trees. By mid-1869, the fungus had spread from a few trees to several acres. Over the next two years, the fungus engulfed the island's coffee farms. "The rapidity with which this coffee leaf disease has spread throughout the coffee districts on the Island," wrote George H. K. Thwaites, the director of the Royal Botanical Garden at Peradeniya, "has been perfectly marvelous." "It is probable," he continued, "that not a single estate has quite escaped, though it appeared in a very slight degree on some."[1] In the years that followed, the rust gradually wreaked havoc on Ceylon's coffee production. The photograph below (fig. 3.1) shows the Madulsima district just a few years after the rust was first reported. It shows some planters and laborers walking through a field of young coffee; the plants are waist high. Looking closely at the photo, the trunks and branches of

Figure 3.1. Planters and laborers walking through a coffee estate, Ceylon. (Samuel Bourne and Charles Shepherd, *View from Mr. Jenkins' Coffee Estate, Madoolseema, Ceylon*, 1872, Hume Collection, Photographs of Southern India and Ceylon, the British Library, Archives and Manuscripts. © Granger)

the coffee plants are visible, suggesting that the plants may have been heavily defoliated.

Farmers in Ceylon had been cultivating and exporting coffee for global markets since the eighteenth century, when the island was under Dutch rule. Ironically, most coffee produced in Ceylon under Dutch rule came from the one part of the island that was *not* directly under Dutch control: the highland Kingdom of Kandy. Under Dutch rule, Sinhalese farmers exported between 37,000 and 100,000 pounds of coffee per year. Coffee production boomed after the British took control of the island after the Napoleonic Wars. Between 1830 and 1880, Ceylon was the world's third-largest producer of coffee. The colonial government eliminated export duties on coffee and exempted coffeelands from tax. They built roads, and later railroads, that linked the highlands of Kandy with the coast.[2]

At first, this sparked a boom in Sinhalese coffee production. At least some of this was produced using traditional farming techniques. Sinhalese farmers tended to farm coffee under shade and at lower altitudes, sometimes as low as sea level. "In these cases," wrote Hull, "the plants will invariably be found growing under the shade of the jack, cocoa-nut, or other suitable trees, without which protection all chance of their thriving permanently would be out of the question." These farms were also "limited in extent, and are generally richly manured and often well watered during the dry season."[3] According to some accounts, they also cultivated coffee in small patches around their villages. James Webb persuasively argues that during the 1820s and 1830s, some Sinhalese farmers adopted more intensive production techniques, supported by a series of policy changes by the colonial government to encourage local production. This intensification involved clearing highland chena lands and forests to take advantage of their rich soils. Webb estimates that they must have cleared some 60,000 acres of forest for coffee production, sometimes bringing them into conflict with British coffee planters.[4]

Although the earliest British estates were established in the 1820s, the estate boom did not began in earnest until the 1840s. Spurred by rising coffee prices in Europe and North America, Europeans (mostly Britons) started aggressively clearing the steep slopes of Ceylon's highland forests. In 1840, the colonial government decreed that Ceylon's highland forests belonged to the Crown. Over the next several decades, much of this land was sold to settlers for coffee production. Most of the colonists had little previous experience with farming coffee, or indeed, farming of any kind. Like estate coffee producers in other parts the world, they sought to maximize productivity and profitability. "It is generally admitted," observed the planter William Sabonadière, "that nothing equals virgin forest land for the cultivation of coffee." The trees were cleared so that coffee could be cultivated on the rich forest soils. At first, farmers often obtained arabica seeds and seedlings from neighboring Sinhalese farms. The estates were usually planted without shade, since shade reduced yields. By the late 1880s, 600,000 acres of forest had been cleared for coffee. "The lovely sloping forests are going," wrote the novelist Anthony Trollope on a visit to Ceylon, "and the very regular but ugly coffee plantations are taking their place." Between 1849 and 1868, annual coffee exports tripled, from roughly 330,000 hundredweight to 1,000,000 hundredweight (16,700 metric tons to 50,800 metric tons).[5]

The "most fruitful coffee districts," according to Edmund Hull, were in the highlands between 2,500 and 3,500 feet (roughly 750–1,050 meters), although estates could be found at altitudes between 50 and 1,500 meters. Like coffee planters everywhere in the early nineteenth century, farmers on Ceylon (both Sinhalese and European) pushed arabica coffee to its ecological limits. They managed the plant as best they could by manipulating the conditions under which it was cultivated. In these respects, Ceylon was just as vulnerable to the rust as other coffee zones around the world. In another respect, however, it was even more vulnerable. Ceylon's climate was unusually wet and windy. The summer monsoon (May–September) and the winter monsoon (December–February) showered the island with rain and exposed it to winds that could exceed 100 kilometers per hour. Rain also fell regularly during the intermonsoonal period. Ceylon's wet climate, then, turned its coffee farms into a vast incubator for the coffee rust. And the strong and regular winds ensured that when the rust appeared, it would spread rapidly through the island and beyond.[6]

The Search for Origins

The early history of the rust in Ceylon remains murky. Some observers contended that the rust fungus was native to Ceylon, arguing that the epidemic had been triggered by the introduction of *C. arabica*. The rust's supposed wild host was a plant then known as *Coffea travancorensis* (now classified as *Psilanthus travancorensis*), a plant closely related to coffee and indigenous to Ceylon and Southern India. Thwaites, who had been studying Ceylon's fungi for almost a decade, argued that this was unlikely because he only found the rust on *C. travancorensis* after the epidemic had already broken out. It was more likely that *C. travancorensis* was infected from *C. arabica*, not the other way around. The naturalist John Nietner, along with several others, suggested that the rust had likely been present on coffee farms for several years before the epidemic broke out. Thwaites countered that if the rust had been present, "it is somewhat remarkable that the somewhat conspicuous orange-coloured spores on the underside of the leaves did not attract attention; and it is equally remarkable that the disease should so suddenly have assumed so very malignant a character."[7] Thwaites could not have known this, but as the rust later spread around the world, it often did pass unnoticed for several years before attracting attention—even when people were specifically looking for it.

This last objection is the most compelling one against an early introduction of the rust to Ceylon: if the fungus had been present on the island for any significant length of time, why didn't the epidemic break out sooner? All the ecological conditions for a large-scale rust epidemic had existed since at least the coffee craze of the 1840s. One possibility is that the fungus *had* been present in Ceylon for some time, but the arabica plants cultivated in Ceylon were resistant to the strain of *H. vastatrix* that was initially introduced. After a time, a new, more virulent strain of the fungus evolved that could overcome that resistance. Later in the story, we shall see examples of this pattern. But as far as we know, most cultivated arabica is susceptible (to a greater or lesser degree) to all strains of *H. vastatrix*, and many, if not most, plants would surely have shown at least some lesions. It is hard to understand how it could have escaped notice altogether before 1869.

The location and pattern of the early rust outbreak in Ceylon strongly suggest that the rust was introduced. It began at a single point—Madulsima—in the interior of the island and spread outward from there. This pattern is characteristic of what plant pathologists now call a "focal epidemic," which typically begins with a low level of inoculum (in this case, spores) at a well-defined location. The fungus then spreads outward from the focus in waves, like ripples in a quiet pond after a stone is dropped in.[8] Had the fungus already been widespread in Ceylon's forests, it is highly unlikely that the disease would have appeared at such a well-defined location; the epidemic would have been generalized across Ceylon's coffee farms from the very beginning. But if we accept that the fungus was introduced, then we need to ask how.

In the mid-nineteenth century, pathogens of all kinds were traveling farther and faster than ever before. The historian David Arnold has aptly described the Indian Ocean basin in those years as a "disease zone" in which pathogens of all kinds followed the ebbs and flows of empire and found new host populations on which to survive and reproduce.[9] Ceylon was tightly linked into a global network of steamships that regularly and swiftly moved goods and people between Asia, Africa, the Pacific, and beyond. New innovations like the Wardian case—essentially a portable greenhouse—made it possible for people to ship live plants anywhere in the world.[10] This increased the risk of accidentally moving diseases and pests that fed on those plants. Newly empowered public institutions, such as the Royal Botanic Gardens at Kew, helped broker the movement of plants and seeds across the global tropics. Private nurseries, such as William Bull and Sons in London and the Horticole Coloniale in Brussels, also supported a global trade in tropical seeds and plants. The geographic and economic barriers that had for several centuries kept the coffee rust contained in Africa had begun to erode.

In the 1980s, the biologist Gordon Wrigley speculated that the spore might have been brought to Ceylon by the Napier expedition, a military expedition that sent troops from India to Ethiopia early in 1868. While in

Ethiopia, the expedition passed through a number of minor coffee-growing areas where the rust may have been present. A number of people on the expedition, including Napier himself, had close connections with Ceylon. Wrigley speculates that they "might have returned with some live or pressed coffee plant material carrying viable spores."[11] This is one possible explanation. But the fungus need not have come from Ethiopia; it was also present on wild coffees in the Great Lakes region of East Africa and in the upper reaches of the Congo. Trade routes for slaves and ivory passed through these regions. These routes linked the East African interior to maritime trade networks spanning the Indian Ocean and beyond. They were heavily traveled by many people, including African slaves, Arab traders, and European missionaries and explorers, among others. Perhaps one of these travelers brushed up against some infected coffee plants and inadvertently picked up some spores on his or her clothing. Then, that person may have gone to Ceylon and inadvertently brushed up against an arabica plant, leaving some spores on the susceptible arabicas. The specifics of how the fungus got from eastern Africa to Ceylon are unknown, and likely unknowable. But the circumstantial case is clear: one way or another, the rust epidemic was triggered by intensifying connections between the interior of East Africa and the Indian Ocean.[12] Taken individually, any given transfer between East Africa and Ceylon was unlikely. But taken together, as ever more people and goods were moving from Africa to Ceylon, there was a greater likelihood that some rust spores stowed away on a journey.

Of course, the spore was just one part of the story. The epidemic in Ceylon was devastating because the island's coffee estates provided the fungus with the ideal conditions in which to reproduce. The outbreak was abetted by Ceylon's climate. The rains that accompanied Ceylon's two annual monsoons showered the coffee plants, providing ample supplies of the water droplets that the fungus needed to germinate. Ceylon's comparatively warm temperatures, especially at lower elevations, also helped the spores reproduce. During a single crop season, the fungus could easily complete several infection cycles. In Ceylon's warm and wet landscapes, much of inoculum survived from one crop season to the next, reinfecting each new crop of coffee. The coffee estates presented few physical or genetic barriers to prevent rust spores from dispersing and reproducing. The intense monsoonal winds—largely unchecked by forest trees or shelter belts—dispersed spores widely across the island. In this context, a vastly greater proportion of the spores released by each lesion landed on susceptible coffee plants, colonized their leaf tissue, and produced new lesions that, in turn, liberated countless new spores of their own.[13] The outbreak in Ceylon was the fungal equivalent of nuclear fission. Just fifteen years after the rust was first detected in Ceylon, the island's once-vibrant coffee industry had collapsed.

Competing Models of Crop Disease

Farmers and scientists alike struggled to make sense of the disease. Crop diseases on this scale were new; the potato blight in Ireland, for instance, had taken place just two decades before. And the coffee rust developed in complicated ways, making it difficult to read. In some years, it seemed far less severe than in others. During the initial attack, "the trees were denuded of their leaves altogether, and the site is then so pitiable that during the early years of the attack experienced planters recommended the abandonment of fields."[14] But the defoliation was not permanent. A few months after the initial defoliation, the trees "had put on a fresh flush of leaves and were bearing several hundredweights of crop per acre."[15] It seemed, at least initially, that the disease afflicted European estates more severely than the farms of Sinhalese coffee planters. "The coffee and plantations and gardens cultivated on the European system seemed likely to suffer most," wrote one government official, "while much of the unpruned coffee surrounding the villagers' huts and houses presented a fair show of berry."[16]

Scientists quickly started searching for explanations and solutions. The farmer who first encountered the disease took some infected coffee leaves to the director of the Royal Botanical Gardens at Peradeniya, George Thwaites. The garden, located near Kandy in the heart of Ceylon's coffee country, was then one of the world's leading tropical botanical gardens. Nonetheless, naturalists at the garden had conducted little research on coffee agriculture. The garden's applied research focused on acclimating exotic crops such as cinchona and tea.[17] Thwaites had spent more than two decades studying Ceylon's flora, but he had never encountered anything like the rust. So he sent the leaves back to Joseph Hooker at the Royal Botanic Gardens of Kew in England.

Hooker immediately forwarded the infected leaves to Miles Berkeley, Great Britain's leading plant pathologist. Two decades earlier, Berkeley had participated in the commission to study the causes of the Irish potato blight (*Phytophthora infestans*). His research on the potato blight convinced him of fungal pathogenicity, a view of plant diseases that was, for the time, quite new. In the 1850s, he had published extensively on crop diseases.[18] Berkeley had begun his scientific career as a specialist on the fungi of Great Britain, but he also developed an expertise in tropical fungi collections from British expeditions around the world, including the voyages of Darwin's *Beagle*. He had previously analyzed the thousands of fungi that Thwaites collected in Ceylon.[19] Given his expertise on crop diseases and his deep knowledge of Ceylon's fungi, it is difficult to imagine anyone better suited to study the coffee rust. Berkeley's collaborator, the microscopist C. E. Broome, created detailed drawings of the fungus.

After seeing the drawings, Berkeley concluded that the fungus appeared to be a completely new species. "The most curious circumstance," he observed, "is that amongst more than a thousand species of Fungi received from Ceylon, this does not occur." The fungus looked like no other, and Berkeley concluded that "it is not only quite new, but with difficulty referable to any recognized section of the fungi." Berkeley concluded it was not only a new species, but also an entirely new *genus*, which he baptized *Hemileia* (Latin for "half-smooth," reflecting the shape of the spores). He named the species, aptly as it turned out, *vastatrix*—the Latin word for "devastator" or "destroyer." His description and drawings of the new fungus were published in *The Gardeners' Chronicle*, a leading publication on pure and applied botany, on November 6, 1869. Just six months after this fungus had been discovered in a remote corner of Ceylon, it had been classified and described in Europe. Its image was published and circulated in one of Europe's leading botanical journals—warning farmers and scientists about this new disease just as "most wanted" posters alerted citizenry and law enforcement officers about fugitive criminals.[20] Berkeley's publication marked the beginning of scientific research into the coffee rust epidemic, but describing the fungus from dried spores was just a start.

As the epidemic in Ceylon became more severe, some of Britain's leading scientists became alarmed. In February 1875, Joseph Hooker surveyed the world's coffee farms to measure the extent of the rust. He sent a circular to all the world's major centers of coffee cultivation.[21] The circular described the nature of the rust infections and their impact on the coffee plants, then asked the local informants to report back to Kew if they had seen such a disease. By the end of 1875, responses had returned to Kew from informants as far afield as Jamaica, Brazil, Réunion, and the Dutch East Indies, all of whom answered in the negative. It appears that in mid-1875 the coffee rust was unknown anywhere beyond Ceylon and Southern India. The reports do, incidentally, indicate that coffee farms around the globe suffered from many local diseases and pests, but nothing on the scale of the leaf rust.[22] In an article in *The Gardeners' Chronicle* discussing the global rust survey, Hooker warned that "unless measures are taken to prevent the introduction of Coffee plants from infected countries into others at present free from it, [the rust] may be expected to spread eventually to wherever Coffee is cultivated."[23]

Hooker also lucidly explained why plantation monocultures were inherently vulnerable to epidemics such as the rust. Wherever large concentrations of crop plants were found, Hooker argued, the conditions would be "extremely favourable for the rapid extension and development of parasitic plants and insects." In the wild, these parasitic organisms did not cause much of a problem since they had "only native plants in small quantities to prey upon." Hooker expected diseases such as the rust to become a regular feature of tropical agriculture, characterizing them as "one of the penalties which man must expect to pay for such an enormous disturbance of natural conditions as implied in replacing a tropical forest of the most varied and mixed vegetation by a plantation of a single economic plant." The problem was not limited to tropical crops; he pointed to the potato blight, the phylloxera of the vine, and the potato beetle as comparable infestations in the temperate zones. Based on this fundamental vulnerability, he predicted that Ceylon's coffee planters would have to bear "the constant loss of a certain percentage in every year, with occasionally the loss of an entire crop," just as the potato farmers in Europe did once the potato blight had become endemic in their fields. Still, Hooker hoped that some measure of control would be possible in order to keep coffee production economically viable.[24]

Some coffee planters did not accept this kind of explanation. In retrospect, it is easy to characterize these planters as intellectually conservative, but at the time, the connections between the fungus and the decline in coffee production were not at all evident. Coffee production, especially estate coffee production, was volatile even without the rust. Intensively cultivated arabica farms follow a biennial production cycle, in which a year of high production is followed by a year of lower production. During high-bearing years, the trees devote so many resources to production that the next year they produce a much smaller crop. The coffee rust exacerbated this biennial cycle. Coffee trees that had been completely defoliated one year—often with the branches left dry, brittle, and seemingly dead—would recover the following year. In good years, coffee production remained high, although perhaps not as high as it would have been without the disease. In the off years, the defoliated trees produced even fewer cherries than they would have in disease-free off years. Production dropped by a quarter in 1869 and 1870 and then dropped precipitously over the next two years. Between 1873 and 1878, coffee production seemed to settle into the biennial cycle that planters were familiar with. During the peak years of the early 1870s, Ceylon produced about 950,000 hundredweight of coffee, just short of the pre-rust production. During the low-yielding years, it produced between 650,000 and 750,000 hundredweight. This stability, or seeming stability, may have given the planters the sense that they had reached some sort of equilibrium with the disease. But there were certainly still causes for concern. While the island's total production had remained stable on average, the yield per acre had declined significantly. The total acreage under coffee cultivation actually *increased* by 50 percent between 1870 and 1878, from 185,000 acres to 275,000 acres.[25]

Planters did recognize a correlation between the fungus and the drops in production but did not necessarily see the fungus as the *cause*. Rather, they argued that the fungus and the drop in production were both the *consequences* of a deeper disease inside the plant. "The leaf disease is not *the* 'disease' but an effect arising upon and from a *diseased* condition already contracted by the coffee trees," argued one planter. "Fungus, blight, mouldiness, appear only upon already diseased subjects. Wherefore surely we are less concerned as to inquiring into how the evil operates . . . than in ascertaining *the cause* of it."[26] The planters had no single theory to explain the disease; most invoked some sort of physiological or environmental explanation. Some argued that the disease was caused by a "poisoning of the juices" of the coffee tree. They suggested that the disease was the result of poor cultivation, inadequate manuring, or climatic disturbances. Some planters argued that the disease was just temporary and that sooner or later it would "wear itself out," as earlier outbreaks of diseases and pests appear to have done.[27] In the end, planters were primarily interested in finding a practical way to manage the disease, however it was caused.

Managing the Coffee Rust

Farmers fought back against the rust, both individually and collectively. Some planters thought that high cultivation could help control the rust and perhaps even cure it. High cultivation involved a holistic approach to farming. The planter Edmund Hull succinctly described it as "careful pruning, manuring, shade, where required, the entire suppression of weeds, [etc.]." He found "a great unanimity of opinion" among planters, who agreed that

while the coffee rust might not be "altogether prevented by high cultivation, [the disease] may be at least checked by it." [28] The discourse of high
cultivation had a strong moral undercurrent. Some European farmers
used the concept to distinguish their farming practices from those of the—
supposedly inferior—local farmers. In this view, any planter who failed
to practice high cultivation, who neglected his farm, was letting his peers
down—and also allowing the disease to spread.

Estate farmers tried a range of solutions, many of which drew on
ideas and technologies imported from abroad. For example, one key
component of high cultivation was manuring—the use of fertilizers. Coffee planters in Ceylon had been interested in fertilizers even before the
coffee rust broke out. This was one area in which the planters had learned
from scientific innovations and adopted science into their farming practice. The German chemist Justus von Liebig had revolutionized the fertilizer industry in the 1820s and 1830s. Liebig, a professor of chemistry at
the University of Giessen, had developed the field of agricultural chemistry. His laboratory produced the earliest chemical fertilizers. Still, the
scientists did not have a monopoly on the study of manures, and coffee
planters used chemical and organic, local and imported fertilizers alike,
choosing whichever they thought would work best. Ceylon planters,
for example, used cattle dung, pig dung, dead animals, bones, castor-oil
cake, and wood ashes (among others) as fertilizers, in addition to the
chemical fertilizers then gaining prominence. Imported fertilizers were
clearly important: between 1874 and 1877—as the rust made serious
inroads into coffee production—the value of fertilizer imports to Ceylon
quadrupled.[29]

In the early years of the outbreak, it seemed that manuring *did* mitigate
the coffee rust, if not cure it outright. Coffee growers who applied manure
to their farms found that coffee yields recovered, at least partially. They
concluded, therefore, that the crop losses were caused by soil exhaustion
and that manuring could cure it. Thwaites, for example, claimed that "high
cultivation, with judicious manuring, enables the tree to better sustain the
attacks of the fungus, and to retain strength and vigour enough to produce
a fair yield of berry." But he worried—correctly, as it turned out—that the
manure might not be a permanent cure for the disease.[30] Recent research
has shown that the relationship between manuring and the epidemic is
complicated. While manuring can offset some of the losses from the rust,
its effectiveness depends on which fertilizers are used, how often they are
applied, and the broader structure of the farm.[31]

Other planters experimented with chemical sprays. They used ideas and technologies imported from Europe. In his initial publication on the coffee rust, Miles Berkeley recommended that planters use sulfur, then the most widely used fungicide, to control the rust. Sulfur—in various compounds— had been used as a fungicide in Europe since the early nineteenth century. Farmers had used it to control mildew on grape vines and fruit trees, so it seemed reasonable to assume that it could also control the leaf rust. Sulfur sprays functioned primarily as preventives rather than curatives. Properly applied, they could prevent spores from germinating but could not cure a plant that was already infected. Berkeley recommended that farmers spray the coffee plants or use syringes to apply the sulfur directly to the infected parts of the leaves. It proved to be difficult, however, to use this imported technology to control the rust. To be effective, sulfur had to be applied at the specific moment the rust was germinating, and scientists had not yet established when this moment occurred. The rust's life cycle had not yet been worked out. A second challenge was physical: Berkeley noted that the disease would be difficult to control since "the fungus is confined to the underside of the leaves, and the mycelium is not superficial."[32] This meant that the fungicide would have to be sprayed *upward* to be effective. Finally, fungicides were also expensive; they required significant investments in labor, chemicals, and equipment.

Farmers and researchers alike began searching for rust-resistant arabicas. They imported coffee plants from around the globe, through public and private institutional networks. The Royal Botanic Gardens at Kew helped facilitate a number of these global transfers, as they did with other crops such as tea, cinchona, and rubber.[33] Private institutions and individual planters also moved live planting material over great distances, often with unprecedented speed. Coffee planters could purchase coffee seeds and plants from newly established British nurseries that specialized in exotic crops, such as William Bull in London and Veitch in Liverpool. Some planters conducted bioprospecting expeditions of their own. The many non-Europeans who traveled to Ceylon as laborers, traders, or migrants of other sorts may have also circulated their own planting materials, as they had done for centuries before the age of European hegemony. Unfortunately, the surviving documents remain frustratingly vague about this possibility. In the end, however, all the imported arabicas promptly succumbed to the rust.[34]

For the first time, coffee farmers also tried to cultivate other plants of the *Coffea* genus. In the early 1870s, some planters experimented with

Liberian coffee, a coffee species native to West Africa. Unlike arabica coffee, Liberian coffee was a lowland plant, better adapted to warm and humid temperatures. The first seeds and seedlings of Liberian coffee were shipped to Kew and to William Bull's nursery in 1872. From there, the plant was disseminated around the world through parallel state and commercial networks. By the mid-1870s, Liberian coffee plants were being "sent safely, in Wardian cases, to any country without removing the native earth from their roots."[35] By 1873 at the latest, Liberian coffee had been introduced in Ceylon.[36] Coffee planters there hoped that the plant's broad and thick leaves would be better able than arabica's to resist attacks of the rust. In 1875–76, some coffee planters from Ceylon traveled directly to Liberia to observe how the coffee plant was being cultivated there, and to collect seeds for themselves. This movement of live plants, seeds, and soil in Wardian cases could have hastened the spread of the rust, although most commentators argue (compellingly) that any crop diseases carried in the cases would have likely made themselves apparent during the voyage itself.

Introducing the plant to Ceylon was just the beginning; farmers also had to determine how well it performed in the field. The initial trials were discouraging: "The Wardian cases had scarcely been opened," noted one report, "when the Liberian plants were attacked by the prevalent plague, *Hemileia vastatrix.*" Undaunted, farmers continued to experiment with the plant and discovered that if the young plants were given proper care, "after 18 months or two years, they seem to be strong enough to withstand the disease and become healthy trees."[37] And even if Liberian coffee plants were susceptible to *H. vastatrix*, they suffered less than arabica. They were not defoliated to the same extent, and "the greater part of the leaf area is left intact and it is enabled in spite of the leaf disease to discharge its functions as an essential part in the economy of the plant."[38] By 1877, on some lowland coffee farms Liberian coffee produced as much as 2 tons per acre.

Even so, however, the crop faced other challenges. The fruit of Liberian coffee had a thicker skin than arabica coffee, so planters had to get special depulping machinery to process it. And there were also broader challenges with the market; Liberian beans had a different flavor from the arabica coffee that traders and consumers were then used to. The market for Liberian coffee remained uncertain through the 1870s, although global demand for coffee was expanding quickly enough that Liberian coffee usually found buyers.[39] In the end, in spite of continued advocacy from its many boosters, Liberian coffee remained little more than an experimental crop. European planters and Sinhalese smallholders alike showed little interest in Liberian coffee. In 1878, at the height of the coffee boom, only about 440 acres of Liberian coffee were under cultivation in Ceylon.[40]

Still, in spite of the rust outbreak, owners of coffee estates remained generally optimistic about their crop through the 1870s. The outbreak coincided with a global spike in coffee prices after 1873, which for several years more than offset the losses in production. Between 1875 and 1881, the price for Ceylon plantation coffee fluctuated between 100 and 107 shillings per hundredweight, almost double what it had been a decade before. In 1877, the best year ever for Ceylon coffee planters, the total value of Ceylon plantation coffee exports exceeded £4,600,000. Profits increased even as production declined. In 1874, for example, when exports were 30 percent lower than they had been in 1870, the total value of coffee exports was 17 percent greater.[41] "This great access of value to [one's] returns," wrote the Ferguson brothers, "more than sufficed to compensate the Ceylon planter for any diminution of his crop."[42] In fact, the high prices triggered a land rush; between 1869 and 1879—as the rust was wreaking havoc on coffee farms—some 100,000 acres of new coffee estates were brought into production, supported enthusiastically by Ceylon's government. Even in the face of such losses, the planters continued to be optimistic. In short, as Thwaites observed, the planters were confident in the fact "there is little, if any, diminution in the anxiety to invest in the cultivation of coffee."[43]

The New Botany and the Origins of Coffee Rust Science

Estate coffee remained profitable though the 1870s, but by the end of the decade, planters began to express some concern. Total production declined steadily during the trough years of each biennial cycle. The editors of Ceylon's *Planting Directory* predicted (accurately) that the coffee harvest of 1878 would be "less by 40% than that of 1869, although the area cultivated has increased to nearly 100,000 acres since that time."[44] In 1879, which should have been a peak year in the biennial cycle, production was 170,000 hundredweight (about 8,600 metric tons) lower than the previous peak year. Planters finally began to panic. They asked the colonial government to hire a scientist who would devote himself exclusively to studying the epidemic. The planter G. A. Talbot wrote that the planters needed "a scientific man to make what researches he can and to give us information from a scientific point of view, so as to help us carry on the experiments. From a practical point of view we know our business, but from a scientific point of view we can get valuable assistance, by investigations with the microscope for instance."[45] Talbot's reference to a microscope is significant. Scientists had, of course, used microscopes to study the coffee rust since it was first reported in 1869. But the scientists who had done so—Berkeley and Broome, principally—lived and worked in England. Their research was important, but they didn't work on living plant material and therefore could only see part of the fungus's life cycle. Talbot was asking for a scientist who could bring the techniques of the laboratory—scientific instruments and experimental protocols—to study living coffee rust in the field.[46] They expected, or hoped, that this innovative kind of fieldwork would uncover some means to control the disease.

The coffee rust outbreak had, in fact, coincided with important innovations in botanical research, known in the English-speaking world as the "new botany." The new botany could equally well have been coined the "German botany" since the discipline was largely developed in German institutions (just as Liebig's agricultural chemistry had been) and then taken by eager students to the rest of the world.[47] Practitioners of the new botany emphasized the study of living plants, in contrast to traditional botany, whose practitioners usually worked with dried herbarium specimens. The new botany emphasized studying the life cycle of plants, both in the laboratory and in the field. The emergent discipline of phytopathology—the study of plant diseases—built on the methodologies and approaches of the new botany. In the 1840s and 1850s, German naturalist Anton de Bary conducted pioneering research on crop diseases, particularly on the potato blight and the rusts and smuts of wheat. Through meticulous research in the laboratory and the field, he reconstructed the entire life cycle of fungi, from spores to mature organisms. He cultivated spores in the laboratory and on plants, and he tried to reproduce disease by systematically inoculating healthy plants with fungal spores. He produced convincing evidence that the fungi were independent organisms, that they had a life cycle, and that they were the cause of plant diseases rather than the consequence. De Bary's approach offered a new way of understanding the coffee rust.[48]

In 1879, Ceylon's planters enlisted the colony's government to hire a scientist to study the rust. William Thiselton-Dyer, the assistant director at the Royal Botanic Gardens in Kew, recommended one of his former students, a young biologist named Daniel Morris. Thiselton-Dyer had previously trained Morris in the techniques of the new botany at the Normal School of Science in London. Morris had been in Ceylon since 1877 as an assistant at the Peradeniya Botanic Gardens. Using de Bary's techniques, Morris carefully studied the rust in the field and reconstructed the fungus's life history. He concluded that the rust had an external "filamentous" stage that lasted several months. He argued that attempts to control the fungus should focus on this external stage because the rust would be exposed and amenable to chemical control.[49] Morris worked directly with the coffee farmers in ways that the other scientists at Peradeniya had never done. He enlisted the help of coffee planters to conduct experimental sprayings of working coffee farms in the Dimbula district using "some of the specifics that have proved so successful in the treatment of the hop and vine mildew." The sprays included mixtures of sulfur, including black sulfur, flowers of sulfur, sulfur and coral lime, and Grison's mixture (sulfur and slaked lime). Morris found that a "mixture of sulphur and lime dusted by hand onto the tree has been found, by experiment, to be the most suitable remedy," at a cost of 16.5 rupees per acre for materials.[50] Although the trials lasted just a single season, the preliminary results seemed to satisfy the planters.[51]

Morris's decision to involve planters paid institutional and political dividends. Before his arrival, coffee planters had doubted whether botany had anything useful to offer them. Thwaites had not done any experimental work on the rust and had offered planters little hope. Morris quickly gained their support by enlisting them in his programs and offering them a compelling explanation for the disease and recommendations for control strategies. "Mr. Morris has been in this country for over a year, Dr. Thwaites more than thirty," observed one coffee planter. "Who has told us the most about leaf disease?"[52] Morris wrote that "there are plenty of good, practical, and hard-headed planters who have been convinced by the logic of *facts* and who intend to take up the cure most thoroughly."[53] The editors of *The Gardeners' Chronicle* in England celebrated "the progress made in ten—we may say for all practical purposes, in three years. It is a justification for the existence of scientific committees, scientific lectures, and practical experiments, and we are heartily pleased to see that Ceylon planters fully appreciate the import of what has been done."[54]

Just as Morris seemed to have established the value of agricultural research, he left his post. In mid-1879, the Colonial Office appointed him as the new director of the botanical garden in Jamaica, leaving the planters once again without the support of a scientist. At first, the island's governor, Sir James Robert Longden, balked at hiring a replacement. He cited Morris's success as a reason for *not* appointing a replacement. Morris, argued Longden, "had exhausted the history of the *Hemileia*." The planters, he continued, "knew what they had to do and the mode of carrying it out." That work "belonged to the practical planters rather than scientific men."[55]

Even as some planters celebrated Morris's achievements, others voiced caution. Morris himself had argued that the results of his experiments could only be confirmed after a full growing season. He had left for Jamaica before this, and over the remainder of the season, it became apparent that the chemical treatments Morris had recommended did not, in fact, control the rust. This did not destroy the planters' newfound faith in science, though. Ceylon's chamber of commerce requested that the home government appoint "another gentleman of possible equal qualifications and attainments to Mr. Morris." The Colonial Office once again asked Thiselton-Dyer at Kew to recommend a suitable candidate. He recommended another young scientist named Harry Marshall Ward, who had studied natural science at Cambridge (where he graduated with a first-class degree in 1879) and Würzburg, where he had studied under Anton de Bary and Julius von Sachs, two leading proponents of the new botany. When he returned to the UK, he worked at the Jodrell Laboratory at the newly founded center for experimental plant biology at Kew.[56] Thiselton-Dyer and Hooker recommended that Ward be sent to Ceylon on a two-year contract. This was enough time, they felt, for Ward to study coffee over several growing seasons. That would allow him to establish where Morris had gone wrong and—they hoped—to find an effective cure.

Ward brought the new botany to bear on solving the problems of the coffee rust. Over 1880 and 1881, he conducted a wide range of systematic and comparative observations and experiments aimed at understanding the fungus's life cycle, its epidemiology, its impact on the coffee tree, and potential control measures. In these two years, he produced three important reports for the government of Ceylon detailing the experiments and his findings. He also produced two scientific papers for the *Quarterly Journal of Microscopical Science* and the *Journal of the Linnean Society*. Although the reports are written in dry, official language, they nonetheless reveal Ward's creativity and energy. He conducted meticulous microscopical studies on the life history of the fungus, isolating the spores and exploring how they germinated and developed through the living leaf tissue. He placed potted coffee trees around the veranda of his house so that he could observe how the disease developed on coffee plants with different exposures to the wind and rain. He hung glass slides from coffee trees to trap airborne rust spores; he deliberately infected coffee plants placed in Wardian cases. He carefully observed how rust epidemics developed in the field.

He also partnered with several coffee growers to conduct experiments on chemical control. Few cultivated plants had been subjected to this kind of systematic field work, and certainly no other tropical crop had received this kind of attention. Ward's experimental rigor matters, then and now, because he transformed scientific and popular understandings of the rust.

The central puzzle was, as it had been with Morris, to determine the full life cycle of *H. vastatrix*. The phases internal to the coffee leaf were, by that point, reasonably well understood, but the phases external to the leaf had still not been settled. Morris had argued that the fungus's life cycle included an external phase in which the fungus covered the surface of the coffee plants in a microscopic mycelial web for several months. Ward quickly cast doubt on Morris's model. He collected samples of these mycelial threads in the field and studied them under a microscope. He concluded that these filaments were produced by four species of fungi, none of which bore any relation to *H. vastatrix*.[57] Furthermore, none of these external mycelia connected with the internal mycelia that *were* definitely *H. vastatrix*. Based on this, Ward discarded Morris's model and the control methods on which it was based.

To clarify the rust's life cycle, Ward conducted experiments on living plants under tightly controlled conditions. He collected rust spores from a lesion on an infected leaf. He then placed them in droplets of water on the leaf of a healthy coffee plant housed in a Wardian case. This glass case reduced the risk that the plant could be contaminated by other fungi. He found that the spores germinated in as little as twelve hours after contact with water, and the mycelium started forming inside the leaf two or three days after that. Within two weeks, this mycelium would produce a lesion visible to the naked eye. Roughly a week after that point—three weeks after the initial infection—the lesion would start producing and releasing new spores. Under ideal conditions, the lesion could continue producing spores for five to six weeks.[58] He calculated that a single lesion, produced by a single spore, could produce 150,000 new spores at a time. And a badly infected leaf could contain many lesions, which could cause the leaves to drop prematurely. Each individual spore thus carried the potential to cause tremendous damage.[59] As Darwin had done on a much larger scale, Ward demonstrated the tremendous cumulative power of small biological events.

Ward's field research shed new light on the rust's ecology. He showed how all the seemingly mysterious phenomena of the disease could be explained by the fungus's life cycle. To determine how the spores spread in the field, he placed sterile glass slides in various parts of the farm, on the ground and attached to trees. In a single water droplet collected this way, he found spores of fifty-one species of fungi (including *H. vastatrix*). His experiments with slides suggested that spores could travel up to 50 feet in a single journey. He carried out other experiments that showed how outbreaks of the rust were connected to wind and rain patterns. He had placed potted coffee trees around the veranda of his house and noted that "the plants placed on the side of the house more exposed to the wind suffered more than those that had been sheltered"[60] Extending these observations to the coffee estates, he argued that "a sudden appearance of the disease is closely connected with the *wind* and this connection is of exactly the same nature as what we should expect if the wind blows spores about."[61] Similarly, the veranda experiment showed that water was also important to the development of the disease: plants "placed on the edges of the verandah, and kept wetter on the whole (from drip, driving rain, etc) appeared to become more diseased than the sheltered ones," an observation that he later confirmed experimentally using coffee plants in Wardian cases.[62]

Using the pathogenic model of disease, Ward explained the patterns of rust outbreaks in Ceylon. He described a field that had been apparently free of the rust in April but was badly infected by June. Using temperature and rainfall records, Ward showed how rains in mid-May would have caused spores across the farm to start germinating. As expected, the first lesions in the field were observed two weeks after the rain. Ward's report discussed a number of real-life examples, showing how each outbreak could be explained mainly in terms of how wind and water shaped the fungus's dispersal and development. He argued that the connection between the fungus and its conditions of existence "were no more mysterious than that between the life of any organism and its environment: sow the spores of *Hemileia* on a proper nidus, and give them air, water, and warmth, and they germinate and flourish as do the seeds of coffee or an similar plant in damp, warm, aerated soil."[63]

Based on this, Ward's recommendations for rust control differed from the ones Morris had made. Ward argued that chemical control would only be effective under limited circumstances. The fungus was only vulnerable during the few hours after it had germinated but before it had penetrated the leaf tissues. To control the rust, then, the chemical had to be applied before the spores germinated. It needed to coat the leaf and stick to it. It had to be soluble so that it could be sprayed, yet it also had stick to the leaf during the heavy monsoon rains. It would need to be toxic to the fungus but not to the coffee plant or the soil. These stringent criteria eliminated most of the chemicals that planters had been trying. Ward enlisted a number of eminent planters in a series of spraying experiments, using various measures (weight of leaves and fruit produced) to assess how farms treated with chemicals fared in comparison to untreated farms. At the time, only sulfur compounds and particularly sulfur of lime met the criteria. In fact, planters found that the lime also acted as a manure, improving the life of the tree. Ward struggled to quantify the amount of benefit that applications of sulfur would give, but most experiments suggested that it offered planters at least some benefit if it was applied at the right time.[64]

Ward argued that the rust could best be controlled through preventive measures. "The problem of combating this disease," he argued, "is not a mere matter of quantity of chemicals and their efficacy in killing the fungus, but also in maintaining the strength of the tree and preventing reinfection."[65] Like some planters, Ward called for the careful cultivation of coffee—judicious pruning and manuring as well as the systematic elimination of infected leaves and trees. A few years before, planters had argued that manuring actually *cured* the rust. Ward argued that it did not; in fact, paradoxically, "of every basket of manure placed at the foot of the tree, a certain proportion must be looked upon as serving the mycelium of *Hemileia* for food."[66] Even so, careful manuring was still worthwhile because it would help the trees produce their leaves sooner and retain them longer, allowing the fruit and branches to develop more fully, which would mitigate the rust's effects. Outbreaks could also be controlled by planting windbreaks that would slow the dispersal of spores.

Ward's research was a scientific success, but it was a practical failure—at least as far as Ceylon's planters were concerned. The planters accepted the basic premise of fungal pathogenicity and Ward's account of the epidemic; most quietly abandoned their earlier models of disease. But from their perspective, Ward had failed to accomplish his main purpose: he did not offer them any tools to effectively manage the rust. He had shown them why most of their treatments would *not* work, but he had given little guidance as to what *would*. So the planters continued to innovate on their own. "We have now," wrote the planter G. A. Talbot, "all that can be taught us by scientific men about *Hemileia*, and it is for practical planters, in working their coffee, to study the disease. I must say, I think there is a good deal to be found out yet."[67]

In 1880, the planters of Ceylon founded a horticultural journal, the *Tropical Agriculturist*, that published reports summaries of horticultural research as well as reports from European planters across the tropics. In this sense, the *Tropical Agriculturist* was a tropical version of *The Gardeners' Chronicle*, which published horticultural pieces from both professionals and amateurs.[68] In the field, some planters continued to experiment with new methods of controlling the disease. One of the most widely reported of these involved the experiments of a planter named Eugene Schrottky who developed what he described as a "vaporization" technique that involved covering his coffee plants with a powder containing carbolic acid. In the local press, however, coffee planters argued heatedly about whether or not Schrottky's method did much to control the disease. In the end, it was never adopted on a large scale.[69]

Both the colonial and the imperial government were reluctant to sponsor any further scientific research into the rust. Ironically, Ward's research was so compelling that it shut down official interest in sponsoring further research. The planters had initially suggested that the government offer a substantial reward—250,000 rupees—to anyone who could find an effective means of curing or controlling the rust. The home government rejected the suggestion because, at the time, Ward was still at work. There did not seem to be any point in supporting private research when a publicly funded researcher was already working on the question. From Kew, Thiselton-Dyer argued that Ward had discovered "all that is practically important to know about the *Hemileia*," so the real question was how best to apply that knowledge. Further research on fungicides was pointless since "none can remedy the difficulty that having killed one crop of the fungus the plantation is still open to fresh infection." No further research was necessary to "enforce the common-sense suggestion to protect the coffee plants from spore-laden winds." He pointed out that when the French government had offered a similar reward for work on the phylloxera of the grapevine, the competition had been an "embarrassment" that had not offered any useful results.[70] After Ward's departure, systematic research on Ceylon ground to a halt, and planters were left to their own devices.

Coffee Collapses

Ceylon's coffee industry collapsed in two phases. Sinhalese smallholders felt the epidemic's impact much more swiftly than the Europeans did. Both the volume and value of smallholder coffee declined almost from the moment that the rust was first detected. According to one British official, during the coffee boom, their "luxuriant" smallholder coffee farms had generated enough revenue that many Sinhalese farmers chose to "regularly and cheerfully" pay their paddy taxes to the government in cash instead of in kind.[71] But in the early 1870s, native coffee farms across Ceylon often failed to produce much coffee at all. In 1871, native coffee production in the Central Province failed almost entirely; the following year, it failed in parts of the Uva and Central Provinces. Sometimes, smallholder production would recover in the following season, but it never returned to former levels. Between 1870 and 1880, total exports of smallholder coffee fell by two-thirds. By 1886, it had declined 93 percent. The epidemic thus ended several decades of Sinhalese entrepreneurship in coffee in which they had enjoyed a small but significant share of the wealth generated by the coffee boom.[72]

This collapse of smallholder production was not caused by the rust alone, but rather by a toxic combination of the rust and government policy. Ceylon's taxation policies had, as the geographer James Duncan observes, "been constructed around a set of environmental expectations that were dashed by disease."[73] Traditionally, the government had allowed local farmers to pay their paddy taxes in cash or in kind. In 1878, the government made it compulsory for peasant farmers to pay their paddy taxes in cash (eliminating the option to pay in kind), just when they were least able to do so. Unlike their European counterparts, they could not draw on outside capital to finance their shift to a different crop. The government expropriated the land of peasants who were in arrears, throwing many families into destitution. "Coffee was the stay of the villager," wrote a contributor to the *Tropical Agriculturist*. "From it he purchased clothes, saltfish, and other commodities that he needed, and he had a few rupees to put by." Burdened by the coffee rust and unforgiving government policy, many of these villagers could "hardly get one meal per day to eat." This transformed the labor situation in Ceylon. Before the crisis, European planters had imported labor from southern India because they could not convince the Sinhalese to work on their coffee estates. "Now," continued the article, "let it be known that labor is wanted, and you are inundated by men and boys at from 25 to 33 cents per day, and, in some districts, gangs of women go regularly to weed and do other work on the estates; shewing plainly the poverty of the people."[74] During the early 1880s, some locals starved, and others stole coffee from estates and other small producers. By 1885, "by far the greater number of the native [coffee] gardens have died out completely," wrote a British official in the Badulla province. "For the most part what was once flourishing gardens is now a wilderness of dry sticks."[75]

There is reason to think, though, that some local smallholders were more resilient than others. To be sure, they could not draw on the range of resources that estate planters could. They were less mobile than European settlers: their farms were often surrounded by coffee estates or Crown Lands, making it difficult for them to shift cultivation to another location (a strategy that estate owners used through the 1870s). And their farms tended to be concentrated at lower elevations, in the hotter and more humid lowlands that favored the growth and reproduction of the fungus. But the collapse of Sinhalese coffee production may not have been caused solely by disease. Rather, in the face of the rust and taxation, local farmers abandoned coffee for other cash crops, including spices, rubber, coconuts, and palm products more generally. According to an 1889 estimate, for example, there were more than thirty million coconut palms under cultivation in Ceylon, covering some 550,000 acres. The entire industry was in the hands of non-Europeans. In 1880, coconuts accounted for 9.4 percent of the value of Ceylon's exports; by the end the century they accounted for 16.4 percent.[76] Later in the 1880s, some local producers also began cultivating tea. So the "collapse" of Sinhalese coffee exports did not mean universal economic disaster. In fact, these producers drove the first important diversification of Ceylon's export economy away from coffee.[77]

The collapse of estate coffee began somewhat later. Until 1879, the value of exports remained comparatively high. Beginning in 1879, both the volume and value of coffee exports started declining rapidly and steadily. Broader transformations in the global coffee industry and a fiscal crisis in the United Kingdom pushed the price of Ceylon coffee below the economic threshold for many planters. Prices for Ceylon's coffee dropped amid a massive increase in global coffee supply, especially from Brazil. Demand for Ceylon coffee in the United Kingdom weakened in the face of a depression that lasted from 1879 to 1884. This turned British consumers toward cheaper (and lower-quality) coffee from Brazil. The economic turmoil in the United Kingdom ultimately contributed to the collapse of the Oriental Bank in Colombo, which financed much of the planting enterprise in Ceylon.[78] Still, coffee estates had weathered worse economic crises than this one; the price of coffee fell only 20 percent from its peak in 1879. The depression "hastened the collapse" of Ceylon's coffee industry, writes Vanden Driesen, "but on its own it could not have dethroned coffee."[79] The combination of economic and environmental crises made it impossible for many estates to survive.

Coffee prices had fallen to the point where, in many places, coffee farming was no longer possible. Planters who tried to sell their estates often found no buyers; abandoned (shuck) estates dotted the island. The untended coffee trees on the shuck lands provided places for the fungus to reproduce and spread to neighboring coffee farms. Daniel Morris had highlighted this as a significant problem in the 1870s, but neither the planters nor the government ever mobilized the resources to deal with it. Furthermore, it is not clear that a massive campaign to eradicate diseased coffee plants would ever have been feasible. There were simply too many infected coffee plants on the island—in plantations, in local gardens, and even semiwild coffee in the forests. In spite of the desperate call for rewards from the planters' association, many coffee planters accepted that it was no longer possible to cultivate arabica coffee profitably. "Why go on cultivating a product that has become unprofitable?" asked one planter. "This is not a financial crisis, nor a market crisis, that has overtaken the colony, but the sure result of the presence of a fatal disease of coffee. The end I would say is sure."[80] The colonial government also refused planters' requests for financial support. Some planters were left destitute, relying on local charities to obtain passage back home to Europe. Others, particularly those committed to growing coffee, migrated to new plantation frontiers in the Indian Ocean basin and beyond.

Figure 3.2 shows how the rust and the changing coffee economy combined to drive the collapse of Ceylon's coffee industry. The figures are expressed in percentages, taking 1870—the year after the rust was detected—as the benchmark. The zig-zag pattern of production shows the pattern of biennial bearing (described in the introduction) that is typical of intensive coffee production. It also shows, more subtly, the growing impact of the rust. Each passing season, both the peaks and the troughs of the biennial cycle were lower than in 1870. Even in the peak years, production never recovered to its 1870 levels. Economically, however, the 1870s were a highly profitable decade for coffee growers; coffee prices rose swiftly and remained high for most of the decade. Because of this, even as production shrank, coffee harvests were significantly more profitable than in 1870. As long as coffee prices remained high, farmers could coexist with the rust— at least over the short term. But when prices fell below a certain threshold, when credit dried up, and when Ward could find no cure for the rust, they quickly abandoned coffee. The lessons of Ceylon are clear: the rust alone seldom causes coffee production to collapse. The rust in combination with low prices, however, could be fatal.

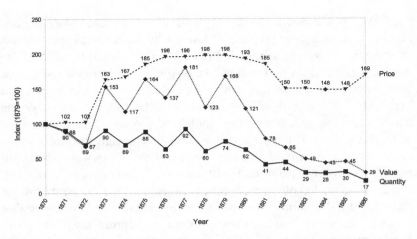

Figure 3.2. The collapse of coffee in Ceylon, showing the complex interplay between the rust and coffee prices between 1870 and 1886.

While the coffee rust signaled the end of coffee's dominance in Ceylon, it did not signal the end of the planting enterprise. Planters looked to other cash crops for salvation. Planters in Ceylon's low country experimented with a wide range of domestic and imported crops, including Liberian coffee, cocoa, vanilla, cardamom, rubber, and other crops. Liberian coffee, as we have seen, also proved to be susceptible to the rust. Ironically, it was the old botany—rather than the new—that ultimately rescued Ceylon's coffee planters. In the 1850s and 1860s, the Royal Botanic Gardens at Kew initiated a program to obtain seeds and seedlings of the cinchona tree, native to the Andes. The bark of the cinchona tree contained quinine, a medication that was used as an antimalarial drug. Some of these plants were sent to the Royal Botanical Gardens at Peradeniya in the early 1860s. Thwaites established a satellite botanical garden at Hakgala, about 80 kilometers southeast of Peradeniya, to acclimate the cinchona plants. Over the 1860s and 1870s, the Hakgala garden distributed more than 3.4 million cinchona seedlings to planters in Ceylon.[81] Many coffee planters planted some stands of cinchona along with their coffee. There was a brief cinchona boom in the 1870s and 1880s, which was only partly related to the collapse of coffee. Ceylon's cinchona boom was driven by more intensive exploitation of existing plants rather than the cultivation of new plants. Cinchona exports from Ceylon expanded from 1.3 million pounds in 1881 to 14.6 million pounds in 1886, before tapering off in the 1880s and 1890s.[82]

Ceylon's planters replaced coffee with tea. As with cinchona, the success of Ceylon's tea industry also depended on the old botany (introduction and acclimation) rather than the new. In the 1860s, a planter named James Morris visited the British-run tea plantations of Assam, with the support of Ceylon's governor, the planters' association, and Thwaites.[83] The Royal Botanical Gardens at Peradeniya propagated and distributed tea plants to anyone who was interested in taking up the crop. Before the mid-1880s, however, estate planters expressed little interest in tea. Tea and coffee were not complementary: they competed for the same land, labor, and capital.[84] Tea processing also required more capital and labor than coffee. But as planters confronted the twin shocks of the rust and declining prices, a space for tea gradually opened.

Some planters began to sow tea and then tear up the coffee plants once the tea trees had reached maturity. Tea cultivation also expanded into abandoned coffee farms and to areas where the forest had been cleared for coffee but had never been brought into cultivation. Furthermore, the tea plant was better suited to Ceylon's ecosystems than coffee. Tea flourished from sea level to altitudes even higher than those where coffee could be cultivated. And since tea was a leaf crop, as opposed to a fruit crop, it could be harvested continually rather than seasonally.[85] As the coffee economy declined, labor also became more readily available—the Tamil labor from India was gradually redirected from coffee to tea. Ceylon's tea industry also received a boost from growing demand for black tea in the United Kingdom, which was produced in India and Ceylon but not in China.[86] By the end of the 1880s, tea accounted for more than three-quarters of the exports from Ceylon's highlands; by 1900 it accounted for almost 99 percent of highland exports, while coffee had declined to just 1 percent.[87] While the leaf rust had been a catastrophe for coffee, plantations (of tea, cinchona, and other cash crops) continued to dominate the island's economy well into the twentieth century. Cinchona and tea "merely took over the edifice which their predecessor had constructed."[88] Planters had solved the crisis generated by the leaf rust through an ecologically radical (and economically conservative) reordering of Ceylon's landscapes.

The Lessons of Ceylon

Some accounts of the rust outbreak in Ceylon claim that the rust explains why the British drink tea instead of coffee. In their 1967 classic *Famine on the Wind*, the plant pathologists G. L. Carefoot and E. R. Sprot argued that "it was natural and loyal, then, for the English to take to tea drinking when the *Hemileia vastatrix* wiped out the coffee plantations of Ceylon."[89] They speculate that, were it not for the rust epidemic, "the English would likely still be using coffee by the hundreds of millions of pounds per year."[90] This compelling story has been widely repeated in academic and popular accounts of the rust ever since. It makes a vivid point about the broader repercussions of crop diseases. Unfortunately, there is not a shred of evidence to support this story, and plenty of evidence to contradict it. First, Great Britain did not import coffee from Ceylon alone. In 1884, for example, less than a quarter of Great Britain's coffee imports came from Ceylon. Second, throughout the period of Ceylon's collapse, Great Britain continued to import at least twice as much coffee as it consumed domestically. In some of these years it imported much more than that. Most of the excess imports were reexported to coffee-mad consumers in continental Europe, especially Holland, Germany, and Sweden. Third, and most tellingly, statistics clearly show that British coffee consumption changed little through the 1880s, even as coffee production in Ceylon collapsed. Between 1879 and 1887, production in Ceylon dropped 80 percent, but British consumption declined just 4 percent below the historical average for the preceding twenty years. Between 1880 and 1886, domestic consumption vacillated between 14,400 and 14,900 imperial tons.[91] In short, Ceylon's booms and busts had no discernable impact on coffee consumption in the United Kingdom. The British did drink considerably less coffee and more tea than people in the United States and continental Europe, but this had nothing to do with coffee production in Ceylon generally, or the rust specifically.

The problem with this story—beyond the fact that there is no evidence to support it—is that it directs our attention to the wrong place in the commodity chain. While rust epidemics often devastated coffee production at the origin, they rarely had any significant impact on global coffee consumption. As the global coffee trade grew and became more integrated over the nineteenth century, consuming countries typically imported coffee from a wide range of origins. According to an 1884 report, for example, Great Britain imported coffee from the Americas (Central America, Brazil, Colombia, the British and Spanish West Indies, Ecuador, Haiti, Mexico), from South Asia (Ceylon, India), from Southeast Asia (Philippines, Straits Settlements), from West Africa, and also from other industrial nations (United States, France, Germany, Holland, Belgium, Portugal).[92] Because major importers like Great Britain sourced their coffee globally, they were rarely vulnerable to production crises in a single origin. They could, and did, offset production shortfalls in one origin by increasing imports from other origins. Brazil, given its outsize role in global coffee production, was the only coffee-producing country whose production problems could disrupt global consumption.

The burdens of the coffee rust have primarily been borne by the farmers and laborers who produce coffee, not the consumers who drink it. This was true of the outbreak in Ceylon, and of every outbreak since then. As the rust spread through Ceylon, many European planters faced bankruptcy. The rust epidemic simultaneously reduced production and increased costs, making Ceylon's estate coffee less competitive in global markets. Planters had to mobilize a range of local and global resources to even sustain production in the face of the epidemic. The farmers who chose to continue producing coffee imported the latest chemical sprays, fertilizers, manures, plants, and other agricultural technologies, some of which offered a measure of relief but all of which meant additional costs. The Sinhalese coffee farmers and laborers suffered even more; they could not draw on the same range of tools as the settlers. And their misery was compounded by punitive government taxes, which came at the worst possible moment. For some laborers, such as indentured Tamils from southern India, the rust meant added labor, and exposure to the host of chemicals (sulfur, carbolic acid, and others) that estate owners applied to their farms. From the perspective of the coffee industry, the rust outbreak in Ceylon was an unmitigated disaster. It is a story of an almost unprecedented collapse, an ill omen to coffee producers around the world. Ceylon's farmers never found a way to coexist with the rust and thus abandoned coffee altogether.

Viewed from other perspectives, however, the rust's legacy is more complex. For example, although coffee production in Ceylon collapsed, the plantation enterprise did not. Science could not cure the rust, but it could offer planters an alternative crop. We can also glimpse the outlines of another story of resilience: the Sinhalese smallholders in the forested lowlands who shifted from coffee to coconuts. Neither large nor small farmers were permanently committed to coffee. If the rust made coffee cultivation unprofitable or burdensome, they were prepared to switch to other crops, where viable alternatives were available. But switching to a new crop was never simple. John Christopher Willis, a later director of the Ceylon Botanical Garden, speculated that "if tea had not then come in [to Ceylon], and proved very profitable, coffee would not have died out so completely as has been the case."[93]

The rust outbreak in Ceylon threatened coffee far beyond the island's shores. Ceylon's coffee farms were, directly and indirectly, connected to coffeelands across the Indian Ocean basin. In just a few short years, the coffee rust fungus had morphed from a local curiosity to a transnational emergency. Ceylon's coffee estates collectively became a vast incubator for the rust. A handful of infected trees unleashed a chain reaction that engulfed the entire island. Each infected tree could produce millions of spores each season. Clouds of rust spores spread across Ceylon's coffeelands and beyond. They would have been impossible to avoid or to contain. Some would have floated high on the air, carried by wind currents far beyond the island. Others would have attached themselves to the clothing of the people who passed through the ecosystem—to sarongs and dhotis, to Norfolk jackets and pith helmets. The spores would then have traveled comfortably by steamship and dhow, by donkey and railway, to other coffee farms, where some of them would have found purchase on coffee plants in their new home. Once the coffee rust had broken out in Ceylon, the global epidemic was inevitable.

CHAPTER 4

Arabica Graveyards

Asia and the Pacific

IN 1876, the American coffee trader Francis Thurber rhapsodized about the coffee landscapes of Java and Sumatra. He praised the "lofty mountains . . . deep gorges, rushing streams, fertile valleys, fine plateaus, jungles and forests, lowlands and highlands, hills and volcanoes, lakes and rivers, all contribute to make these islands the most attractive spots in the world." He recalled "the delightful picture" of the "hill slopes of Preanger, near Buitenzorg, with their thousands of shapely and luxuriant coffee trees in all stages of bearing."[1] In the late nineteenth century, picturesque and productive coffee landscapes like this dotted hillsides and mountainsides around the Indian Ocean basin.

The future prospects of coffee in the Eastern Hemisphere seemed good: global coffee consumers had developed a seemingly insatiable thirst for coffee. In 1889, the food writer Peter Lund Simmonds predicted that "the continued increase in the demand for coffee . . . will of necessity extend the present area of its cultivation largely into those belts of land which are favourable to the production of the plants."[2] At the time Thurber was writing, coffee was cultivated along an archipelago of coffeelands that ran from Madagascar through South Asia and out to Oceania. The Dutch East Indies, especially Java, was the heart of the region's coffee industry. In the latter half of the nineteenth century, this colony accounted for between 50 and 85 percent of coffee production in Asia and the Pacific.[3] Ceylon, southern India, and the Philippines also produced and exported signifi- cant amounts of coffee. Some of the region's coffees set a global standard for quality: Thurber described Javanese coffee as having "the highest place in the estimation of the American public, and with the single exception of Mocha, commands the highest price."[4]

By 1910, the rust epidemic had reduced many of these once-booming farms to arabica graveyards. The rust reached Java less than a decade after Thurber's visit; ten years after it was introduced, the island's arabica farms were in ruin. The same forces that produced the coffee boom also drove the coffee rust epidemic. Between roughly 1885 and 1905, coffee cultiva- tion in Asia and the Pacific declined sharply as farmers struggled to cope with global competition (especially from Brazil) and the coffee rust. They might have been able to cope with one or the other, but they could not cope with both.

Entwined Diasporas

The coffee rust epidemic was just one of many colonial epidemics that struck Asia and the Pacific in the nineteenth century. European colonial projects—and the technologies associated with them—had altered all three facets of the disease triangle in ways that promoted large-scale epidem- ics. European steamship and railroad networks moved pathogens farther and faster than they had ever traveled before, breaking down barriers of distance that had previously protected host populations from infection. The same networks had accelerated the diasporas of susceptible hosts— people, plants, and animals alike. And finally, colonialism had created new ecological and social conditions in which epidemics could flourish. In these years, epidemic diseases such as cholera, rinderpest, and the bubonic plague spread across the Indian Ocean and across the globe.[5]

The rust first traveled in a northern arc from Ceylon through India. The epidemic first appeared in Travancore, the southernmost coffee zone of India (and the one closest to Ceylon) in 1872, just three years after it had first been recorded in Ceylon. From Travancore, as one planter recalled, "the malady gradually travelled northward [along the Western Ghats] until it reached Wynaad, Coorg, Mysore, and the most northern limits of the industry" in the early 1880s.[6] Planters, laborers, and countless others regularly moved between the coffeelands of Southern India and Ceylon, providing the fungus with many opportunities to cross the Gulf of Mannar to the Indian mainland. From Travancore, it likely spread both anthropogenically and naturally.[7]

Ceylon's rust-wracked coffee farms threatened coffee farms thousands of kilometers away. The coffee rust traveled outward from Ceylon in two ways. The first was by wind. The infected coffee plants of Ceylon produced countless millions of spores, rising in invisible plumes above the farms. Some may have floated high into the atmosphere, and a tiny handful may have landed on coffee farms thousands of kilometers away. Such events were likely rare but have since been recorded for many kinds of rust.[8] The wind likely moved the rust to Western Sumatra. When it was first detected on the island in August 1876, it was already present over a large area, which suggests that many spores may have been transported. In March 1879, the rust appeared in West Java "in several very distant spots simultaneously," according to Rudolph Scheffer, director of the Buitenzorg Botanical Garden in the Dutch East Indies. This may simply be a reporting error, but coffee farmers and scientists alike would have been keeping a close watch for the disease.[9]

The pattern of outbreaks—along with some secondary evidence—suggests that humans were primarily responsible for the long-distance dispersal of the rust. Long-distance dispersal by the wind was possible, but at this historical moment, anthropogenic dispersal was almost certain. By the mid-nineteenth century, people were traveling regularly from infected regions to susceptible ones, moving spores and infected planting material along with them. The spores found rich populations of susceptible plants and the ideal environmental conditions in which to germinate and propagate, spreading the infection even further.

The parts of the Indian Ocean became much more tightly connected after 1850, and even more so after the Suez Canal opened in 1869. A series of technological and institutional innovations increased the speed and frequency of shipping connections in the region's ports. John Ferguson, editor of the *Ceylon Observer*, described Colombo as "the great central mail and commercial steamer port of the East." It was a major maritime hub: according to Ferguson "all the large steamers of the P. and O. Company, the British India, Star, Ducal and most of the [French] Messageries [Maritimes], the Clan, Glen, and other lines for Europe, India, China, the Straits, and Australia, call at Colombo regularly."[10] Voyages that had once previously taken months now took a matter of days or weeks.[11] The fungus could comfortably travel throughout this shipping network as a stowaway (see map 4.1). It could travel as spores attached to the clothing and goods that accompanied people traveling between distant coffee zones, or on the live coffee plants that some farmers regularly carried. Reviewing the rust situation in 1900, the French plant pathologist G. Delacroix—head of the plant pathology station at France's Institut National Agronomique—argued that the disease was primarily spread by "recently infected young plants."[12]

In some cases, the pattern of outbreaks points unambiguously to anthropogenic spread. Two of the first places where the rust was detected were the British colonies of Natal (1878) and Fiji (1879). They lay at the opposite poles of the British Empire in the Old World. Natal is in southern Africa some 6,800 kilometers to the southwest of Ceylon; Fiji is in Oceania, some 11,000 kilometers to the east. Even so, the fungus initially bypassed many other coffee-producing regions that lay closer to Ceylon. If the fungus had been spread primarily by the wind, then Fiji and Natal should have been among the last areas to be infected, not among the first. But both colonies had strong ties with Ceylon. In the 1870s, British planters migrated from Ceylon to both places. So too did migrant laborers from India, many

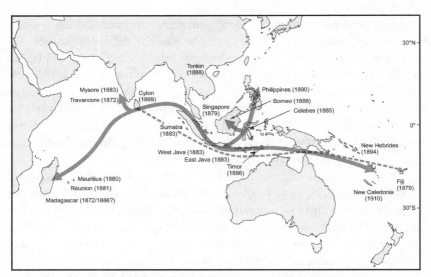

Map 4.1. Spread of *H. vastatrix* in the Indian Ocean basin. (Map by Marie Puddister)

of whom found work on coffee farms. Migrant laborers also inadvertently carried smallpox and cholera to Fiji in 1879, the same year that the coffee rust broke out there.[13]

In a little over a decade, from 1884 to 1895, the rust raced through the Indonesian archipelago and into the Pacific. The outbreaks followed the routes of the Netherlands India Steam Navigation Company, a costal shipping service that linked the main islands of the Dutch East Indies. From West Java (1884), the rust spread northward to Celebes and Borneo (1888), then Luzon in the Philippines (1890). It likely reached the Portuguese colony of Timor around 1886, New Guinea in 1892, and German Samoa and the French New Hebrides in 1894. Just twenty-five years after the initial outbreak in Ceylon, the rust had spread through the Indian Ocean basin and into eastern Oceania.[14]

The rust even reached as far as the Americas, although it was identified and destroyed before it could establish itself in the coffee farms there. In 1903, the fungus made its way from Java to Puerto Rico. Early in 1903, a Wardian case containing about a hundred coffee seedlings from Java arrived at the Mayagüez experiment station, recently established by the island's American colonial government.[15] The shipment was inspected by O. W. Barrett, an American scientist who worked at the Mayagüez experiment station. Barrett found that most of the coffee plants were badly infected with *H. vastatrix*. He sent a few infected leaves to the US National Herbarium, which confirmed that the infection was indeed *H. vastatrix*. Barrett immediately burned the infected plants and everything that had come with them, and he treated the remaining plants and soil with formaldehyde. Scientists later inspected the island's coffee zones and found them to be free of the disease.[16] This is the earliest documented example of a coffee rust outbreak being eradicated. It was possible because Puerto Rico had an effective infrastructure to detect and destroy crop diseases. The infected plants were identified quickly and the infection never got the chance to establish itself in Puerto Rico's coffee farms. It remained contained to the grounds of the Mayagüez experiment station.

While this event is now little more than a footnote, it reminds us that the vast coffeelands of the Americas were also vulnerable to the rust. If the rust outbreak in Puerto Rico had not been contained, the history of coffee in the Americas would look significantly different. Even at this early date, the world's coffeelands were tightly enough connected that the Americas were at risk. Had the rust managed to establish itself in Puerto Rico at that point and then spread to the mainland (as it surely would have), the course of coffee cultivation in the twentieth-century Americas, and the course of the global coffee economy, might look quite different. As later events showed, the rust, if left untreated, could cause substantial losses—as much as 30–50 percent in Brazil. Although it would have been a disaster for individual farmers, it may have helped the global coffee economy. By the early twentieth century, Brazilian overproduction had depressed coffee prices around the world, and would continue to do so. This rust, then, could have caused a shortfall that would have pushed up global prices, much the same way that frosts would do later in the century. But unlike the frosts, which were episodic problems, the rust would have been a permanent one.

Rust Belts in Asia and the Pacific

Although the rust had reached virtually every corner of Asia and the western Pacific, its impacts on coffee production varied widely. It is notoriously difficult to calculate losses in production, particularly for a crop as volatile as coffee. It is also, frequently, difficult to isolate the impact of the rust from other factors that also affected coffee production.[17] But some numbers can give a sense of the epidemic's scale. In the lowlands of Java and Sumatra, the rust reduced production by 30–50 percent in a single season.[18] Between 1883 and 1887, coffee exports from the Dutch East Indies dropped by half, even while the expansion of arabica coffee cultivation in the highlands offset some of those losses. In 1910, coffee exports in the Dutch East Indies were just 15 percent of what they had been in 1883.[19] The arabica coffee zones of coastal Madagascar and Réunion suffered a similar fate. Production in Réunion's already ailing coffee industry declined by 75 percent in the 1880s and 1890s.[20] After the rust appeared in the Philippines in 1892, exports plummeted from 16 million pounds to virtually nothing. In the early 1880s, the Philippines had been the world's fourth-largest exporter of coffee, but by the early twentieth century it was a net importer.[21] The rust appears to have been just one of several diseases and pests that afflicted coffee in the Philippines; reports also discuss infestations with worms and with a root borer.[22]

In each place, the outbreaks—and responses to them—tended to follow broad patterns. The severity of an epidemic at any given place depends on many factors, as Harry Marshall Ward had eloquently shown. It was dictated by rainfall, wind, topography, and cropping patterns, among other things. But we can focus on altitude as the key variable because altitude in the tropics is closely correlated with temperature, which in turn is a major factor in spore gemination. We can consider the rust's impacts at three altitudes—low, medium, and high belts. The specific altitudes that defined each belt varied from location to location, but the patterns remained consistent.[23]

At the highest altitudes, temperatures were cool enough to keep the rust in check without significant intervention. In Java, according to a survey conducted in the 1930s, this belt began at about 1,200 meters above sea level. The rust was not noxious between 800 and 1,200 meters, but yields were lower. On Java, this zone was limited to the area around the Ijen plateau in East Java; in Sumatra, it included the highlands near Padang in West Sumatra. Smaller enclaves of arabica could also be found throughout Asia and the Pacific.

In the middle belt, the rust—if left unchecked—could cause significant drops in arabica production in some years but good harvests in other years. Farmers learned to coexist with the rust, uneasily. In India, rust levels were low enough that coffee production remained commercially viable in the Nilgiri Hills, Coorg, and Mysore, where cooler temperatures and a dry season helped keep outbreaks in check. Significantly, other environmental and agricultural factors helped limit the rust's impact in India. Many, if not most, estate planters and smallholders there planted coffee under forest cover or artificial shade. The planter Robert Elliot argued that "the leaf disease may be reduced within practically speaking harmless limits if the coffee is judiciously shaded with good caste coffee trees." He also noticed that the long dry season in Coorg seemed "to kill off large numbers of the spores, and so mitigate the damage arising from the disease."[24]

Even so, production in the middle belt could be volatile. A wet season could provoke strong rust outbreaks and produce heavy losses. In 1883, an unusually heavy monsoon in Coorg triggered such a heavy outbreak that the coffee harvest failed almost completely. "I notice with pain a persistent increase in leaf-disease over the country," lamented one planter. "The trees are in the height of the sickness now; bare, leafless branches on withered stems and high easterly winds gripping and whirling way a few green leaves that were making an attempt to stem the shocks of the disease."[25] Scenarios like this could be dispiriting, even if the farm recovered and produced a full crop the following year. The need for effective control mechanisms was greatest in the middle altitudes; at the lowest altitudes control was virtually impossible.

The rust's impacts were the most devastating in the lowest belt, where the warm temperatures and rainfall favored the fungus's growth and dispersal. In many parts of Asia and Oceania, farmers had extended arabica cultivation almost to sea level. While these warm regions were marginal for the arabica plant, they were ideal for *H. vastatrix*.[26] In Java, farmers abandoned coffee cultivation at altitudes below 1,000 meters, while in the Philippines, the rust made it impossible to cultivate coffee at altitudes below 800 meters, which included most of the island's coffee farms.[27] In India, the rust wiped out the arabica farms in Wynaad and Travancore, the southernmost and warmest coffee zones, but it was less severe north of the city of Coimbatore (latitude 11° N), including the rich coffeelands of Mysore and Coorg.[28] "Such an affliction as this leaf disease," lamented one British planter in Travancore, "at once so rapid, devastating, and ruinous in its nature, I had never before seen, nor even dreamt of."[29] In Madagascar, the rust virtually wiped out European coffee estates on the island's humid eastern coast. Arabica coffee could still grow in these low, humid regions. But as the scientist P. J. Wester observed, "there is a very great difference between being able to merely *grow* coffee and to *produce it in such quantities that its cultivation becomes profitable*."[30]

As in Ceylon, those farmers who could do so abandoned coffee for other crops, typically cash crops. The economies of the Dutch East Indies and the Philippines had never depended quite as heavily on coffee as Ceylon's had. At middle and high elevations, farmers switched to cinchona, tea, and food crops.[31] In the humid lowlands, where the rust was the most severe, they switched to cocoa, pepper, and other cash crops. Most of these crops were, in any case, better suited to lowland environments than arabica. Rubber was a particularly popular alternative in places like Sumatra and the British colony of Malaya (whose coffee industry had never been particularly strong in the first place). In a curious parallel, the global rubber industry was itself shaped by debilitating commodity disease. The rubber plant is native to the Amazon River basin, but a fungus, the South American leaf blight, defeated all attempts to establish large-scale rubber cultivation in Brazil. Rubber flourished much better in the landscapes of Southeast Asia—then free of the leaf blight—than in the Americas.[32]

Individual and Collective Responses

In the early years of the rust outbreak, few places in Asia and the Pacific had the scientific or administrative infrastructures to manage a crop disease on this scale. Few places anywhere did; even in Europe and North America these infrastructures were still in their infancy. Large-scale, global crop diseases were a fairly new phenomenon, although they generated a lot of concern. Diseases and pests such as the potato blight and the phylloxera of grapes, among many others, mobilized farmers and governments to start seeking collective responses to collective agricultural problems. In the colonial context of South Asia and the Pacific, however, farmers—locals and settlers alike—received little support at first.

Even so, farmers quickly started to search for effective ways to control the rust. The documentary record for European planters is strong, which in itself is telling. If they could not find much help from local governments, they drew on global networks in their search for solutions. They tracked the spread of the rust, locally and regionally. As in Ceylon, they experimented with many different forms of chemical control, often imported from Europe and adapted to local conditions. They assembled collections of coffee varieties—both cultivated and wild—from across the tropics in the hopes that some might be rust resistant. They discussed disease-control practices in memoirs, manuals, and publications like the *Tropical Agriculturist*. It became apparent, however, that the rust did not have a simple, short-term solution. The rust was clearly a collective problem, not an individual one, and so required a collective response. In some places, farmer organizations—usually European farmers—lobbied their governments to study the rust and to provide farmers with an effective means of managing it.

Government responses to the rust epidemic were, in most places, limited and improvised. Government officials were often reluctant to support sustained agricultural research institutions, even though crop diseases and other agricultural problems were getting worse. Official responses to the epidemic were often haphazard and halfhearted, and almost always ineffective. When the rust arrived in Fiji, for example, the colony's chief medical officer was charged with studying and controlling the disease. One planter, under orders from the government, handed his estate to the care of the government, which "kept the estate in strict quarantine, and no one was allowed on it without having his clothes boiled, and his hat dusted with sulphur before leaving again, when the disease was at the same time all over the group." The government officials tried a range of fungicides and other techniques to control the disease, to no avail. The irate planter whose farm had been subjected to the quarantine argued that in fact, the chief medical officer likely "carried the disease with him to those places which before were free from it."[33]

States were slow to recognize and adapt to the new waves of agricultural diseases and pests that swept across the tropics in the nineteenth century. Previously, state-sponsored biological research—like that carried out at botanical gardens—had focused on introducing and acclimating crops and conducting inventories of flora and fauna. As events in Ceylon showed, the naturalists at botanical gardens had neither the training nor the resources to confront these large-scale outbreaks. While botanical gardens had a long history, agricultural experiment stations were comparatively new, even in Europe and North America. The first dedicated agricultural experiment stations were established in Germany in the 1830s; in the following decades, governments founded experiment stations across Europe and North America. Scientists at these stations used the tools of emergent scientific disciplines such as agricultural chemistry, economic entomology, and plant pathology to solve practical problems in the field. But in the colonial world, the infrastructure for agricultural research was not as well developed or as well funded.[34]

Governments in the British colonies were, on the whole, disinclined to offer support for coffee research. Even in the throes of a catastrophic outbreak, the government of Ceylon had only reluctantly agreed to hire Daniel Morris, then Harry Marshall Ward. And Ward's reports seemed so compelling that some governments dismissed any further research as futile. In British India, coffee planters organized and lobbied their local governments for research support. The Madras presidency and the Kingdom of Mysore maintained small research centers, but these focused primarily on acclimating exotic plants rather than studying diseases of existing plants. The smaller provinces of India often could not afford anything in the way of agricultural research.[35] Planters' associations in Wynaad and Coorg asked their respective governments to contract experts to study the rust and were rebuffed. The government of Madras "declined to incur any expenditure in engaging an expert. This decision will probably not recommend itself to the [growers'] association in particular, nor to the coffee planters in general," argued the editors of the *Tropical Agriculturist*, "but the emphatic opinion of Dr. Cunningham that no benefit was likely to accrue to the planters from the proposed investigation no doubt justified the government in refusing to extend its support in the direction indicated."[36]

The climate for agricultural research was much stronger in the Dutch East Indies. In 1817, the colonial government had founded a botanical garden in West Java: the 's Lands Plantentuin in Buitenzorg (Bogor) near Batavia (Jakarta). In 1870, the garden—under the directorship of the botanist Rudolph Scheffer—started to research key agricultural problems, partly to support the growing European plantation enterprise in the colony. When Scheffer died in 1880 (at age thirty-six), he was succeeded by the dynamic Melchior Treub. Under Treub's leadership, the Buitenzorg garden became the leading global research center for tropical botany, both pure and applied.[37]

From 1876 onward, the Dutch colonial gardens employed at least one permanent coffee researcher. In 1876, the year the rust appeared in West Java, Scheffer hired the colony's first dedicated coffee specialist, William Burck. For several decades Burck, in close collaboration with coffee estate owners, studied virtually every facet of the rust and surveyed its spread through the colony. Like his contemporary Harry Marshall Ward, Burck used the experimental and field techniques of the new botany. He explored a range of disease-control strategies, some of which I discuss below. In 1893, Treub obtained a grant of land and funding to establish experimental fields and a research laboratory dedicated to studying coffee hybrids and varieties. European coffee planters provided some of the operating costs. In 1900, a coffee research station was established at Bangelan in East Java, closer to Java's coffee district. In 1905, another scientist—P. J. S. Cramer—began working on coffee and coffee diseases. Cramer, who had studied under the pioneering geneticist Hugo de Vries, came to Java with cutting-edge experience in botany, breeding, and genetics. Burck, Cramer, and their colleagues inaugurated the first long-term programs of coffee research.[38]

The Promise and Limits of Chemical Control

Early in the rust epidemic, farmers—especially settlers—experimented with chemical controls. In principle, chemical control seemed like a good idea since an effective control would allow them to continue farming coffee. The chemical industries in Europe were making an ever-wider array of chemicals available, some of which had proved useful in treating crop diseases in Europe. In practice, however, finding a chemical that was effective against the coffee rust in the field proved to be challenging. To be effective, the chemical had to kill or contain the fungus without harming the leaf or the plant. In the earliest experiments, infected trees were treated with powdered or vaporized acids, as well as various sulfur compounds (which Daniel Morris and others had used in Ceylon), mercury, and tobacco juice.[39] In Java, Burck conducted experiments with "chloride of iron, sulphate of copper, nicotine, boric acid, sulphate of quinine, extract of cinchona bark, cupric hydroxide, mixtures of lime and sulphur, and cupric sulpho-steatite" with varying degrees of success. One of Burck's experiments involved having laborers use small glass tubes to apply sulfuric acid directly to lesions on infected coffee leaves. This experiment proved problematic, however, because "the quantity of acid cannot be regulated, and it is also liable to get upon and burn the hands of the operator." This observation points to a broader issue that the literature only discusses in passing: the impact of these chemicals on the laborers who would apply them in the field. Regardless, none of these chemicals seem to have been widely adopted by farmers.[40]

In Ceylon, a planter named Eugene Schrottky developed a system for dusting trees with carbolic powder. In Fiji, a German planter named Jacob Storck claimed to have cured infected coffee trees on his farm using a vapor of carbolic acid. Storck used fixed vaporizers (tins placed on top of poles) to disperse carbolic acid vapors through the farm. Storck claimed that, nine months after having been treated, his coffee trees had "grown three times the size, are in full spike, and splendid condition."[41] The editors of the *Tropical Agriculturist* greeted Storck's claims with some caution, noting that the "success of the plant depends upon very many circumstances" and recommending "cautious experiment on a small scale before embarking on a large one."[42] Planters elsewhere tried these and other remedies (fig. 4.1) without much success. A committee of planters in Ceylon conducted field trials using Schrottky's remedy and concluded that "carbolic acid, as hitherto applied, cannot be regarded as supplying any practical cure for leaf-disease." They concluded that "it would be far more practical to spend money on pruning or manure than on any topical treatment that has yet been suggested."[43] In 1900, the French plant pathologist Georges Delacroix reviewed these various chemical treatments and concluded that "if none of these substances were wholly inefficient, the results they achieved were inadequate."[44]

In 1885, a newly discovered copper fungicide seemed to offer coffee growers just what they were looking for. The Bordeaux mixture, a blend of lime and copper sulfate, had been developed in southern France in the early 1880s to control the downy mildew of the grapevine. Like *H. vastatrix*, the downy mildew (*Plasmopara viticola*) was a fungal disease that spread through spores and infected the plant by germinating and penetrating the plant tissue. The Bordeaux mixture prevented the spores of the downy mildew from germinating. In Europe, the Bordeaux mixture was quickly and widely adopted to control other fungal diseases—most significantly the

Figure 4.1. Spraying sulfur in a coffee estate, Dutch East Indies. (Nationaal Museum van Wereldculturen, Netherlands, collection no. TM-30000136)

potato blight.[45] Richard Sadebeck, the director of the Hamburg Botanical Garden, conducted laboratory experiments demonstrating that the Bordeaux mixture could kill *H. vastatrix* spores in minutes. In the early 1890s, some planters in India sprayed the Bordeaux mixture on their coffee "with promising result."[46]

The Bordeaux mixture performed acceptably in areas like India, where rust levels were moderate, but it proved ineffective in areas where rust was severe. The Bordeaux mixture was most needed during the rainy season, argued Delacroix, yet the "violent downpours" would "wash the leaves and rapidly carry off the deposits of copper that protected them from infection."[47] The French botanist Edouard Raoul disagreed, arguing that most of the rainfall would run off the upper surface of the leaves and have little impact on the lower surfaces. On the other hand, Raoul noted that if the rains did not wash the fungicide off the plants, then the monsoon winds often would.[48] At the turn of the century, scientists and planters were working to develop a copper-based fungicide that could adhere to the coffee leaves even during the monsoon rains. One option was the "sweet mixture" developed in 1889 to control the mildew of vines in France. This new mixture consisted of the Bordeaux mixture further mixed with an adherent of

1 percent molasses. Experiments with the sweet mixture in Réunion and Madagascar found that it showed "an extraordinary adherence," the blue spots (characteristic of the compound) persisting "in spite of the violence of the rains in this region."[49]

Experiments such as these were promising, but chemical controls were an almost complete failure in the field before the 1920s. Some challenges were technical. Technologies developed in Europe—the chemicals, the equipment, and the knowledge about how best to use them—could not simply be transferred wholesale to a different context. They had to be adapted to reflect the particularities of the crop, the disease, and the ecosystem. Sprayers developed to treat diseases of the vine in Europe delivered the spray downward. The coffee rust, which infected the underside of the coffee leaf, required a sprayer that could deliver the spray upward. Furthermore, the sticky chemical sprays developed to adhere to the underside of the coffee leaves were so thick that they often clogged the sprayers' nozzles. Still, such technological obstacles were not insurmountable. In India, Matheson and Company imported Strawsonizer spray engines that, in combination with the right sprays, were effective in controlling the rust. Planters in Java imported Broquet sprayers, which had been developed to control diseases of the grapevine in France. Those worked reasonably well but required a high volume of liquid. In response, Java's chief engineer of public works and the chief inspector of railways developed a new device adapted for the coffee farms, which "had a stronger pump and used less liquid," meaning that it would be easier for laborers to carry. So foreign technologies could, in principle, be adapted for local conditions, or new technologies could be developed on the spot.[50]

But the main difficulty with chemical control was financial, not technical: it was too expensive for most coffee farmers. Chemical control required a considerable investment in technology, in chemicals, and, above all, in labor. In Réunion, for example, it was estimated that treating a hectare of land with a copper spray would require six man-days of labor and 300 liters of spray. And for the sprays to be effective, at least in Réunion, they would need to be applied at least three times per year. The specific amounts and cost of labor varied across Asia and the Pacific, but the fundamental challenge remained the same. In Réunion, farmers abandoned the copper sprays, finding that "the result did not cover the expense of spraying."[51] Planters in India found that while spraying could help control the rust, it was "quite impracticable" to treat whole estates, "both from the cost and the immense amount of labour that would be required."[52] Georges

Delacroix concluded that "the excess of labor required by some of these operations renders them quite onerous, and has inhibited their broader spread."[53] Before the mid-1910s, these challenges meant that only a few coffee planters adopted chemical control on a large scale.[54] Even today, cost remains a chronic problem for chemical control, although not always an insurmountable one.

Costs also made other control methods impracticable. For example, Burck developed a device—essentially a hole punch—that was designed to cut out infected spots on leaves, leaving behind nothing but healthy tissue. The British scientific journal *Nature* celebrated this discovery: "The economic value for Java of the discovery of these remedies, should they prove successful, can scarcely be over-estimated . . . perhaps Dr. Burck has saved Java." Farmers, however, greeted this innovation with derision. "How practical is this remedy[?]" asked the editors of the *Tropical Agriculturist*. "A coolly would take a week to a bush, and then the leaves would drop off to make room for another crop of the spores to fasten on."[55] In Réunion, the French agronomist J. Buis noted that this procedure "worked perfectly in a greenhouse or a garden, but is unworthy of attention from the perspective of the farm, because its excessive cost, and the need to repeat it several times each year, render it essentially impractical."[56]

These economic challenges were aggravated in the mid-1890s, when global coffee prices plummeted after Brazil enjoyed several bumper harvests. Even as prices fell, the costs of labor and inputs tended to remain stable, increasing the relative costs of disease control. Buis found that such challenges produced "a certain despair that paralyses that spirit of enterprise among the creoles, because for many years they have seen all of their crops suffer in the agricultural and economic domains."[57] And while Buis was speaking specifically about the farmers of Réunion, his words could apply equally to coffee farmers throughout Asia and the Pacific. They had experimented and innovated continually through the 1880s and 1890s, but the combination of technical and economic challenges in the early years of the twentieth century discouraged further innovation in chemical control.[58]

The Quest for Resistant Coffees

Resistant arabicas were—and remain—a holy grail for farmers since, in principle, they would not require costly control measures. Rust-resistant arabicas would allow farmers to continue farming arabica the way they had always done, and to continue producing the high-quality coffees that fetched high prices on the international markets. So—just as Ward had done in Ceylon—farmers and scientists in Asia and the Pacific imported cultivated arabicas from around the world in the hopes that one of them would resist the rust. In India, the trading house Matheson and Company "went to great expense in introducing coffee seed from Brazil, Venezuela, Costa Rica, and Jamaica" to see whether any of these would be resistant to disease, to no effect.[59] In Java, Burck inoculated "all sorts and varieties [of coffee] cultivated in the East Indies, or introduced from Brazil, and all species in cultivation" and found that they "are equally liable to the attacks."[60] Still, farmers and scientists continued their search for resistant coffees.

Farmers in India found several varieties of arabica that appeared to show resistance to the rust. The botanical history of arabica coffee in India differs from that in other parts of the Indian Ocean basin. The coffee plant had been brought to India and cultivated there long before Europeans arrived. According to one legend, it was introduced to it by a Muslim monk, Baba Budan. Whether or not the legend is true, Muslim pilgrims likely transported arabica seeds or plants from Yemen across the Arabian Sea to the Malabar Coast. These arabicas were of a slightly different genetic stock from the ones later introduced by the Europeans. Indian farmers cultivated these in the shaded forests of Mysore, and in household gardens and village plots.[61] When European settlers established farms in the Western Ghats, they often obtained seeds and seedlings from these gardens near the plantations. For example, a planter named Sandy Bain explained that in order to ensure that he had "good caste [coffee] trees," he "visited the native gardens and marked the trees he wished reserved for seed which, when ripe, he personally saw picked and carried to the estate."[62] So the European farms were built on coffee germplasm that generations of indigenous farmers had selected and adapted to local conditions.

European planters, in turn, circulated these indigenous cultivars through their own informal social networks.[63] Before the rust arrived, they preferred one local cultivar in particular known to them as Old Chik, an affectionate nickname that indicated its origin near the city of Chikmagalur. This cultivar, however, proved to be highly susceptible to the rust. As Old Chik plants failed, planters turned their attention to other indigenous arabica cultivars. They appropriated several other Indian arabica cultivars: the Nalknaad, the Munzerabad, the Coorg, and the Golden Drop. The Coorg coffee had originated in the same stands of coffee as Old Chik, noted the author E. G. Windle, but "somewhere, at some time, a type of arabica was produced [that was] decidedly superior to the original 'Chik.'"[64] Significantly, the Coorg arabicas seemed to be more rust resistant than the other varieties. After 1880, coffee planters in India began to replace Old Chik coffee with Coorg coffee, which remained the dominant variety planted in India until the early twentieth century.[65] Coorg coffee was cultivated across the coffee farms of Mysore and Coorg until the early decades of the twentieth century, when it, too, began to lose its resistance to the rust.[66] The Coorg coffees were also taken to some other parts of the Indian Ocean basin but were never cultivated on a large scale.

Farmers elsewhere in Asia and the Pacific also experimented with new coffee species that Europeans had collected in Africa. Before the 1790s, arabica coffee was the only coffee known to Europeans. As Europeans began to explore and colonize the coast and interior of Africa, they encountered new species of coffee. In 1876, the British botanist William P. Hiern listed fifteen species of coffee, eight of which were new. In the following decades, Europeans continued to collect, name, and distribute other species of coffee. Most of these coffees remained little more than botanical curiosities, but a handful showed commercial promise. The first species other than arabica to be cultivated on a large scale was Liberian coffee, *Coffea liberica*.[67] This species was a wild lowland coffee, native to the tropical lowlands of Western Africa. When former slaves from the United States colonized Liberia, they found large stands of this plant growing wild. It seems that they first harvested the coffee for local consumption. From the 1830s onward, they exported modest but growing quantities of this coffee to the United States, where it was primarily used as a cheap filler coffee. But before the 1870s, it was not cultivated commercially anywhere else, and it accounted for only a microscopic fraction of the global coffee trade.[68]

Liberian coffee—both as a crop plant and a commodity—made its global debut in the 1870s. French botanists had collected the plant in Gabon in 1865 and sent it to the Muséum d'Histoire Naturelle shortly thereafter. Joseph Hooker at the Royal Botanic Gardens of Kew obtained seeds from Liberia later in the 1870s and distributed Liberian coffee to colonial botanical gardens across the empire. The London-based nurseryman William Bull imported Liberian coffee separately and started offering it for sale in 1873. European coffee planters and botanical institutions sometimes acquired Liberian coffee through both public and private distribution networks. Liberian coffee remained little more than a curiosity until the rust started to threaten lowland cultivation. At that point, coffee farmers—particularly European estate owners—started to take an interest in it. Figure 4.2 is from a small book promoting Liberian coffee, touting its advantages over the smaller and sicklier arabica plant.[69]

Unlike arabica, Liberian coffee was a hardy lowland plant. It flourished much better than arabica in lower and warmer areas, the very kinds of places where the rust had attacked arabica most severely.[70] In the field, *C. liberica* proved to be less susceptible to the rust than arabica. Infected plants showed some lesions but seldom suffered the same level of defoliation as arabica. The species also had other agronomic advantages. The coffee expert Frederick Wellman later described Liberian coffee as "a plant that can produce crops under some of the crudest and most thoughtless management"; it was commercially viable even where "Hemileia, worn out soils, and other growing conditions have driven out Arabica."[71] If it did receive adequate care, it could yield 25–50 percent more coffee per acre than arabica.

But Liberian coffee also presented some new challenges. The plants were much more variable than arabica. The problem was genetic: Liberian coffee is allogamous, meaning that it can only be fertilized by pollen from a different Liberian coffee plant. "The planter therefore accustomed to the cultivation of [arabica coffee] was little prepared for the boundless variety of the Liberian species," wrote an anonymous contributor to the *Tropical Agriculturist*. "The different specimens differ from each other in every possible way: taking one hundred plants grown from seed, put out on the same day, in the same soil, and treated exactly the same in every way, for two-and-a-half years, there is a vast range of variety in the height at which they begin to branch . . . then there is a vast range in the size, form, and colour of the leaf. . . . So in crop yielding they are as unlike as in other respects."[72] Planters, traders, and roasters had to learn how to cope with this variability, both on the farm and farther up the commodity chain.

Traders had to find a place for Liberian coffee in global markets. The plant's variability made it difficult to produce a consistent product; the tree produced unevenly sized beans that were difficult to mill. The drink it produced tasted different from the arabica that consumers knew; traders were, at first, not sure what to make of it. Late in the nineteenth century, a Dutch journalist observed that Liberian coffee was "more fragrant than the common variety [arabica], but when it is tried for the first time there may be something peculiarly unpleasant about it." Still, all was not lost: "after a couple of days this difference is no longer perceptible."[73] Taste mattered a

Figure 4.2. Liberian coffee plant, as compared with Arabica coffee. (In Crüwell, *Liberian Coffee in Ceylon*, frontispiece. Image © Royal Botanic Gardens, Kew)

great deal because buyers paid a premium for produce that met or exceeded accepted standards of taste (and conversely, paid less for produce that did not meet those standards). But taste is, to a certain extent, mutable. So like arabica coffee itself, carefully cultivated and processed Liberian coffee fetched high prices as a fancy coffee through the 1880s and 1890s. Some coffee estates on Java could sell their entire crop to American buyers at a higher price than arabica. Poorly processed Liberian coffee was sold as filler, especially to the US market, but also in the United Kingdom, Holland, and France. This paralleled the global markets for arabica, where washed arabicas from Java fetched much higher prices than cheap Brazilian "Rio" arabicas.

In spite of Liberian coffee's uncertain promise, the coffee rust epidemic drove lowland farmers almost everywhere in Asia and the Pacific—from Madagascar to New Caledonia and almost everywhere in between—to experiment with Liberian coffee. Planters in Ceylon experimented with Liberian coffee in the lowlands; some farms were established in the late 1870s but were abandoned in the mid-1880s, seemingly because the plants there had succumbed to the rust. The crop was most successful in the lowlands of Java, whose arabica farms had been particularly hard-hit by the rust. Between 1893 and 1901, Liberian coffee production in Java grew from 37 metric tons to 1,840 metric tons. For a time, it seemed that Liberian coffee would be a commercially viable replacement for arabica.[74] In 1896, the planters' association in West Java proclaimed that in their region "Liberian coffee has taken the place of Arabian coffee almost completely. There is a strong likelihood that, as a consequence, this part of our beautiful island will reach the same degree of prosperity it enjoyed during the flourishing period of Arabian coffee."[75] Their optimism about Liberian coffee's future was, however, misplaced.

Liberian coffee's heyday ended all too soon. In the mid-1890s, simultaneous economic and ecological crises struck. First, in many places, Liberian coffee plants appeared to lose their resistance to the rust, just as Coorg coffee had done. In retrospect, it appears that *H. vastatrix* had adapted to Liberian coffee. Problems were reported in India in 1887 and then in British Malaya in 1894. The breakdown of resistance there coincided with the opening of a steamship connection between Malaya, Ceylon, and South India. In the Dutch East Indies, the rust first appeared sporadically on Liberian coffee farms in the mid-1890s, and after 1897 it started causing serious losses.[76] Observers noted that the rust behaved differently on Liberian coffee than it did on arabica. Some individual Liberian coffee trees were almost completely defoliated, while others escaped unscathed. This reflects Liberian coffee's greater genetic variability, which meant that on any given farm some trees would be much more resistant than others. Even so, the effects of the rust were cumulative; Cramer noted that by the time a field of *C. liberica* was "12 or 15 years old, the majority of the trees had become valueless."[77]

Just as Liberian coffee was succumbing to the rust, coffee planters also faced an economic crisis. Liberian coffee had prospered during a time of high coffee prices in the 1880s and 1890s largely caused by instability in Brazil. By 1897, however, Brazilian coffee was flooding the market, driving global coffee prices downward. Over the 1890s, the price of Liberian coffee dropped from twenty cents per pound to six cents per pound; prices continued to slide in the following decade. Faced with these simultaneous economic and ecological challenges, many planters abandoned Liberian coffee and switched to tea or cinchona in the highlands, and to rubber in the lowlands. Liberian coffee's brief heyday as a major alternative to arabica had come to an end, although farmers across the lowlands of Africa, Asia, and the Pacific continued to cultivate it on a small scale.

Host and Pathogen Transformed

The rust epidemic in Asia and the Pacific left some curious genetic legacies in the form of new kinds of coffee and new strains of the fungus. In places where Liberian coffee had been planted near arabica coffee, farmers in Asia and the Pacific—in India, the Dutch East Indies, Réunion, and Ceylon—reported finding spontaneous hybrids of *C. arabica* and *C. liberica*. In the wild, these two species were unlikely to hybridize because they inhabited different landscapes and flowered at different times. But when they were naturalized into new environments, exposed to similar environmental conditions (especially rainfall, which shaped flowering patterns), and planted close to one another, the chances of cross-pollination became much higher. Research in New Caledonia has since found that in areas where several coffee species were cultivated together, up to 4 percent of the individuals were hybrids. This percentage is small but significant.[78]

In India, a planter named Brooke Mockett first noticed some hybrids on his farm in the late 1880s, and he began to collect seedlings from them. When John Cameron, the superintendent of the nearby Lal Bagh Botanical Garden, visited Mockett's farms, he concluded that "the variation in the different seedlings now in fruit is truly remarkable, and leaves me in no doubt as to the interspecific nature of their origin." Significantly, some of these plants "showed no sign of being attacked by leaf disease. In fact, all hybrids appear to be proof against the latter type."[79] At about the same time, farmers in the Dutch East Indies had also identified a spontaneous *arabica* × *liberica* hybrid, which came to be known as the Kalimas hybrid after the estate in Central Java where it was first discovered. Like the hybrids in India, the Kalimas hybrid seemed to remain free of the rust while neighboring arabica and Liberian plants were badly affected.[80] Coffee planters in the Dutch East Indies sometimes found such hybrids on their farms and forwarded them to the coffee experiment station at Bangelan for further research. Some of these hybrids showed promise; their taste supposedly united "the strength, 'body' of the liberica with the aroma of the arabica. Small lots of these hybrid coffees often obtained a premium on the local market."[81] But the Kalimas hybrid's commercial potential proved limited; after a few years it also succumbed to the rust.

So farmers and scientists continued their search for a rust-resistant arabica or some acceptable substitute. The supposedly resistant arabica cultivars did not prosper over the longer term. Liberian coffee's variability presented both agricultural and commercial problems, although—given the right economic conditions—these problems were not insurmountable. For a brief moment in the late nineteenth century, an agricultural and economic niche for Liberian coffee had opened. But as Liberian coffee succumbed to the rust, and as Brazilian arabica production surged and prices dropped, that niche largely disappeared. The *arabica* × *liberica* hybrids represented a wholly new kind of coffee with considerable potential, in theory. In practice, they remained experimental. Among other things, hybrid coffees were difficult to propagate, a problem that would challenge breeders for decades to come.

Research on the supposed breakdown of rust resistance in Liberian coffee revealed that the rust fungus itself was changing. This was one of the first significant scientific insights about *H. vastatrix* since Ward's work in Ceylon. Planters had argued that Liberian coffee had succumbed to the coffee rust because the plant itself had degenerated and its resistance to the rust had broken down. This thinking was common among tropical planters at the time. On newly cleared forest lands, their crops often performed well for a generation or so before yields began to diminish and various diseases and pests began to appear. They attributed this to a gradual weakening of the plant. In response to the apparent breakdown of Liberian coffee in the Dutch East Indies, planters argued that the solution was to import more vigorous strains of the plant from Africa, to bring "new blood" into the supposedly degenerated population.[82]

In Java, the Dutch botanist P. J. S. Cramer conducted a global experiment to better understand degeneration. He imported Liberian coffees from equatorial Africa and also from the colony of Dutch Guiana (present-day

Suriname) in South America. These plants had all prospered in their native range, but when introduced to the rust-infected zones of Java, they all proved to be equally susceptible to the rust. In fact, the plants grown from seed collected in South America "suffered from heavy attacks of leaf disease in the nursery, often to such an extent that it was deemed necessary to remove them, since they threatened to infect neighboring Liberian plants (in the nursery) from domestic seed." Cramer concluded that the problem did not lie in the plant. When he sent seeds from "so-called degenerated *C. liberica* in Java . . . to Dutch Guyana . . . they produced excellent plantings with no signs of deterioration." Based on this simple yet elegant global experiment, Cramer concluded "that if the equilibrium between the plant and the fungus had been broken in favour of the latter, it was not because the coffee had become weaker, but because the fungus had become stronger and had adapted itself to the new coffee."[83]

Cramer's insight reflected innovations in the discipline of plant pathology. In the late 1890s, researchers in the United States and Sweden independently discovered strains of wheat rust (*Puccinia graminis*). Although the strains could not be distinguished under the microscope, each strain specialized in attacking some grasses but not others. In the 1890s, the Swedish botanist Jakob Eriksson identified six different strains of *Puccinia graminis*, differentiating them according to their various host varieties and species. In Europe and North America, the study of these strains (commonly known as "special forms" or "physiologic races") developed considerably in the early twentieth century. The American plant pathologist E. C. Stakman published pioneering work on the origin and development of races of wheat rust. Stakman's work revolutionized wheat farming, as breeders developed new varieties of wheat that were resistant to particular races of rust. Stakman's innovative work also shaped the whole field of plant pathology.[84]

Cramer's discovery showed how the switch from arabica to Liberian coffee produced genetic changes in the population of *H. vastatrix*. The host (the coffee plant) and the pathogen are in a continuing, dynamic relationship. Changes in the host plant population induced changes in the pathogen population, and vice versa. In the fields of Liberian coffee, as with arabica coffee, the fungus epidemic produced countless millions of spores. Over the years, a small proportion of these spores spontaneously mutated, which is normal in such large populations. Few of these mutations produced any significant changes, but just one of them was enough to overcome the S_H3 resistance gene in Liberian coffee. This new race of rust then reproduced far more successfully on Liberian coffee than the original race(s) did, causing greater defoliation and economic damage as it gradually made its way through growing regions. The coffee rust fungus had become, at the genetic level, at least partly anthropogenic.[85]

Like Harry Marshall Ward's work, Cramer's groundbreaking scientific insight did not suggest any practical control measures. Cramer argued that it would be possible to develop rust resistance in *C. liberica* through selective breeding: by collecting seed from "healthy trees in badly-infected fields" and then propagating and selecting the offspring for resistance over several generations. But the pathogen evolved quickly, and coffee breeding was slow and expensive. As coffee-breeding efforts later in the twentieth century showed, it could take a decade or more to develop an agronomically and commercially viable new coffee variety. The farmers who cultivated Liberian coffee did not have the time; Cramer's insights came too late to save Liberian coffee. By about 1910, planters in Asia and the Pacific, faced with seemingly intractable economic and ecological problems, abandoned Liberian coffee, although small-scale production did continue in many places.

Arabica Graveyards

By the eve of World War I, the coffee rust had contributed to the dramatic contraction of the coffee industry in Asia and the Pacific. The region produced less than 5 percent of the world's coffee, down from almost 30 percent in the mid-nineteenth century. In part, this reflected a relative decline amid the explosive expansion of coffee production in Brazil during the latter half of the nineteenth century. Coffee producers in the Old World simply could not compete with Brazil's seemingly endless supplies of primary forest, its expanding transportation infrastructure, and its ample pool of labor, as well as its rust-free farms. The coffee rust epidemic was not the sole cause of this decline—other factors such as scarcities of land, labor, and credit also contributed—but by reducing production and increasing costs, the rust epidemic made it harder for coffee producers in Asia and the Pacific to compete in global markets.[86]

The rust had also contributed to an absolute decline in production. It drove many farmers out of coffee production altogether, which likely accounts for the largest decline over the long term. It checked any further expansion of coffee cultivation in the lowlands. And even in the places where coffee production did survive, it continued to cause losses—at least episodically. The rust outbreaks had also slowly started to transform coffee-cultivation practices in Asia and the Pacific. Farmers had imported new varieties and species of coffee into the region and had started experimenting with chemical control. It had become clear that the booming years of pioneering coffee cultivation—in which farmers benefited from the rich soils of newly cleared forests and from landscapes free of diseases and pests—were now over. After thirty years of trial and error and systematic research, scientists and farmers in Asia and the Pacific had yet to find an economically viable method of managing the rust.[87] But they had learned about coffee and about the rust. After about 1910, some of this research produced results that would provide farmers with new tools for dealing with the rust and—over the long term—transform the global coffee industry.

CHAPTER 5

Robusta to the Rescue

BETWEEN 1905 and 1940, coffee production in much of Asia and the Pacific began to recover. In part, the region's coffee economy was buoyed by the stabilization of global coffee prices, largely the result of control schemes developed by Brazil. But the recovery was not driven by higher prices alone. The coffee rust, now endemic across the region, made it impossible to cultivate arabica coffee on the scale that it had been before the outbreak. After 1905, however, coffee farmers—in conjunction with scientists—developed effective ways of coping with the rust. The most significant of these was the development of the rust-resistant robusta coffee (*Coffea canephora* var. *robusta*) as a commercially viable replacement for arabica coffee. By the 1930s, coffee production in Asia and the Pacific had more than doubled from its early twentieth-century nadir, and the region had also doubled its share of global coffee production.[1]

Part of this recovery was driven by changes in the global coffee economy. Coffee prices had collapsed during the mid-1890s as new production from Brazil flooded global coffee markets. In some years, global coffee production exceeded global demand, even as demand continued to grow. At the beginning of the century, Brazilian producers, in conjunction with state and federal governments, tried to unilaterally control global coffee prices using a strategy known as "valorization." Brazil had a large enough market share of the global coffee production (more than two-thirds) that the state could control supply, and therefore prices, by warehousing their excess production in years when production was high. In years when production was lower, they could then release the stored coffee onto global markets. The Brazilian state of São Paulo, one of the largest coffee producers, banned the planting of new trees and encouraged farmers to diversify into cotton. The first valorization scheme was launched by the coffee growers of São Paulo to address the global oversupply caused by the bumper crop of 1906. This succeeded in its short-term goals, so the national government underwrote other valorization schemes. In the 1920s, valorization became a permanent feature of Brazilian coffee policy. Over the short term, Brazil's coffee-defense policies did shore up global coffee prices, which remained comparatively high until the mid-1930s. The average price of coffee doubled between 1899 and 1911 and had doubled again by 1925.[2] By shoring up prices, Brazil was also, unintentionally, underwriting the expansion of its competitors. Between 1910 and 1937, Brazil's share of global coffee production declined by slightly more than 20 percent, although that still left Brazil with almost half of global coffee production.[3] The most important beneficiaries were the producers of "mild" arabicas in Colombia and Central America, but Brazil's control schemes also benefited coffee producers in Africa and Asia.

In those rust-ravaged regions, stable prices gave coffee producers some breathing room to develop effective strategies for sustaining and even expanding production amid the coffee rust and a host of other environmental challenges. Farmers could no longer count on fertile landscapes or environments free of diseases and pests. It became apparent that dealing with the rust would require constant innovation. Farmers in Asia and the Pacific had, of course, been innovating constantly since the rust epidemic first broke out, but only with mixed success. In the early twentieth century, farmers' organizations in India and the Dutch East Indies started to provide sustained funding for coffee research. Governments in each colony—under pressure from farmers—also initiated or expanded coffee research programs of their own. Although these stations may, in retrospect, seem comparatively small, they drew on an expanding global infrastructure of science. Globally, the agricultural sciences were flourishing; between 1900 and 1930, some six hundred agricultural experiment stations were founded. Scientists at the coffee research stations regularly drew on ideas, techniques, and tools developed at these other agricultural experiment stations and research laboratories. For example, they paid close attention to how scientists in Europe and North America dealt with the stem rust of wheat. They also built on the lessons learned from other tropical commodities, especially rubber and sugar cane. Commercial nurseries also continued to play a critical role in circulating coffee germplasm.

Preserving Arabica in India

In the early decades of the twentieth century, Indian coffee entered a long period of decline. Coffee farms were buffeted by the rust, as well as volatile international prices and demand, and growing competition from other producers of high-quality "mild" arabicas—especially British East Africa, Colombia, and Costa Rica. From 1896 to 1916, the acreage under coffee production dropped by a third, from about 300,000 acres to around 200,000 acres. The volume of exports also declined steadily. Nonetheless, in the 1920s the acreage under coffee stabilized as rising internal demand offset volatile international demand. Declining global coffee prices also helped stimulate domestic demand. Indian producers were "relying more and more on the local Indian markets and less and less on the export trade," wrote India's trade commissioner in London, since "better prices have secured at home than abroad." By the 1930s, as much as two-thirds of coffee produced in India was consumed domestically. Over the 1920s, then, farmers had a strong incentive to keep producing coffee and, where possible, to increase production. To do this, they had to address the coffee rust.[4]

Coffee research focused on maintaining the production of high-quality arabicas in the face of the coffee rust, a plague of the borer beetle, and other challenges. After decades of official indifference to research, coffee planters organized the United Planters Association of Southern India (UPASI) in 1893. As coffee prices recovered after World War I, the UPASI opened a coffee experiment station at Siddapur in the Western Ghats. Between 1919 and 1926, the station carried out research on spraying. Gradually, the government of Mysore—the major coffee-producing state—also started funding coffee research. In 1925, it founded the Mysore Coffee Experiment

Station in Balehonnur, in the heart of coffee country in India: the Chikmagalur District in the Western Ghats. It received part of its funding from the UPASI and the rest from the state, through a tax on coffeelands larger than 15 acres. Significantly, its board of directors included Indian and European planters, and the station said explicitly that "it is our intention to enable every coffee planter, large and small, to make use of the information and results which are being so carefully collected, by intensive scientific work," a claim that its research work demonstrated in practice.[5] The UPASI closed its station in Siddapur and instead funded the salary of a coffee research officer at the Mysore station. The association hired a young British botanist named Wilson Mayne, who arrived at the coffee research station in 1928 and helped launch a wide-ranging research program to help coffee planters in Mysore cope with the endemic rust.[6]

In the early twentieth century, farmers in India continued to search for a rust-resistant arabica. They watched their fields for interesting varieties and also imported coffees from abroad. Individual farmers had nurseries where they cultivated promising varieties. They were particularly interested in hybrids of Liberian and arabica coffee because, in principle, they could combine the taste of arabica with the partial rust resistance of the liberica. In practice, as researchers in the Dutch East Indies had already found, these hybrids often produced coffee beans of uneven and poor quality. One hybrid, known as Jackson's coffee, seemed promising but in the end proved to be too irregular. "No hybrid that had ever come into our notice," wrote the planter E. G. Windle, "had succeeded in producing a regular bean, that is to say a bean regular in size and comparable in market value, to good arabica."[7] Windle succinctly described the basic threshold for a new variety to succeed in India. While Indian coffee could not compete with Brazil in terms of quantity, it could compete in terms of quality. Farmers were therefore unwilling to cultivate any coffee that would harm the quality—and therefore the profitability—of Indian coffee in international markets.

Another Mysore variety, known as Kent's coffee, enjoyed more success. A farmer named Kent discovered a resistant arabica tree in one of his fields. He collected seeds from this tree and established nurseries to propagate and sell it. Planters in India preferred Kent's coffee, perhaps because it yielded "an average of over 2 ½ times as much as Jacksons." Kent coffee plants produced more-regular, better-tasting beans.[8] This is one of the first times that we see an attempt to sell (to "privatize") a particular strain of coffee. It was a commercial success and was planted widely across India after 1918. Kent arabicas resisted the rust fungus reasonably well until the late 1920s, when they too began to lose their ability to resist the disease.[9]

Like P. J. S. Cramer in the Dutch East Indies, Mayne reframed the series of breakdowns in resistance as the emergence of new races of rust, each specialized in attacking particular cultivars.[10] It was the pathogen that had changed, not the host. Whereas Cramer had shown this using experiments in the field, Mayne furthered Cramer's insights with experiments in the lab. He collected leaves of Coorg and Kent arabicas (and other selections) and inoculated them with spores of *H. vastatrix*. He found that some coffee varieties would resist *H. vastatrix* completely, while others were highly susceptible. He identified two distinct strains of the rust; Coorg coffee was susceptible to both, while Kent coffee was only susceptible to one. He argued that susceptibility to the rust was controlled by two genetic "factors" in the coffee plant. The discovery was significant enough that it was published in the journal *Nature* in 1932. Mayne subsequently identified four races of *H. vastatrix*, which corresponded to different combinations of these two resistance factors. These factors seemed to follow Mendelian patterns of inheritance.[11] Later researchers correlated Mayne's factors with the $S_H 3$ gene (which is derived from *C. liberica*) and the $S_H 2$ gene. Researchers have since identified more than twenty races of rust, which correspond to combinations of nine resistance genes.[12]

Since the pathogen was mutable, the prospect of finding a perfectly and permanently resistant arabica plant was unlikely. "Resistant coffee selections are never completely immune to infection," wrote Mayne, "and there is always the risk of a 'breakdown' if a previously rare strain of the fungus becomes common or a new strain develops."[13] The planter E. G. Windle took some—perhaps unjustified—comfort in Mayne's discovery, expressing "a slight feeling of relief that it is not all equally virulent."[14] But Windle and his peers did understand the broader challenge: "however strong and outstanding in good qualities, a strain of coffee may be, continual in-breeding and universal use must tend to gradually weaken its disease resistance and bring it to the point where its productive value is eclipsed by some younger and stronger rival." After World War II, Mayne's insights provided a critical intellectual foundation for research programs into breeding for rust resistance. But over the short term, breeding did not provide farmers with any solution that would allow them to coexist with the rust.

By the late 1920s, chemical control seemed to be more promising for coffee farmers in India. In principle, spraying did offer farmers a short-term solution to the rust. But in the previous decades, chemical control had remained largely experimental. Spraying was expensive, difficult, and labor-intensive. Global coffee prices were too low to make any of this worthwhile. Interest in spraying had revived between 1912 and 1917 when a researcher named T. Narasinga Rao found that spraying gave "dramatic results" in controlling another coffee disease—the black rot.[15] Mayne's colleague M. J. Narasimhan had also found spraying to be effective in controlling a catastrophic disease of the palm tree. Innovations in spraying technology also helped make chemical control viable. Mayne and his team did comparative studies of coffee-spraying equipment, of fungicidal chemicals, and of the chemical adhesives necessary to ensure that the fungicide stuck to the bottoms of the coffee leaves.

Sometimes these innovations were adapted from other plantation industries. In the early 1930s, coffee planters in Mysore started using a kind of sprayer that had previously been used in the rubber industry. Mayne recalled that this technology transfer had taken place through a personal relationship: "a progressive planter from Malabar married a coffee estate proprietress in Mysore, and it was from that happy union that the equipment imported for the control of one disease was adapted for the control of another."[16] While this makes for a compelling—and possibly true—story, this was likely not the only way that spraying technologies moved from the rubber industry to the coffee industry. The relative fortunes of the rubber and coffee industries also helped fuel these transfers. When the rubber industry in southern India collapsed in the early 1930s, coffee farmers bought up used sprayers from rubber farms at steep discounts.[17]

Mayne also studied the seasonal behavior of the coffee rust in the field, to determine the optimal time for spraying.[18] Ever since Harry Marshall Ward's research in Ceylon, farmers and scientists alike had understood the general principle that sprays had to be applied before the spore had germinated. But in practice, it was difficult for farmers to know when, exactly, germination took place. Before Mayne's work, they usually determined the timing through trial and error—often error. "Who was to tell the farmer," asked the planter E. G. Windle, "that however well and truly he had sprayed a field, spore inoculation had taken place a week before?"[19] Over several seasons, Mayne developed statistical studies of the rust's behavior over several seasons, which allowed him to correlate rust outbreaks with patterns in Mysore's climate and rainfall. He concluded that the epidemic went through four major periods over the course of a year. Mayne's research on the seasonal periodicity of *H. vastatrix* offered farmers practical guidelines about when it was best to spray, and it also provided specific data for the immediate locale of the experiment station.[20]

With these new scientific and technological tools, farmers across Mysore took up spraying in the early 1930s. At that particular time and place, spraying almost seemed to be a panacea. It could control the coffee rust, the black rot, and dieback. Leslie Coleman, Mysore's director of agriculture, estimated that a well-conducted spraying regime could increase production by 200 pounds per acre at a cost of twenty-five rupees per acre. With coffee prices at forty-five rupees per hundredweight in the early 1930s, planters who sprayed stood to earn an additional sixty-five rupees per acre. "This is a development almost wholly confined to the past ten years," wrote Coleman, "and it has played an important role in enabling Indian coffee-planters more especially in the less-favored areas, to withstand the very severe strain of the economic depression from which this crop along with almost all others, has suffered in recent years."[21] Some planters were equally enthusiastic. "I cannot imagine anyone," wrote the coffee planter E. G. Windle, "who has once seen the effect of proper spraying at the right season thinking of discontinuing it, but, supposing that expenses had to be cut down, I would sooner stop manuring than spraying."[22]

Spraying—and other technological inputs—exacerbated the gulf between smallholders and estate producers. Mayne recognized that "the profitability of spraying varies from district to district," and that "there are probably estates and areas where the value of increased crop will not greatly exceed the cost of spraying." But he concluded that it "may prove to be the only means of economic salvation in a period of low prices, such as the one through which we are passing."[23] And spraying did seem to offer economic salvation—to planters who could afford to spray. It seems that larger farms did become more productive: over the 1930s the acreage in coffee farms larger than 10 acres increased by almost a third, while total production increased by 60 percent. But economic salvation was not as readily available to smallholders: between roughly 1910 and 1940, the number of coffee smallholdings declined by more than half.[24] While large farmers could offset the challenges of diseases, pests, and declining prices by intensifying production and boosting their overall productivity, many smallholders could not. As would happen in Latin America several decades later, spraying programs (and intensified production generally) magnified the differences between small and large producers.

The Robusta Revolution

Coffee production the Dutch East Indies also declined sharply in the early twentieth century. The rust had devastated coffee farms; by 1908, the production of "government" coffee had declined by two-thirds from its nineteenth-century peak. The rust, among other things, contributed to the decline and ultimate abolition of forced coffee cultivation in 1905. In Java, the highland arabica estates remained largely unaffected by the rust. But in the middle belt, where periodic rust outbreaks could still wreak havoc, the long-term future of coffee production was much less clear. Liberian coffee was not the solution that farmers had hoped it would be, and they gradually stopped planting it. Exports continued to decline; average exports from 1905 to 1909 were just 60 percent of the previous five-year average. Along with this absolute decline, the colony's share of global coffee production also declined. For most of the nineteenth century, the Dutch East Indies had been the world's second-largest coffee producer. By 1910 it languished in seventh place, surpassed by producers of high-quality arabicas in the Americas: Colombia, Guatemala, Mexico, El Salvador, and Haiti.[25]

Planters in the Dutch East Indies had, from the very earliest days of the epidemic, worked closely with state scientists at the Buitenzorg (present-day Bogor) Botanical Gardens—although sometimes their interests clashed. Melchior Treub, the director of the Buitenzorg garden, had convinced planters' associations to fund commodity research stations, which were nominally private but had research agendas largely under his control. The Society for the Improvement of Coffee Agriculture in Amsterdam had helped finance the first dedicated coffee experiment station in the Dutch East Indies in 1896. Between about 1900 and 1930, the network of coffee research centers on the island expanded rapidly. The state and private planters alike clearly felt that science had a critical role in sustaining coffee production. Private organizations founded three stations: the Malang Experiment Station in the highlands of East Java, the Boeski Experiment Station in the lowlands of East Java, and the Experiment Station of the General Union of Rubber Planters of East Sumatra. In 1911, the colonial Department of Agriculture established the Government Coffee Experiment Station at Bangelan, about 50 kilometers from Malang. Beyond these four major institutions, some of the larger coffee estates had large experimental gardens of their own. Most coffee research in the Dutch East Indies focused on coffee breeding and improvement; researchers spent little time exploring other methods of rust control. Coffee breeding included a range of activities, such as acclimating wild and cultivated coffees, selecting viable cultivars, hybridizing different coffees, and addressing the challenges of propagating these new coffees. This network of public and private research stations made the Dutch East Indies the world's leading center for coffee research.[26]

These breeding efforts focused on replacing the failing arabica and Liberian coffees with new, improved coffees. Researchers experimented with some of the new varieties and species of wild coffee from Africa that began to circulate globally in the late nineteenth and early twentieth centuries. After the Berlin West Africa Conference (1884–85), Europe's leading colonial powers moved swiftly to consolidate their territorial claims in Africa. As Europeans consolidated their control of the interior, they encountered many wild species of coffee. Between 1890 and 1920, many of these wild coffees were taken to botanical gardens and commercial nurseries in Europe and then disseminated elsewhere in the tropics.[27] These plants, as in earlier periods, traveled through vast and complex commercial and scientific networks in their journey from Africa to other parts of the world. For example, between 1890 and 1910, the Cultuurtuin in Java received new coffee species from colonial botanical gardens such as the Botanical Gardens at Singapore, the Royal Botanic Gardens at Kew, and the French Jardin Coloniale in Nogent-sur-Marne. It also received coffees from commercial nurseries, such as the Horticole Coloniale and Serres Coloniales in Belgium. Other coffees were introduced to Java directly from Africa, either from institutions such as the Jardin d'Essai in Libreville (Gabon) or from individuals.[28] These coffees were little more than botanical curiosities as long as arabica and Liberian coffee remained economically and ecologically viable. But as arabica and then liberica succumbed to the rust, people started to take a closer look at the new species.

One of these, then known as *Coffea robusta*, attracted the interest of coffee growers on Java. The Horticole Coloniale in Brussels marketed this coffee under the "robusta" name to reflect the plant's "great hardiness, its vigorous growth, and most of all its resistance to all coffee diseases."[29] Robusta has since been reclassified as a variety of the species *C. canephora*, a species with several varieties of commercial interest. Like Liberian coffee, *C. canephora* is not self-fertile, which helps explain its wide diversity of forms. Its wild range spans western tropical Africa, the Congo basin in west-central tropical Africa, and eastward to the Victoria-Nyanza in modern-day Uganda and Tanzania. It was primarily a lowland coffee, growing best from just above sea level up to 1,500 meters.[30] The plant had been naturalized by some African peoples long before European colonialism; in

Uganda, robusta beans had been used in religious rituals and as an energy food.[31] Europeans collected plants of *C. canephora* in a variety of locations, including Bukoba (modern-day Tanzania) and Uganda at the eastern end of the plant's range, and along the Congo and Gabon Rivers at the western end. The *C. robusta* marketed by the Horticole Coloniale had been collected in 1893 on a small European farm in the interior of the Belgian Congo. Just a few years later, it had arrived in Java, via Brussels.[32]

The first robusta coffees were planted in Java in 1900, both by private planters and at the government station. An agent of the Soember Agoeng estate had seen robusta plants when he visited the Horticole Coloniale in 1900. Later that year the estate imported some 150 seedlings to Java. Other coffee farmers quickly followed suit. This introduction involved more than passively moving a plant from one place to another. From the beginning, farmers conducted systematic field tests on robusta, observing how it performed at different altitudes and in different soil conditions. They selected and propagated plants that performed well in the fields, eliminating unpromising seedlings from the nurseries.[33]

At first, there was little to distinguish robusta from the many other coffees then being brought to Java, although it did seem to have one key feature of interest. The catalog of the Horticole Coloniale had advertised it as being resistant to the rust. In the field in Java, it proved to be not wholly rust resistant, but still tolerant. For a few years, researchers worried that this tolerance might break down, much as it had with arabica and Liberian coffees. But it did not. Robusta coffee had other agronomic and commercial advantages. It could be planted at comparatively low altitudes, and the plants produced significantly more coffee than either Liberian or arabica coffee. Its fruit was smaller than that of Liberian coffee, with a thinner skin, which made robusta considerably easier to process. And robusta beans, if processed properly, had a mild flavor that (as it later turned out) would work well in blends with arabica.[34]

As robusta's promise became apparent, coffee research started to focus on acclimation and improvement. Breeders at the two private stations tried to develop commercially viable hybrids of arabica and robusta. Their goal was to produce a plant that combined arabica's flavor with robusta's disease resistance. Although simple in theory, this goal proved difficult to achieve in practice. Breeders at the Government Coffee Experiment Station, under the leadership of P. J. S. Cramer, devoted most of their attention to improving robusta coffee—particularly to developing high-yielding strains. At first, scientists used breeding techniques that were little different from those used by coffee farmers. But in the mid-1910s, they started to develop more complex techniques for selecting and propagating coffee plants. These included large-scale grafting and controlled pollination. All three stations released improved robustas to planters.[35] Looking back on this research, the Dutch scientist F. P. Ferwerda concluded that "the result of more than thirty years of this selection work is that families have been obtained which exceed the original material in yield by 50% to 100%, and which can always be reproduced pure by means of . . . clonal seed-gardens."[36]

As robusta's advantages became apparent, planters in the Dutch East Indies quickly replaced their surviving stands of arabica and liberica coffee with robusta (see fig. 5.1). Robusta was first planted as an estate crop in 1905. Between 1907 and 1912, wrote Cramer, "most of the estates with arabian in the middle belt cut out the old species and replaced it with robusta." Figure 5.2 shows just how quickly this transition took place. By about 1915, Cramer wrote, "this coffee crop passed the highest figure ever reached by *C. arabica*" in the Dutch East Indies.[37] Robusta coffee had, for estates the middle belt, solved the problem of the coffee rust. And robusta production continued to expand even after the rust-wracked middle belt

Figure 5.1. Contract workers in a robusta farm, Java, 1912. (Nationaal Museum van Wereldculturen, Netherlands, collection no. TM-30001892)

had been replanted. Robusta coffee, which had first been deployed as a replacement for arabica, had taken on an agricultural and economic life of its own. Estate owners started to cultivate robusta in lowland environments where arabica had never been cultivated before. Rubber planters started cultivating robusta as a catch crop, which would provide some short-term revenue while they waited for their rubber trees to reach maturity. Robusta coffee shifted the geography of coffee cultivation in the Dutch East Indies, moving it largely from the highlands to the lowlands.[38] By 1935, robusta accounted for almost 94 percent of the coffee cultivated in Java and 93 percent of coffee cultivated in Sumatra.[39]

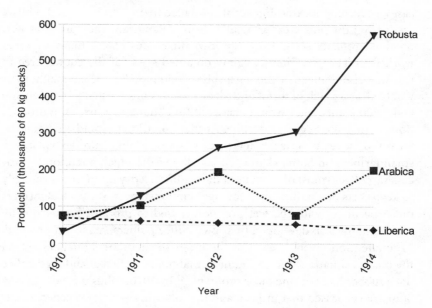

Figure 5.2. The robusta boom in Java, 1910–14. Robusta production quickly overtakes arabica and Liberian coffee production, while arabica stagnates and Liberian coffee virtually disappears.

Although robusta had been introduced and developed as an estate crop, it was quickly adopted by local smallholders, especially in Sumatra. In 1917, the Dutch finally abandoned their efforts to force local communities to cultivate coffee. But the end of forced coffee cultivation did not mean the end of smallholder coffee production. While smallholders resisted forced coffee cultivation, they were more than happy to cultivate it freely when it was worth their while. They did so even without the benefit of the scientific support that estate producers received. Most of the research on robusta had focused on intensive production methods, characteristic of the Dutch-owned estates. Leslie Coleman, on visiting the Dutch East Indies from India, observed that "European coffee interests are, at present, very much better served from a scientific standpoint than are native ones."[40] Even so, smallholders on Java and Sumatra realized that robusta's agronomic characteristics—its rust-resistance, its suitability to warm environments, and its low labor requirements—all made it appealing.

In Sumatra, smallholders began cultivating robusta around 1915, after they had seen how the crop performed on European estates.[41] In some cases, government extension agents provided them with improved robusta seeds from the public experiment station at Bangelan. They probably also obtained robusta seeds from the lowland estates where many of them worked as laborers. They certainly obtained seeds of the rubber tree in this way, simultaneously fueling a rubber boom on Sumatra. Smallholders would clear a patch of forest and plant robusta coffee, usually between 200 and 1,500 plants. They would harvest it for about five years, until production on that site began to decline. At that point, they would abandon the farm and move on to clear a new patch of forest. Unlike European planters, small farmers on Sumatra did not usually devote much attention to processing coffee—most of them used the traditional dry method, presumably to keep costs down. But given the right circumstances, some local farmers did experiment with the wet processing used to produce higher-quality coffees. Some also developed their own coffee pulpers, made out of wood. "The attention given to each of the crops seemed largely dependent on the market situation," wrote Cramer; smallholders often abandoned coffee once rubber had become more profitable.[42] By 1926, robusta production in Sumatra surpassed that in Java, and the following year it exceeded 1 million piculs (a picul is roughly equivalent to a 60-kilogram sack of coffee), or about 60,500 metric tons. Commentators suspect that this figure understates smallholder production because records were so poor.[43]

For all of robusta's many agronomic virtues, it had some significant commercial limitations. Like Liberian coffee, it encountered challenges because of its taste. In the early 1920s, Arno Viehover at the USDA's Bureau of Chemistry asked various "representatives of the American coffee trade" for their thoughts on robusta. One said, dismissively, that robusta coffee "should be taken out and dumped in the Chesapeake Bay," while others—somewhat more diplomatically—found robusta to be "tasteless and bodyless," concluding that "it has not the value that we desire in our coffee."

But this negative opinion was not universal. Others described robusta as having "wonderful cup value" and as being "fancy in style and cup quality." One common theme—and an important one for the fate of robusta in the US market—was that robusta was "really better than low grade Santos or Rio" coffees or even "better than Rio, Victoria, and Central American coffees." Unlike the low-grade Brazilian arabicas, in particular, robusta "has no objectionable features."[44]

Global markets quickly found a place for robusta coffee. It was a cheap alternative to the arabicas, whose prices were being propped up by Brazilian valorization schemes. Buyers in the United States had purchased robusta coffees from the first moment that they came onto the market. They received something of a setback in 1912, when the New York Coffee Exchange refused to take delivery of robusta coffees from the Dutch East Indies. The official USDA trade definition of "coffee" included only seeds of *C. arabica* and *C. liberica*.[45] That same year, for the same reason, the New York Coffee and Sugar Exchange decided to stop trading in robustas. These decisions likely reflected concerns over the adulteration of coffee (and food more generally) that had led to the Pure Food and Drug Act of 1906. The Dutch scientist C. J. J. Van Hall saw darker commercial forces at work: he suggested that the New York Coffee Exchange was boycotting robusta because merchants saw it "as a dangerous competitor of the Santos coffee, over which the American merchants have a control, while robusta imports are not under their control."[46] Clearly, not all buyers in the United States shared the coffee exchange's disdain for robusta. In 1919, the United States imported about 1 million bags of robusta (61,000 metric tons), which amounted to about half the Dutch East Indies' coffee exports and 10 percent of US coffee imports.[47] The robustas also found markets in Europe: by the 1930s they accounted for more than a third of French coffee imports.[48]

Robusta's commercial success was also made possible by companies who started marketing coffee in roasted and ground blends rather than whole beans. Supermarkets such as A&P and large coffee roasters such as Chase and Sanborn promoted packaged blends in large advertising campaigns. In this market, the coffee's brand mattered more than its origin.[49] To produce these blends, coffee companies employed expert blenders whose task was to produce a final product with consistent aroma and taste, using a combination of coffee beans from various origins. Price was also an important consideration in developing a blend, and this was where robusta found its niche. Since robusta coffee consistently fetched a lower price than arabica, roasters started using it in inexpensive blends. Previously, they had used commodity-grade Brazilian arabicas to save costs, but by 1935 the robustas from the East Indies were, according to coffee expert William Ukers, "being used in many instances in place of Brazils." He described "typical low-priced coffee blends" in the United States as consisting of "50 per cent washed Robustas and 50 per cent Colombian Consumos."[50] Roasters in Europe did the same thing. "The consumer as a rule does not possess the palate of a connoisseur," wrote one Swiss coffee merchant, "thus making it easy to mix Santos with Java robusta . . . instead of with the more expensive varieties. Such a blend makes it possible to gain a good profit."[51]

Viehover concluded that "the time when coffee could be limited to beans obtained from plants of *Coffea arabica* and *Coffea liberica* has passed." He argued that "*Coffea robusta* has established its own" because of its "rapid growth, early and prolific yield, resistance to coffee blight, and many other desirable qualities."[52] Because the Bureau of Chemistry scientists decided that robusta coffee was "a true coffee," it could be sold as such under the Food and Drugs Act, with the caveat that it "should not be sold as Java coffee or under any other form of labeling which tends either directly or indirectly to create the impression that it is *Coffea arabica* so long and so favorably known as Java coffee."[53] Even so, it was not until 1929 that the USDA—after lobbying from the Dutch government—officially revised its commercial definition of coffee to include robusta.[54]

Robusta's success in the Dutch East Indies encouraged farmers across Asia and the Pacific to give it a try. Robusta coffee was introduced all across the region: in French Indochina, the Philippines, and Portuguese Timor. The French Jardin Coloniale at Nogent-sur-Marne distributed seedlings of *C. canephora* (both the robusta variety and others, such as Kouilou) to French colonies in Asia and the Pacific, as did commercial nurseries such as the Maison Vilmorin. The Jardin Coloniale sent a shipment of Kouilou coffee to the Pacific colony of New Caledonia in 1910, the year that the coffee rust was first detected there. The following year, the planters on the island also imported 300 kilograms of robusta seed directly from Java.[55] In Madagascar, the introduction of two varieties of *C. canephora*—robusta and Kouilou—triggered a boom in coffee production. Between 1910 and 1930, coffee exports from Madagascar—mostly robusta—expanded from 10 tons to 6,000 tons. Robusta production in the French colonies increased even further in the early 1930s after the government established a preferential colonial tariff and began subsidizing coffee planters.[56]

Farmers in parts of southern India also started to cultivate robusta, seemingly on their own initiative rather than because of any state directive. Robusta coffee was first introduced to India from Java in about 1910, and then several times after that through a variety of routes. It remained experimental until the 1920s, apparently because large planters preferred to stick with the high-quality arabicas and felt that "only those unprincipled would resort to planting Robusta."[57] Robusta production expanded significantly in the mid-1920s, in part because it solved a number of pressing environmental and economic problems, of which the rust was only one. K. M. Povaiah, secretary of the Coorg Planters' Association, recalled that during the 1920s, farmers found that robusta "could manage to exist in comparatively poor soil and under indifferent cultivation practices. Labour shortages, money scarcity, poor yields . . . and declining prices led planters in South Coorg to indiscriminately interplant their second-class arabica with robusta. And thank God they did!"[58] As on Java, robusta cultivation also spread into lowland regions where coffee had never previously been cultivated.[59]

The growing supply of cheap robustas also fueled domestic coffee consumption within Asia and the Pacific. Robusta coffees found a market among poorer local consumers who could not afford arabica coffee. According to Cramer, consumers within the Dutch East Indies consumed at least a third of the colony's coffee production, and likely even more than that. It is difficult to get precise estimates for domestic consumption in the Dutch East Indies because official statistics did not capture much of the coffee consumed locally.[60] In India, most of the robusta crop was consumed locally; little was exported at all. As in the United States, robusta was rarely sold as beans. Rather, it was silently incorporated into canned (tinned) coffees and into coffee tablets, which were marketed by their brand name rather than their variety or origin. It was also sold in India's many coffee hotels. Starting in the late 1920s, domestic coffee consumption in India expanded in parallel with robusta production.[61]

In 1947, the coffee expert Antonio di Fulvio wrote that "the introduction of the robusta species to the Dutch East Indies, which resists the attacks of the formidable coffee leaf rust, saved coffee farming in Asia."[62] The statistics certainly support his claim. By the early 1920s, the robusta boom had propelled the Dutch East Indies back up to third place among the world's coffee producers, after Brazil and Colombia. This increased market share (5.3 percent of the world's total) came largely at the expense of Brazil, although the Dutch East Indies also surpassed major American producers such as El Salvador, Venezuela, Guatemala, and Mexico. Coffee production in Asia and the Pacific, fueled largely by robusta, more than doubled between about 1900 and 1940.[63] But robusta was not a simple substitute for arabica. Robusta changed the geographical and economic structures of coffee production—first in Asia and the Pacific, and later around the world—and it also subtly transformed global coffee commodity chains.

BY THE 1930s, coffee researchers had helped farmers in Asia and the Pacific develop two main strategies to preserve and expand coffee production in the face of the coffee rust. Each strategy had its own economic and ecological niche, which depended on a range of ecological, economic, scientific, and other factors. The first strategy focused on preserving traditional arabica production by using chemical sprays to control the disease and boost production. It was primarily suitable for large estates that produced high-quality arabicas. Chemical control was expensive, requiring significant investments in technology, materials, and labor, but it could be cost-effective if the farm gate price of coffee was sufficiently high and the cost of labor and other inputs was sufficiently low. At the time, India was one of the few places in Asia and the Pacific where spraying was commercially viable on a large scale. Even there, it was only viable because of the work of scientists at the Mysore experiment station. Spraying was also viable because most Indian coffee was cultivated under forest cover, which helped keep the rust levels in check. Planters who chose to spray on a large scale had, in effect, exchanged productivity for vulnerability. With spraying programs, their farms were more productive. But they were also more vulnerable than before to sudden drops in the global price of coffee, and to any increase in the cost of production that could disrupt the spraying program.

The second strategy was to switch to robusta, the first commercially viable rust-resistant coffee. Resistant coffees like robusta did not require any additional inputs to coexist with the rust, so they helped keep the cost of production down. The economic and ecological niches for robusta were much wider than the niche for chemical control. Robusta could be produced profitably both on estates and on small farms. Dutch planters and research institutions first promoted it as a plantation crop; many of the scientific research programs in these years sought to enhance robusta's productivity on plantations. Planters also developed techniques for processing robusta to make it appealing to global markets. While robusta coffee could flourish as a plantation crop, its greatest success was with smallholders, who adopted it on a large scale in the Dutch East Indies. Producers elsewhere in Asia and the Pacific quickly emulated the Dutch model, although not quite on the same scale. Robusta appealed to smallholders because it was rust resistant, was productive, required few inputs, and could withstand neglect. In short, it could be produced profitably with low investments in land, labor, and technology. Robusta's low prices also helped generate demand, both internationally and locally. In India, and also to a certain extent in the Dutch East Indies, the domestic demand for robusta helped insulate farmers from the volatility of the global coffee trade. Robusta coffee producers effectively created a new commercial niche for coffee.

CHAPTER 6

The "Malaria of Coffee"

Africa

THE COFFEE rust was not a significant problem in nineteenth-century Africa for the simple reason that the continent did not export that much coffee. The nineteenth-century boom had largely bypassed Africa. Continental Africa had provided the germplasm—the seeds and seedlings—upon which the global coffee industry had been built. Before the Berlin conference, Ethiopia was almost the only place in Africa where arabica coffee was cultivated on any significant scale. But Ethiopia's coffee zones were comparatively isolated and, at times, wracked with conflict. It is hard to measure Ethiopia's output because it was often sold as Mocha coffee from Yemen. European settlers had also established tiny pockets of arabica in Natal (South Africa) and the Portuguese island colonies of São Tomé and Principe. In western Africa, local peoples gathered or cultivated small amounts of other coffee species for export. Since the 1830s, farmers in Liberia had exported small quantities of *C. liberica*, mostly to the US market. In Angola, also in the 1830s, Portuguese colonists, Brazilian farmers, and Africans alike started domesticating and cultivating several wild coffee species, one of which would turn out to be robusta.[1]

The Berlin Conference of 1884–85 opened a new phase of coffee cultivation in Africa. European powers had been jockeying over their spheres of influence on the continent. The Berlin Conference defined the political parameters for staking territorial claims in Africa, emphasizing the principle of "effective occupation." European settlers—and some Africans—began to cultivate coffee for export. Before World War I, coffee cultivation across Africa expanded slowly. Between World War I and World War II, coffee production across Africa grew explosively as European colonial powers consolidated their hold over the interior and started to build the infrastructure to connect it to global markets. The rally in coffee prices during the 1920s also helped. At the beginning of the twentieth century, Africa accounted for about 1 percent of global coffee production; by the late 1930s, it accounted for more than 9 percent. Arabica cultivation dominated in the highlands, especially in the eastern part of the continent: Kenya, Tanganyika, Ruanda, Urundi, and the eastern Congo. Robusta cultivation dominated in the lowland coffeelands of Uganda, the Congo River basin, Angola, and West Africa.[2]

The coffee rust developed differently in Africa than it had in Asia and the Pacific. Planters in Asia and the Pacific benefitted from landscapes initially free of the fungus, which allowed them to establish arabica farms on a wide variety of landscapes. In most of Africa, however, from the earliest days of commercial cultivation, the rust was either already present or nearby. So coffee farmers in Africa always faced the risk of infection from wild coffees or from existing stands of cultivated coffee. By the late 1880s, they also had to contend with the rust introduced from the infected coffee farms of Asia and the Pacific. The ports of British East Africa (Kenya) were well connected with the infected coffee zones of Ceylon and Southern India. In Africa, the rust did not primarily destroy existing plantations; rather, from the very beginning it defined the contours of coffee production—especially arabica production. The rust limited arabica cultivation to highland areas where the disease could be managed.

The Scramble for Africa

The coffee rust was present across much of Africa long before European colonization. Most coffee species show resistance to some strains of *H. vastatrix*, which suggests that they coevolved with *H. vastatrix* in a process of antagonistic coevolution. In the wild, the rust fungus faced selection pressure to overcome resistance from the coffee plants. In turn, the coffee plants faced a reciprocal selection pressure to respond to new strains of the pathogen. Over time, then, the fungus developed a range of virulence genes, and coffee plants developed a corresponding range of resistance genes. The presence of these resistance genes thus provides indirect evidence for the existence of the fungus. "It is difficult to explain," wrote the rust expert Albertus Eskes, "why rust resistance would have evolved in the absence of *H. vastatrix*."[3]

The populations of *H. vastatrix* were highly variable because the wild coffee species were themselves highly variable, dispersed across a wide range of environments that either promoted or inhibited the fungus's development. This variability helps explain why some kinds of coffee (such as strains of *C. canephora* from the humid lowlands where the fungus flourishes) are highly tolerant to the rust while other coffees (especially those that grow in drier or cooler environments less favorable to the fungus) are comparatively susceptible. Coffee farms in Africa, then, were often at risk of being infected by *H. vastatrix* from wild "forest" coffees—although this risk was not apparent until well into the twentieth century.[4]

The coffee industries of central and western Africa, from the Ivory Coast to Angola, were initially built using local coffees, particularly different varieties of *C. canephora* and, to a lesser extent, *C. liberica* and its relatives. In the Lake Victoria (Victoria Nyanza) region, African farmers had harvested robusta coffee—and other wild coffees—long before Europeans arrived. They used green beans for rituals and for food. They also moved *C. canephora* outside its native forests; they cultivated it extensively on the Ssese Islands in Victoria Nyanza and farther south in what is now the Bukoba District of Tanzania. The first written description we have of robusta coffee in East Africa comes from the explorer James Grant. Writing from Bukoba in 1861, he described being "sheltered [from] the rays of the sun by the bough of the coffee-shrub, then with clusters of green berries bowing down its branches till within reach."[5] In Victoria Nyanza the rust was seemingly widespread, but not serious. African farmers kept the rust in check by cultivating the coffee at comparatively low density, on farms with great diversity. They also, over the years, likely selected rust-resistant varieties of robusta.

Over the nineteenth century, European settlers and Africans established small centers of commercial coffee production along Africa's Atlantic seaboard. At first, they cultivated the coffees they found growing wild in the forests; one of these was Liberian coffee. Early farmers, and even some early naturalists, initially assumed that these forest coffees were varieties of arabica. When the Austrian botanist Friedrich Welwitsch visited Angola in the 1850s, he found African and European farmers alike cultivating a coffee whose seeds they had collected from the surrounding forest. This plant was initially classified as *C. welwitschii* (and later reclassified as a variety of *C. canephora*).[6] In the following decades, European settlers along the west coast of Africa found several other wild coffees, some of which they cultivated on a small scale. In the 1880s, European settlers in the French Congo and Gabon encountered a plant they called the Kouilou coffee. In 1885, a French priest named Alexandre Le Roy discovered yet another kind of coffee farther inland "while bathing near the post of Agouma on the Rembo Nkoius." The coffee tree "grew in the forest gallery alongside the riverside and its branches—heavy with red cherries—hung over the river." Specimens of the plant were sent to Paris, where the botanist Jean-Baptiste Pierre classified it as *C. canephora*.[7]

These early coffee farmers preferred to cultivate local coffees because they were well adapted to local conditions. "Success is certain," wrote the French planter F. Sargos in 1899, "especially if you want to use the indigenous [coffee] plant, and why wouldn't you?" Sargos had tried Liberian coffee with little success, but "the wild [Kouilou] coffee only produces fruits during the dry season," which made them easier to process. And in terms of quality, the Kouilou coffee was classified at the same rank as the coffees from "Cazengo, Rio Nunez, and African Mysores."[8] Although these coffees were not highly prized by coffee markets, they were sufficiently profitable to be worthwhile. Africans would, according to one report, "bring unpulped coffee seeds to the factory" from time to time. Some Africans established small farms "constituted by coffee trees ripped out from the forest and transplanted around the house." French and Dutch companies established coffee farms of their own, cultivating seedlings from seed. By 1897, the French house of Ancel-Seitz had sown one hundred thousand coffee plants in the Kouilou River valley of the French Congo (now the Republic of the Congo) and exported more than 2,400 kilograms of Kouilou coffee to France.[9] In these early coffee frontiers, there was little interest in arabica coffee. The local environments were not suitable for arabica coffee.

In contrast, the commercial coffee industry in the highlands of East Africa was initially built on susceptible arabicas. The early colonial coffee farmers in East Africa were seemingly unaware of the hard lessons then being learned about the coffee rust in Asia and the Pacific. Although arabica coffee is native to Ethiopia, the arabicas first cultivated in East Africa were introduced from coffee farms in Asia and the Americas. Arabica coffee was first brought to East Africa by the French Catholic mission of the Congrégation du Saint-Esprit et du Saint-Cœur de Marie (better known in English as the Holy Ghost Fathers). They had a mission at Bagamoyo, on the African mainland near Zanzibar. The mission experimented with many different crops and found coffee and coconuts to be the most successful. They obtained their coffee plants from Aden and from the French colony of Réunion, where they also had a mission. These seedlings were of a variety of arabica known as Bourbon. In the 1880s and 1890s, the Bourbon cultivar was then circulated from the Bagamoyo mission to other Catholic missions in the highlands of German East Africa (Tanganyika, later Tanzania), Kenya, and Uganda.[10] A second variety of arabica—the so-called Typica variety (*C. arabica* var. Typica)—was introduced to British Nyasaland (Malawi) in the 1870s as well; this was likely Jamaican Blue Mountain coffee, introduced from Jamaica either directly or indirectly. In East Africa, this variety came to be known as Nyasa coffee. Like the Bourbon coffee, Nyasa coffee gradually circulated through East Africa's small coffee farms in the 1880s and 1890s, readily crossing colonial boundaries.[11]

Many of the early arabica farms in East Africa, like those in Asia and the Pacific, were established in areas that were, for one reason or another, ecologically marginal for the arabica plant. These pre–World War I commercial plantings of arabica were small and often plagued with agricultural and economic problems, of which the coffee rust was just one. The first significant arabica farms in British Nyasaland were established in the 1870s but had been all but wiped out by 1900 because of inadequate rainfall, attacks from pests, and plummeting global coffee prices. The British coffee expert A. E. Haarer later cited these poor choices of environment and cultivation practices as reflecting a "lack of cultural knowledge" on the part of the European settlers. "The roving [estate] managers," one of whom had been Haarer himself, "were seldom qualified in either horticulture or agriculture."[12]

The rust first broke out in German East Africa during the 1893–94 growing season. It was discovered on a plantation in the Usambara Mountains that belonged to the German East Africa Company. There were two comparatively large plantations in the affected area: one of 150,000 trees and one of 350,000 trees. The company sent specimens of diseased leaves to Kew for identification; the botanists there confirmed the planters' fears. The German government sent a botanist—one Dr. Heinsen—to try to control the disease, to no avail. At first, the company and the settlers feared that the coffee crop might be wiped out entirely, as it had been in Ceylon. "Every effort is being made to exterminate the disease," wrote a German named Gosselin, "but if it spreads it will naturally throw back the cultivation of what promised to be one of the most successful crops in the Colony."[13] Over the next few seasons, however, they discovered that the rust levels were low enough in many areas to keep coffee production viable.

From the Usambara Mountains, the epidemic appears to have gradually spread north and west through the coffee zones of German East Africa (see map 6.1). By 1907, "European settlers on Kilimanjaro were already complaining of the danger of disease spreading to their plantations from African-grown coffee," a complaint that was to be repeated by settlers elsewhere in Africa in the years to come. By 1910, the disease had spread throughout the Kilimanjaro District.[14] It is entirely possible that the rust *was* present on African farms. But in blaming the African farmers, European settlers discounted their own role in moving plants and people (and inadvertently the pathogen) through East Africa, as well as the role their cultivation practices played in the development of rust outbreaks.

By the 1890s, a series of global crop epidemics—including the coffee rust—had sparked a debate about the global movement of plant germplasm. For much of the nineteenth century a cosmopolitan model of botanical exchange had prevailed, in which plant germplasm (plants and

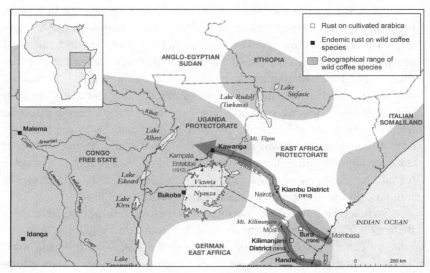

Map 6.1. Spread of *H. vastatrix* in East Africa. (Map by Marie Puddister)

seeds) had circulated around the world with few restrictions. But it became apparent that this botanical cosmopolitanism had also contributed to the global movement of diseases and pests. In response to these problems, some planters, scientists, and government officials began to call for more botanical protectionism, asking for states (and scientists) to more closely regulate and control the movement of plants and seed.[15] Almost as soon as large-scale commercial coffee production began in British Central Africa, for example, the planters' association asked the colony's government to pass an ordinance prohibiting the importation of coffee plants and seeds from "prohibited" countries where the coffee rust was present, including everywhere in the Indian Ocean basin and the Pacific. Commenting on the proposed legislation, William Thiselton-Dyer at Kew expressed his reluctance to "concur in regulations which must have a restrictive effect, however small, on commerce," a view reflecting the prevailing wisdom of the day. In spite of this, Thiselton-Dyer supported the regulations, arguing that it was "impossible to accept the risk of ruining an important and developing industry."[16] He had seen the rust's impact on Ceylon's coffee industry the decade before. The colony's government duly passed the ordinance in 1894, the very year that the coffee rust first appeared in neighboring German East Africa. The colonial government of British East Africa passed an almost identical ordinance in 1900, adding German East Africa to the list of prohibited countries.

While some people argued that botanical exchanges should be strictly regulated, others argued against any significant controls. Some farmers argued that such exchanges were necessary for innovation and improvement. Planters in British Central Africa chafed under the regulations that they themselves had requested. In 1900, for example, they complained that the quarantine regulations "acted as a practical bar to the importation of new seeds by private planters." They argued that new germplasm was necessary in order to "reinvigorate" their failing coffee farms.[17] Whether or not their judgement was correct in this case (it now seems likely that their farms were failing for other reasons), this debate reflected a broader tension between cosmopolitanism and protectionism in the global coffee industry, and in global botanical exchanges more generally.[18]

Even so, Thiselton-Dyer doubted whether quarantines could protect Britain's African colonies from the rust. He pointed to phylloxera's inexorable spread across the Atlantic and the coffee rust's "inexplicable" outbreak in Natal as examples where diseases and pests had leapt across huge natural barriers. The case of Natal, he wrote, "leads me to take a gloomy view of the whole position, and to incline to the belief that sooner or later the disease will establish itself through the coffee cultivation of the whole world despite every precaution."[19]

The pattern of early rust outbreaks in eastern Africa suggests that the fungus was introduced from Asia and the Pacific. The outbreaks moved, along with European settlements, from the coast to the interior. As we saw above, the first recorded outbreak took place in the Usambara Mountains of German East Africa. At that time, the region was still isolated from western Victoria Nyanza, where the rust was endemic on wild coffees. But it was well connected to Zanzibar and the networks of trade in the Indian Ocean basin. The emergent coffee farms of Kenya and Uganda were linked to the Indian Ocean basin by the Uganda Railway (built 1896–1901), which connected Kenya's port city of Mombasa with the Kenyan highlands and later Victoria Nyanza. A network of lake steamers connected the lake's major port cities with the railroad and the world beyond. Heinrich Brode, a contemporary German author, observed that the Kilimanjaro and Lake Victoria regions of German East Africa "owe[d] their development more or less to the Uganda Railway."[20] Coffee producers in both regions found it more practical to ship their coffee through the British steamship and railway network rather than through their own colony, whose transportation network was much less developed. So given this pattern of trade, one might expect that the rust would have moved from western Victoria Nyanza (where it was endemic) down to the coast.

In fact, though, the rust followed the Uganda Railway from the coast inward and then radiated outward from the railway to coffee farms connected to these focuses. The railhead at Mombasa was connected to transportation and trade networks in the Indian Ocean basin. Mombasa was linked to India by regular steamship connections on the British India Steam Navigation Company, and several other lines. The Uganda Railway was built using laborers and goods brought from India, and it is certainly possible that some spores of the rust traveled along the same route. In 1906, the rust was first recorded at the Catholic mission in Bura, just 40 kilometers from the Voi railroad station. This station, roughly 150 kilometers inland from Mombasa, had been completed in 1897.[21] The Bura mission was located in the humid and warm coastal lowlands, where the rust flourished. The outbreak caused severe losses, and the colonial government ordered planters in Bura to "tear up all its coffee."[22]

The disease also seems to have spread laterally from the railroad. In 1910, it appeared in Kilimanjaro, 100 kilometers east of Bura. Although the infected farms were on the German side of the border, they shipped much of their coffee to global markets through Bura.[23] It remains unclear whether Kilimanjaro was infected via British East Africa, or vice versa. In any case, the disease continued to spread inland along the railway. In 1912, it was discovered in the Kiambu District just north of Nairobi. That same year, A. C. Anderson, the protectorate's director of agriculture, toured the colony's coffee farms. He found the rust on three farms and suggested that it was even more widespread. In one of the farms, he concluded that the disease had been present for at least three years. In the following few years the rust seemed to spread outward from Nairobi to farms elsewhere in the Kenyan highlands.[24]

In Uganda, the rust was first recorded on arabica in the 1912–13 growing season, shortly after it had been detected in Nairobi. The obvious explanation for this is that the rust continued to spread inland along the Uganda Railway, and that probably did happen. But Uganda's arabica farms were *also* vulnerable to rust already endemic in the colony, on the cultivated robustas and forest coffees in the regions surrounding Victoria Nyanza. European planters had only begun to cultivate arabica on a large scale in 1909; the rust struck in 1912, just as this crop was reaching full maturity.[25] Uganda's government entomologist sent some diseased coffee leaves to Kew for identification, where researchers confirmed that this was a "very bad case of the coffee-leaf disease."[26]

Uganda's director of agriculture concluded that "there can be no doubt but that the disease has been present in this country for many years. . . . Old residents were well acquainted with the disease and called it the 'native coffee leaf disease' under the impression that it was not *Hemileia vastatrix* and that it had been identified at Kew some years ago as something different."[27] The 1912–13 outbreak was widespread and reduced the colony's arabica crop by a third. Uganda's government botanist argued that the rust fungus was endemic and that "its appearance in the form of an epidemic in 1913 may be attributed to the fact that it was suddenly provided with a new host plant."[28]

The rust's impact was strongest in comparatively hot and humid areas, as it was elsewhere in the Indian Ocean basin. The disease was particularly strong in the coastal missions in Bura (British East Africa) and Bagamoyo (German East Africa)—making it effectively impossible to continue cultivating arabica coffee there.[29] The disease was also comparatively severe on arabica coffees in Uganda, although other coffee species were not as seriously affected. Many of Uganda's coffee-growing zones did not have a distinct dry season, and the constant rainfall and humidity provided perfect conditions for the growth and spread of the rust. The disease was generally less damaging—or at least more manageable—in the cooler highlands of Kenya and Tanganyika, especially around Mount Kilimanjaro.

As the rust spread through British and German East Africa, it was met by a small but dedicated cohort of government scientists. Their presence reflected shifting state attitudes about the role of the agricultural sciences in colonial development. In the 1880s, Ceylon's colonial government had only grudgingly funded a single scientist to study the rust, and that was done on just a two-year contract. In the last decade of the nineteenth century, European colonial officials articulated an ideology of "improvement" (*mise-en-valeur* in the French colonies). One of the keystones of this ideology was that the sciences would promote the effective use of tropical nature. Furthermore, at least in principle, these sciences would not necessarily focus exclusively on the agricultural problems of settler plantations; they would also focus on "improving" indigenous agriculture.[30]

The Germans had sent scientists to East Africa from the very beginning of their colonial venture. In 1902, they established a biological and agricultural research institute at Amani whose researchers included the coffee expert Franz Stuhlmann (who directed the institute in the early twentieth century) and the plant pathologist Hermann Morstatt. While the British colonies could not boast any institution as eminent as Amani, in the first decades of the twentieth century most British colonies in Africa established departments of agriculture, which included scientific experts. In 1913, British East Africa's department of agriculture employed at least four scientists, including a mycologist (an expert on fungi). Uganda's government employed about a dozen scientists, divided between the department of agriculture and the botanical, forestry, and scientific department.[31] These government scientists tracked the rust outbreak and studied its impact as it swept through the region; they also started to explore means of controlling the disease.

Walter J. Dowson, Kenya's government mycologist, found that the disease could easily be controlled through careful cultivation and, in some cases, light application of fungicides.[32] His counterpart in Uganda, William Small, wrote confidently in 1913 that "despite the prevalence of this disease, the outlook is favourable, for the indications are that its virulence will be less in the future than in the past; the fungus, being endemic in Uganda, cannot be expected to work the havoc that it has wrought in other countries to which it was introduced."[33] Not everyone, however, was as optimistic as Small. In 1913, Wyndham Dunstan of the Imperial Institute argued that colonial scientists still had a lot of work ahead of them: "Systematic work with a view to the discovery of a means of eradicating this fungus (*Hemileia vastatrix*) is one of the pressing needs of tropical agriculture, and the discovery of a fungoid resistant Coffee ought not be beyond the skill of modern Science. The failure of all attempts so far made alone stands in the way of Coffee cultivation in many promising countries."[34]

On the eve of World War I, commercial arabica production in East Africa remained comparatively small, and the coffee trade economically insignificant. The rust, then, had only a modest economic impact. Scientists seemed to be confident that they could manage the disease. East Africa's high-quality arabicas were fetching correspondingly high prices in Europe. High coffee prices, indirectly propped up by Brazilian valorization, helped ensure that the coffee industry remained profitable in spite of any losses. Anderson concluded that "this hitherto dreaded disease has, on closer acquaintance, proved not so disastrous as was feared when less was known on the subject."[35] So even in the face of the rust, African and European farmers alike continued to open new coffee farms.

Colonial Consolidation

World War I marked a watershed in East Africa's coffee industry. The war disrupted markets and shipping, making it difficult for farmers to get their coffee to market. Many European settlers and scientists returned to Europe to fight in the war; many of them never returned to the colonies. And East Africa itself became a theater of war. Great Britain and Germany fought a brutal war, involving a small number of European troops and a much larger number of African troops. According to the Treaty of Versailles, Germany's former colonies in Africa became mandates of the League of Nations, and each would be administered by one of the victorious nations. Most of German East Africa (renamed Tanganyika) was administered by Great Britain. The former province of Ruanda-Urundi became a separate mandate administered by Belgium, which had occupied it during the war. Other administrative changes followed. In 1920, the protectorate of British East Africa became Kenya Colony. The highlands of the colony were reserved exclusively for white settlers. Uganda remained a protectorate, and there the British promoted agricultural production by Africans.

In the decade following the war, coffee production in Kenya, Tanganyika, and Uganda exploded; between 1913 and 1930, exports from these colonies grew from 2,000 tons to 30,000 tons. In Kenya, the area under coffee cultivation expanded from 5,000 acres to 97,000 acres. In the same period, the area under cultivation in Tanganyika reached 95,000 acres, and that in Uganda reached 39,000 acres.[36] Coffee production was stimulated in part by growing global demand for coffee (especially in the United States) and also by stable global coffee prices brought about by Brazil's coffee-defense policies. The character of coffee production varied considerably from one colony to the next, depending on the nature of the colonial relationship in each place. In Kenya, the best coffeelands were reserved for white settlers, who cultivated high-quality arabicas. In Uganda, African producers gradually came to dominate coffee production by the mid-1920s. The picture in Tanganyika was more complicated. Around the slopes of Kilimanjaro, European estates and African smallholders competed to produce arabica coffee. In western Tanganyika, near Bukoba, African robusta producers dominated coffee production.[37]

In East Africa, the struggle against the coffee rust was part of a larger struggle against a host of diseases and pests. The postwar coffee boom had produced, in the words of a British journalist, "vast new opportunities for natural forces inimical to coffee," of which the rust was only one.[38] Kenya's coffee planters complained that "each year since 1922 has produced a fresh pest of coffee."[39] Coffee farmers in Africa had to contend with many endemic diseases and pests already present on wild coffee in the forest or on the small stands of cultivated coffee. The most serious insect pests included the Antestia bug, which "suck[ed] the juices from the developing coffee beans, flower buds, and young shoots"; the coffee thrip (*Diarthrothrips coffeae*), which could completely defoliate the coffee plant; and the coffee berry borer (*Hypothenemus hampei*), which burrowed into the coffee cherries and hollowed out the seeds.[40]

In addition to these insect pests, farmers had to cope with other diseases. In East Africa, the most serious of these was the coffee berry disease (*Colletotrichum kahawae* Waller and Bridge). The coffee berry disease was a fungus that infected the berries and caused them to become "dark in colour" and "hard and brittle." The beans at the center became "brown, dry, and withered." It first appeared in the West Rift district of Kenya in the early 1920s and caused losses of up to three-quarters of the crop. At that time, it caused "more loss than any other coffee disease in Kenya" including the rust.[41] Whereas coffee rust was a disease of low altitudes, the coffee berry disease favored higher altitudes, above 1,600 meters.[42] The disease "changed prosperous coffee farms into liabilities within a single year," recalled Haarer. Later losses were much smaller—not because scientists had developed effective control methods, but rather "because many of the estates so badly affected in the 1922–35 period [were] no longer in production."[43] By the late 1920s, diseases and pests of all sorts had become a key feature of East Africa's coffee farms, large and small alike.

This onslaught of diseases and pests made East African coffee producers—both European and African—increasingly dependent on the agricultural sciences. After the war, the British revived the former German colonial station in Tanganyika, renaming it the East African Agricultural Research Station. In spite of the grand ambitions suggested by the new name, the station received only a minimal operating budget through most of the early 1920s.[44] The most important coffee research in East Africa was conducted by the departments of agriculture in Kenya, Tanganyika, and Uganda. Uganda's department of agriculture created a dedicated position of coffee scientific officer. During the 1920s, this position was filled by scientists who had experience working in the coffee zones of the New World.[45]

In Kenya and Tanganyika, scientists focused on strategies to coexist with the rust. Early work on the coffee rust focused on understanding disease patterns, particularly the relationship between altitude and the severity of rust infestations. In Kenya, Dowson's research "affirmed that meteorological conditions supply the key to the solution of the problem of the relations of host and parasite." Dowson determined some critical thresholds for coffee cultivation, arguing that it was "useless to try and grow coffee" below 1,200 meters "as *Hemileia* cannot be controlled." The government mycologist George Wallace found a similar pattern in Tanganyika.[46] In highland areas above 1,800 meters, such as the coffee zones to the northwest of Nairobi, the rust was present but not a significant problem. Just as scientists in the Dutch East Indies and India had found, the biggest problem was in the middle altitudes—in this case between 1,200 and 1,800 meters above sea level—where arabica production was viable, but where rust outbreaks could be severe if left unchecked. The question was how best to manage it.

Chemical spraying was one option, especially where farmers were committed to growing arabica. With the rise of coffee prices in the 1920s, spraying with copper fungicides had become cost-effective once again.[47] As in India, spraying was a particularly attractive option for farmers who wanted to preserve or increase the production of high-quality arabica coffees. Still, it was a major expense, especially for planters who depended on paid labor. The cost is reflected in some farm budgets from the period.

One account from Arusha, Tanganyika, estimated £252 for "upkeep" that included "weeding, pruning, spraying, pest control, [etc.]" and a further £35 for "chemicals"—fungicides and pesticides. Together, then, upkeep and chemicals cost £287, or about a quarter of the total cost of production.[48] And for farmers who were working on narrow profit margins, these costs could make the difference between making a profit or a loss. In Uganda, the government entomologist concluded that "the margin of profit is so narrow that planters are unable to afford the additional expense" of spraying.[49]

In light of the economic challenges of spraying, government scientists in Kenya and Tanganyika recommended that farmers manage the rust by using appropriate cropping practices. A. E. Leechman, director of the East Africa Experiment Station, likened the coffee rust to malaria. Just as "constant vigilance and first class sanitation are essential to prevent malaria from regaining the upper hand in Africa," wrote Leechman, "so unwearying watchfulness and the cleanest cultivation are necessary to combat *Hemileia*."[50] The elements of "clean cultivation" included "good tillage, giving careful attention to mulching, systematic soil renovation, not forgetting an occasional dressing of lime, and well-planned drainage."[51]

The way that Leechman spoke about "clean cultivation" brings to mind similar moralistic discussions of high cultivation in nineteenth-century Ceylon. Leechman argued that it was "just as criminal for a planter to have neglected, dirty, and diseased patches on his estate as it is for him to allow mosquito-breeding pools near his house." Pursuing the analogy between human disease and crop disease, he stated that just "as starved and enfeebled human beings fall easy victims to fever, so coffee plants grown on exhausted land are the first to succumb to Leaf Disease."[52] Still, even supposedly virtuous planters could not always escape the ravages of diseases and pests. Uganda's warm and wet coffee zones were ideally suited for the rust, as well as many other diseases. European settlers did attempt to cultivate arabica coffee in Uganda, but regardless of whether they practiced "clean cultivation," their farms simply could not withstand the attacks from the rust and (more significantly) the Antestia bug. The bug, the rust, and the high cost of transportation contributed to the decline of arabica cultivation in Uganda. In 1920, the colony had some 20,873 acres under arabica production. By 1935 that figure had shrunk to 6,286 acres.[53]

But while Uganda's arabica industry was in decline, its robusta production increased. Robusta coffee was native to parts of Uganda and much better suited to the prevailing environmental conditions. It was at least partially resistant both to the coffee rust and to the Antestia bug. Some estates replaced their failing arabica plants with robusta. "Experience has shown," wrote scientist A. S. Thomas, "that robusta, in spite of its low market value, is more profitable as a permanent estate crop than Arabica below 4,500 feet, as yields are larger, and it is comparatively free of pests and diseases."[54] Robusta also had new commercial potential in the global markets because of Dutch efforts through the previous two decades. Even so, it was Africans, rather than settlers, who quickly came to dominate robusta production in Uganda. The colonial government supported this effort by distributing robusta seedlings to farmers. Uganda's government botanist, T. D. Maitland, had begun breeding experiments on robusta in 1918 using local robustas and also strains imported from Java.[55] He selected them for "vigor, yield, and size of bean." Vigor, as Maitland defined it, included resistance to diseases and pests. The local trees he was using as raw material were, of course, the result of generations of selection by African farmers. In the years before commercial agriculture developed, African farmers did not necessarily have the same priorities as Maitland—particularly with respect to yield and size of bean. Still, they likely selected their trees for resistance to endemic diseases; Thomas observed that "a tree which attains to great age and large size can be little affected by *Hemileia*."[56]

By the 1920s, the rust had reached all of eastern Africa's commercial coffeelands, decisively shaping the contours of coffee cultivation—especially arabica cultivation. The rust, in conjunction with other diseases and pests (and volatile global coffee prices), sharply curtailed arabica production in the lowlands. Arabica cultivation expanded rapidly in the highlands, but only within a constrained area. The rust also helped create a commercial space for robusta production, which in the following decades became dominated by African farmers rather than European estates.

Depression and War

During the Great Depression, metropolitan demand for colonial commodities declined. European demand shifted toward cheaper coffees, like the robustas. Coffee producers were briefly insulated from the worst of these problems by Brazil's coffee-defense schemes, which reached a crisis and finally collapsed in the mid-1930s. Europe's colonial states responded to this economic uncertainty by exerting greater control over the production, marketing, and trade of colonial commodities. These measures included incentives for providing credit to farmers, distributing coffee seedlings at little or no cost, and offering technical support. Often, these incentives were also accompanied by greater control—marketing boards set strict grading standards for all coffee destined for export, set the local price paid to producers, and centralized the purchase, processing, and export of coffee.[57]

These strategies had the intended effects; the coffee frontier in Africa expanded rapidly between the mid-1920s and the late 1930s. Production grew the fastest in the robusta-producing zones of central and western Africa, especially Angola, the Belgian Congo, and the Ivory Coast in French West Africa. During these years, coffee production in the Ivory Coast grew 7,700 percent; in the Belgian Congo, 1,730 percent; and in French Equatorial Africa, 1,300 percent. The volume of production in those colonies began to match those of more established arabica producers in East Africa.[58] From the beginning, these new coffee pioneer fronts were based almost entirely on varieties of *C. canephora* (especially robusta coffee) and *C. liberica* rather than *C. arabica*. The decision to plant *canephora* varieties in these regions was not driven primarily by concerns about the rust; it was rather about adaptation to the prevailing environments.

The robusta boom in central and western Africa depended on improved robustas. Robusta was a highly variable species, so researchers focused on developing highly productive cultivars that were adapted to local ecological conditions. Coffee experimentation in the Belgian Congo began in 1911, when the Belgians opened an experiment station at Stanleyville (Kisangani). In 1926, the colonial government organized a Plantation Service (Régie des Plantations) to support coffee and other colonial crops; in the early 1930s, the Belgians created the National Institute for the Agronomic Study of the Belgian Congo (INEAC), which included a coffee research station at Yangambi. Researchers there developed improved selections of robusta based on improved cultivars imported from the Dutch East Indies and Ceylon.[59] These INEAC cultivars were, in turn, circulated to the Ivory Coast and other parts of Africa. In the mid-1930s, French researchers in the Ivory Coast also started systematic research on robusta coffee. They experimented on local wild coffees and also imported INEAC selections from the Belgian Congo. Rust resistance did not figure prominently in robusta research, since rust was not a major problem on robustas. Over the short term, this frontier expansion does not appear to have caused any corresponding expansion of the coffee rust, at least none serious enough to draw alarm from the planters.

In British East Africa, arabica coffee production also grew during the 1930s, supported by similar protectionist measures. But it did not expand as quickly as in central and western Africa, in part because arabica production was constrained by a range of diseases and pests. The British expanded their agricultural research infrastructure during these years. In 1933, they established a coffee research and experiment station in Tanganyika, at Lyamungu on the slopes of Mount Kilimanjaro. The Lyamungu station was meant to address the immediate needs of coffee producers, while the East Africa Research Station in Amani dealt with longer-term research projects.[60] At the same time, government researchers at Kenya's Scott Agricultural Laboratories began a systematic program of arabica selection. Breeders developed a number of selections, known as S. L. selections, that had good reputations for quality and yield but were all susceptible to the rust. These higher-yielding coffees did, however, contribute to the growth of Kenya's coffee production in the 1930s. As breeding work continued, Kenyan planters continued to control the rust using sprays, as their counterparts in India did at the time.[61] In Uganda and Tanganyika, robusta production—mostly by Africans—continued to expand, while arabica production was limited to a few highland enclaves.[62]

In 1930, Leechman wrote confidently that "*Hemileia* in the light of modern knowledge and planting techniques has lost most of its terrors; and for coffee planters in East and Central Africa the prognosis, as a doctor might say, is in respect to this disease, good—even excellent."[63] But Leechman was overly optimistic about the power of modern science. The rust—and other diseases—had sharply limited the contours of arabica cultivation in East Africa. Between 1885 and 1940, farmers had pushed arabica cultivation in Africa about as far as it could go. Farmers had opened an archipelago of arabica zones in the highlands of eastern Africa and in a handful of other privileged environments elsewhere on the continent where climates favored the coffee plant but not the rust. Arabica cultivation has never spread beyond these privileged spaces. Endemic rust was an obstacle to large-scale arabica cultivation outside these spaces, much as endemic South American leaf blight prevented the development of rubber plantations in Brazil. Robusta coffee was not constrained by the rust in the same way. The highly variable robusta plants were mostly tolerant to the rust, and also suited to a much wider range of environments than arabica. Robusta cultivation in Africa would continue to expand after World War II. This expanding robusta front made it easier for the coffee rust fungus to circulate to parts of western Africa where it had not previously been detected, and to threaten the coffee farms of Latin America.

CHAPTER 7

Coffee, Cold War, and Colonial Modernization

ONE MORNING in August 1952, the American botanists Frederick "Fritz" Wellman and William Cowgill set out from Douala, the main port city of French Cameroon. Their destination was the city of Nkongsamba, in the heart of Cameroon's coffee zone. "When we stopped in our first field," recalled Wellman, "Cowgill stepped to a tree I was looking over for Colletotrichum injuries, and turning over the leaves said, 'Here you are, Fritz. Your friend *Hemileia vastatrix*!'" They found the rust spread through the entire coffee district. This was an unwelcome surprise. "I did not recall," Wellman wrote, "any report in [the] literature of occurrence of *H. vastatrix* so close to the Atlantic Coast in West Africa."[1] Over the next several days, they found rust on eleven species and varieties of coffee at the French Station Agronomique in Nkongsamba and at the Station Qunquina in Dschang, some 70 kilometers to the north. The arabica plantings around Dschang were in poor shape; defoliation in unsprayed arabica trees ranged from 20 to 80 percent. Wellman was not primarily concerned about the rust's potential impact on

French Cameroon. There, as in much of western Africa, the main crop was robusta.[2] Most of the robusta cultivars Wellman found were infected by rust, but none of them were "specially injured" by it. Wellman's main concern was epidemiological. The presence of *H. vastatrix* in West Africa dramatically increased the risk that the fungus would spread to the vast arabica coffee farms of the Americas, which had so far escaped the coffee rust.

This small moment captures broader transformations in agriculture, development, and science in postwar Africa, and in the Cold War world as a whole. For the European colonial powers, the late 1940s and 1950s were the apogee of colonial developmentalism—partly driven by the desire to earn badly needed hard currency for reconstruction after World War II and also to justify the continuing colonial project in Africa. During the 1950s, Great Britain, France, and Belgium strengthened their existing colonial research institutions in Africa and created new ones. These technocratic schemes of colonial development used science and technology to modernize traditional farming and to increase the productivity of food crops and export crops.[3] As the threat of the Cold War loomed larger, the United States launched technical cooperation programs with countries around Africa, Asia, and Latin America. New multilateral agencies, especially the Food and Agriculture Organization of the United Nations (FAO), also promoted international collaboration in agricultural research.

These organizations joined with colonial and national institutions in the struggle to control coffee rust. In the postwar years, the United States started to play a greater role in bilateral and multilateral development initiatives. Wellman and Cowgill's "Coffee Rust Survey Mission," sponsored by the USDA's office of Foreign Agricultural Relations, was an initiative of Harry Truman's Point IV program, designed to offer technical assistance to developing countries.[4] Wellman and Cowgill's goal was to explore the impact of the coffee rust in Africa, Asia, and the Pacific in order to help coffee producers in Latin America prepare for any potential outbreaks. In their journey through Europe and the leading coffee research institutions in the Eastern Hemisphere, the two men started to build a global network of coffee researchers and to develop networks for sharing ideas and, especially, germplasm—both of coffee and the coffee rust fungus.

Boom and Rust in West Africa

In West Africa, as in other parts of the world, the coffee rust epidemic followed an economic boom. The global coffee trade had slumped during

World War II as the European market effectively disappeared. After the war, European demand gradually recovered. For a few years during the late 1940s and early 1950s, global demand for coffee exceeded supply. This situation—an unusual one in the twentieth century—drove coffee prices upward. A frost in Brazil's coffee zones in 1953 compounded this gap between supply and demand. Between 1949 and 1954, even the price of robusta coffee tripled from eighteen cents a pound to more than sixty cents a pound. Colonial states across Africa encouraged farmers to sow more coffee, most of which was robusta. "To the coffee farmers, whether European or African," wrote Wellman in 1952, "it appears that the future of coffee is bright."[5]

Colonial states promoted coffee production to generate economic surpluses that could help underwrite reconstruction in Europe. African politicians saw coffee production as a path to economic improvement for small farmers. In the Ivory Coast, Félix Houphouët-Boigny—a coffee planter and emergent nationalist leader (and later president)—told his fellow Ivorians that "if you don't want to vegetate in bamboo huts concentrate your efforts on growing good cocoa and coffee. They will fetch a good price and you will become rich!"[6] His compatriots heeded his call. By 1956, the Ivory Coast had become the world's largest producer of robusta coffee and the world's third-largest coffee producer overall, after Brazil and Colombia. Between 1950 and 1960, coffee production doubled in Angola, tripled in the Ivory Coast, and quintupled in the Belgian Congo. In the late 1930s, only one African country, Kenya, was among the world's top ten. By the end of the 1950s, five African producers—the Ivory Coast, Uganda, Belgian Africa (Congo and Ruanda-Urundi), Angola, and Ethiopia—were in the top ten, and Kenya had fallen off the list.[7] By that point, Africa as a whole produced between a fifth and a quarter of the world's coffee, up from just 5 percent at the beginning of the century.

Most of this coffee—almost 80 percent—was robusta, which worked well both as an estate crop and as a smallholder crop. Most arabica cultivation was concentrated in eastern Africa, in Ethiopia, Kenya, the eastern Congo, and Ruanda-Urundi. Fueled by robusta, the center of gravity of coffee production in Africa shifted to Central and West Africa. African smallholders embraced robusta for many of the same reasons as smallholders in Asia and the Pacific. Robusta could be intercropped with other cash and food crops, and it could produce an adequate revenue stream without expensive inputs or additional labor. Colonial agronomists often complained that smallholders were reluctant to cultivate robusta more intensively or to adopt a full technical package that would have increased yields. Only in the Belgian Congo and Angola did robusta thrive as an estate crop, although even in those places, smallholder production increased in both absolute and relative terms during the 1950s.[8]

Demand for robustas had also been growing, reflecting rising global demand for instant coffee. Known in the coffee trade as soluble coffees, the first instant coffees had been developed in the early twentieth century. Instant coffee is a dried, powdered coffee extract that dissolves quickly in boiling water. It gained a significant market share in the 1940s as Nestlé perfected techniques for processing the coffee and producing a product with consistent flavor. During World War II, the US Army included soluble coffee in military rations. In the postwar years, large coffee companies like Maxwell House and Nestlé manufactured and marketed instant coffees on a large scale. In full page magazine ads, Jackie Gleason proclaimed "Mmm-BOY! New NESCAFÉ IS GOOD COFFEE!" The bottles announced that they contained "100% pure coffee," quietly concealing the fact that this coffee was mostly robusta. Coffee roasters also continued using robusta in their blends of roast and ground coffee.[9]

The coffee rust followed the course of the postwar coffee boom. The path of *H. vastatrix* in central and western Africa is difficult to track with any precision. Because most of the coffee produced in these areas was the rust-tolerant robusta, the rust did not cause the same kind of dramatic losses as it had elsewhere. Farmers and scientists paid it little attention. In the Belgian Congo, for example, Wellman found *H. vastatrix* present almost everywhere, but he noted that it was "of practically no importance." In fact, it "was of such little importance to the growers that many of them, including a few specialists, did not even know what the disease looked like, although their fields were attacked."[10]

The picture became clearer in the 1950s, as coffee researchers began systematically looking for the rust. The rust spread outward from the Congo River basin in two arcs: northward from the Congo Basin into West Africa, and southward into Angola. The rust was first recorded in English Cameroon in 1951 and in French Cameroon in 1952. From Cameroon, the disease appears to have spread to West Africa. It bypassed a number of other coffee-producing zones to reach the Ivory Coast's vast coffee farms in 1952–53. The infection seems then to have spread from the Ivory Coast to its neighbors, reaching Dahomey (Benin) in 1952, British Togo (now part of Ghana) in 1953–54, and Liberia in 1955. After a pause, the rust was reported in Guinea and Nigeria in 1962.[11]

Wellman speculated that Cameroon's coffee farms may have initially been infected by rust spores carried from an infected region on the wind, although this would have involved a flight of at least 1,000 kilometers.[12] He contended that the rust could not have been circulated on infected plants or seeds because all West African countries had "rigorous quarantines."[13] This assumes, however, that the quarantines were completely successful in identifying and eradicating infected plants. The coffee expert A. E. Haarer did not share Wellman's confidence in quarantines, arguing that "illegal or irresponsible importation of seed or planting material" likely helped circulate the rust through West Africa. He also signaled the "danger of air travel transporting the microscopical spores."[14]

Angola was the only major coffee zone of Africa to remain free of the rust. This was surprising; Angola's forests were home to many wild coffee species, it had a long tradition of commercial coffee cultivation, and it bordered the Belgian Congo, where the rust had been present for a long time. Like other countries in the area, it had greatly increased production in late 1940s and early 1950s. Angola produced both robusta and arabica coffees, mostly destined for markets in Portugal and the United States. The colony had a well-developed agricultural research infrastructure, including a technical service of the Junta de Exportaçao do Café Colonial (Colonial Coffee Export Board), a national experiment station, and a private experiment station operated by the Companhia Angolana de Agricultura (CADA). During the 1950s, experts at these stations scoured the colony looking for signs of coffee rust, but they found none. Wellman and Cowgill found many other kinds of plant rusts growing in Angola, so the environment was clearly favorable to fungi. "The reason for [the coffee rust's] absence is not exactly clear to me," mused Wellman.[15] As map 7.1 shows, the world of coffee—like the world of politics—seemed be divided into two blocs: a rust-infested eastern bloc, where robusta dominated, and a rust-free western bloc, where arabica still dominated.

Coffee's Partial Green Revolution

In the postwar decades, governments and multilateral organizations in the Global North began promoting agricultural modernization in the Global South. Development experts argued that agricultural modernization would help countries in the Global South overcome problems of hunger and poverty and would promote overall development. The best known of these programs is the Green Revolution, which focused on food crops—wheat,

Map 7.1. Coffee areas of the world, in relation to the rust, 1952. Most of the coffeelands east of the line were infected with the rust. Robusta production dominated in those zones. Arabica prevailed in the regions to the west of the line, which were still rust-free. (From USDA Foreign Agricultural Services, *Foreign Agriculture* 16, no. 9 [September 1952]: 170)

maize, and rice. While the specifics of these postwar agricultural modernization programs varied widely, most of them sought to rapidly increase productivity by encouraging farmers to adopt modern agricultural practices, which included replacing traditional cultivars with improved hybrid cultivars and applying chemical fertilizers and fungicides.[16]

In Africa, development officials launched a number of agricultural modernization schemes, led by scientific and technical experts. As in other parts of the Global South, these development schemes were often overambitious or poorly adapted to local environmental and economic conditions. Sometimes, the colonial states forced farmers to adopt new cultural practices. In contrast, the modernization of coffee farming in central and western Africa took place more gradually and, partly because of that, with greater participation from African smallholders.[17]

The major European colonial powers in Africa all strengthened their coffee research institutions, often as part of larger colonial modernization initiatives. In 1944, the French government founded the Office of Overseas Scientific and Technical Research to coordinate research in its colonies. One of the principal coffee centers under this office's purview was the Centre de Recherche Agronomique de Bingerville (Bingerville Agricultural Research Center), in the Ivory Coast. The French also maintained a series of smaller agricultural research stations in the Ivory Coast, French Guinea, Dahomey, Cameroon, and Madagascar. In the Belgian Congo, the INEAC continued to carry out research on both robusta and arabica coffee, at Yangambi and four regional coffee stations. The French and Belgian stations were largely concerned with the problems of robusta and excelsa coffee (a variety of Liberian coffee), so the coffee rust was only of secondary interest. The coffee rust played a much larger role at the British coffee research stations in Tanganyika (Lyamungu-Moshi) and Kenya (Coffee Research Station at Ruiru), which were centrally concerned with arabica coffee.[18]

Coffee researchers in central and western Africa had to confront more serious problems than the rust. An epidemic of fusarium wilt (tracheomycosis, caused by the fungus *Gibberella xylarioides*) broke out in Oubangi-Chari (now the Central African Republic) in French West Africa in the 1920s and 1930s. In the 1940s and 1950s it spread through the Belgian Congo, Cameroon, and the Ivory Coast. Unlike the coffee rust, the wilt was fatal to the coffee plant; it killed infected trees in a matter of months. The disease proved to be particularly virulent on several varieties of coffee widely cultivated in the region: excelsa and Indenie (both varieties of *C. liberica*) and the Kouilou variety of *C. canephora*. Over the 1930s, it had destroyed excelsa production in Oubangi-Chari, reducing coffee production there from 20,000 tons to just a few hundred. In the 1940s and 1950s, it caused losses of about 30 to 40 percent in the Ivory Coast, although other regions remained only lightly infected.[19]

The region's colonial governments and agricultural services responded swiftly. In 1956, the Belgian Congo's INEAC hosted a conference on the coffee wilt. Scientists from the Ivory Coast, Oubangi-Chari, Cameroon, and the Belgian Congo all participated. They found that in each place, the coffee wilt was more serious on local coffee varieties than on introduced varieties. This suggested that, like the rust, there were races of the wilt that had adapted to the prevailing coffee varieties in each region. In the Ivory Coast, the colonial agricultural services distributed wilt-tolerant INEAC robustas developed in the Congo, which proved to be comparatively resistant to the wilt in West Africa. Ivorian coffee farmers also had technical and economic support from the colonial state; the state paid coffee farmers to destroy infected plants and plant resistant ones. Between 1950 and 1957, farmers replanted some 100,000 hectares of coffee—roughly a quarter of the area under cultivation—with resistant varieties. It is, in some respects, lucky that the wilt epidemic took place when coffee prices where high and colonial developmentalism was at its peak. Colonial states had both the resources and the interest in keeping such diseases under control. By the 1960s, replanting programs had virtually eliminated the wilt as a threat.[20]

In the arabica zones of eastern Africa, rust research remained a significant priority. In the postwar years, researchers there focused on refining chemical control strategies. During the Depression and the war, planters in Kenya and Tanganyika had reduced chemical spraying or abandoned it altogether. Rising coffee prices in the early 1950s, however, prompted new research into chemical control. Frederick Wellman argued that, without spraying, "Kenya could not produce coffee as a major money crop." For that reason, it was in Kenya that "spraying has been developed to its greatest perfection, in the whole of Africa."[21]

Scientists there built on the work of Mayne and his collaborators in India. Over the 1950s, researchers at Kenya's Coffee Research Station conducted thorough field studies of spraying for rust: they compared the impacts of different fungicides, different spray concentrations, the volume per acre, the methods of application (spraying the upper or lower surfaces of the leaves), the means of application (spraying technologies), and timing of application. The coffee expert R. W. Rayner and his colleagues found a strong correlation between the concentration of the fungicide and the effectiveness of control. This effectiveness came at a cost to the farmer, though, since "for each equal additional decrease in percentage of diseases rusted, the concentration had to be doubled."[22] In Africa, as in Asia and the Pacific, chemical control was a viable option for only a tiny proportion of the continent's farmers.

The Coffee Rust Research Center

One of the main goals of Wellman and Cowgill's coffee rust survey was to develop a global network of coffee researchers and institutions. While traveling through Europe, they visited Portugal's National Agricultural School (ENA) at Oeiras. The fascist Estado Novo government had established the ENA in the late 1930s as part of a program of state-led technocratic development. It also funded scholarships to send promising young Portuguese scientists to train in some of the best laboratories in the world.[23] One of these was a young plant pathologist named António Branquinho d'Oliveira. He had received his PhD from Cambridge, for research on cereal rusts. His interest in the coffee rust began during a visit to the Portuguese colony of São Tomé in 1951. He brought samples of the rust and coffee varieties back to Portugal and began testing them at the

ENA greenhouses. Wellman and Cowgill recognized that d'Oliveira's lab would be an ideal place to establish a global center for coffee rust research. In Portugal, unlike in coffee-growing countries, there was no risk that a virulent strain of the rust might escape the experimental greenhouses and infect surrounding coffee plantations.[24]

The Coffee Rust Research Center (better known by its Portuguese acronym CIFC) was established in 1955, headed by d'Oliveira. It was a hybrid institution, at once colonial and multilateral. On the one hand, it was part of a larger expansion of Portuguese colonial science in the 1950s, as Portugal's fascist Estado Novo government sought to consolidate control over its colonies and make them more economically productive. The agricultural sciences were a key part of these developmentalist initiatives, overseen by the Junta das Missões Geográficas e de Investigações do Ultramar (Board of Overseas Geographical Missions and Research).[25] On the other hand, it was a multilateral institution that promoted knowledge exchange across the Global South. Portugal had joined the United Nations in 1956 and sought to participate in multilateral development projects. The CIFC embodied these contradictions in Portugal's political projects, strengthening the empire while also promoting multilateral developmentalism.[26]

From its inception, the CIFC was a global hub in coffee rust research. D'Oliveria and his colleagues built one of the world's largest collections of wild and cultivated coffee varieties, as well as the largest collection of live rust samples. These collections depended on transnational cooperation; they drew from networks of exchange with national and colonial research institutions around the world, as well as Portugal's own large colonial network. The CIFC received coffee varieties from across Africa, Asia, and the Americas, and samples of the coffee rust from infected regions in Africa and Asia. By 1965, the CIFC had received some 2,101 accessions of coffee plants and 783 samples of *H. vastatrix* from around the world.[27]

With these unique global collections, d'Oliveira and his colleagues could conduct research on the rust that would not previously have been possible. They identified and classified the physiological races of the rust, which in turn shed light on the genetics of rust resistance in the coffee plants. Building on a technique that Wilson Mayne had developed in India, scientists at the CIFC would cultivate each accession of rust and inoculate a range of coffee varieties with it. On some varieties, the rust fungus would not grow at all, showing that the variety was resistant to that strain of rust. On other varieties, the rust would develop fully, showing that the variety was susceptible. Similarly, each new accession of coffee was tested against a range of known rust races.[28]

By systematically comparing how different samples of rust behaved on different coffee plants, the CIFC researchers identified new races of rust and new resistance genes in the coffee plant. They grouped coffee plants according to their resistance to the rust races. By 1960, CIFC researchers had identified ten races of rust and grouped each known coffee variety into one of nine groups. Plants from group A (which included no arabicas but a number of varieties of *C. canephora*) were resistant to all known races of rust. Significantly, plants from group E—which included all the arabica cultivars grown in the Americas—were "fully susceptible to every rust race which can attack arabica coffee."[29] This refuted a widely held but unfounded assumption that the coffeelands of the Americas had remained free of the rust because the coffee varieties cultivated there were resistant.

The CIFC also began a breeding program to develop rust-resistant coffees. Before World War II, most coffee breeders used classical selection techniques to develop improved strains of arabica. They identified plants with desirable traits (for example, yield or disease resistance) from a given population and collected and planted their seeds. The progeny of that generation would be evaluated in the following years, and the process of selection would continue. But the populations of cultivated arabica were too homogeneous for selection programs to make any significant difference over the short term, especially with respect to rust resistance. After World War II, breeders shifted their efforts from selection to hybridization—crossing arabica cultivars with other arabica cultivars or, in the case of breeding for rust resistance, with other coffee species. The Dutch had done some work with hybrids before the war, but the results were unsatisfactory. The offspring were too variable to be useful or were problematic in other ways. In the 1950s, though, scientists at the CIFC obtained a coffee—known as the Timor hybrid (Hibrido de Timor) which proved ideal for breeding programs.[30]

The original Timor hybrid plants were an accidental legacy of the rust epidemic and Portuguese imperialism. Robusta plants had been introduced to Portuguese Timor—a Portuguese enclave in the Dutch East Indies—in the early twentieth century. They had been cultivated alongside arabica, and at some point, plants from the two species had spontaneously interbred. The Timor hybrids were discovered on a plantation of arabica coffee in the 1920s. They showed a "notable vigor, well covered with leaves, contrasting visibly with the rest of the plantation, which showed weak vegetation and almost entirely defoliated."[31] They remained a local curiosity until Portugal recovered Timor from the Japanese after World War II. In the 1950s, Timor's Coffee Export Board (Junta de Exportaçao do Café) developed plans for developing and modernizing the colony's coffee industry. The coffee rust had reached Timor early in the twentieth century and limited arabica cultivation to altitudes above 1,000 meters. The Timor hybrids seemed to offer a potential solution to this problem, but the plants were unsuitable for commercial cultivation; they were highly variable, reflecting their mixed botanical heritage. Timor's Coffee Export Board sent a packet of Timor hybrid seeds to the CIFC in 1957, followed by further shipments in 1960 and 1966.[32]

Researchers at the CIFC set about studying and improving the Timor hybrid. They tested the plants for resistance to the known races of rust, selecting plants whose phenotype was closest to arabica. The Timor hybrid coffees proved to have a critical genetic advantage over earlier spontaneous hybrids of arabica and robusta. The spontaneous hybrids discovered in India and Java in the early twentieth century were all diploids, and self-sterile. Because of this, they did not breed true from one generation to the next. But the Timor hybrids were tetraploids like arabica, and self-fertile. Genetically, they behaved like arabica, which made it easy to backcross the Timor hybrids with arabicas. The goal of backcrossing is to transfer particular genes from one population to another. The offspring of the first cross (the F_1 generation) would then be crossed with the arabica parent, producing the F_2 generation, which would in turn be evaluated and crossed with an arabica parent.

Backcrossing the Timor hybrid with arabica would, over several generations, produce plants that combined the agronomic and cupping qualities of the arabica parent with the rust resistance from the Timor hybrid. Breeders at the CIFC crossed Timor hybrids with important arabica cultivars from the Americas. Over the 1960s, the CIFC sent selections of the Timor hybrid selections to breeding programs at experiment stations in India, Tanzania, Angola, Brazil, Timor, Colombia, and Costa Rica.[33] While coffees based on the Timor hybrid showed some promise, the first generations could not match the cupping quality or some agronomic characteristics of the traditional arabica cultivars. Even with a good foundation, it could take decades to develop a commercially viable new cultivar. But it was a promising start, offering some hope that commercially viable, rust-resistant arabica would be possible.

The Rust Decolonized

While Africa's coffee production was booming, the political and economic contexts began changing. In the late 1950s, most of sub-Saharan Africa was still under colonial rule; by 1970, only a handful of colonies remained. The formal process of decolonization in sub-Saharan Africa began with Ghana's declaration of independence in 1957. Within a decade, most European colonies in Africa—with the significant exception of Portugal's colonies—had achieved independence. Portugal's African colonies, including Angola, did not achieve independence until 1975. The pathways to nationhood varied; in some places, such as the Belgian Congo, decolonization was violent and disruptive. Elsewhere, such as in French West Africa (including the Ivory Coast), decolonization was more gradual and showed considerable institutional continuity before and after independence.[34]

Coffee exports remained a key part of economic development strategies for many of the new nations. But the economic outlook for coffee had worsened since the mid-1950s. As the trees planted in the boom of early 1950s came to maturity, the global supply of coffee once again exceeded demand, and prices began to fall. By 1960s, robusta prices had dropped almost to their pre-boom levels. To avoid renewed cycles of boom and bust, producing countries and consuming countries made a series of agreements that aimed to shore up coffee prices. In 1962, coffee-producing countries—including the newly independent nations in Africa—and coffee-consuming countries signed the first International Coffee Agreement (ICA). The ICA sought to balance global supply and demand for coffee by setting export quotas for coffee-producing countries. The goal was to keep coffee prices high enough to provide a living for coffee farmers while preventing prices from getting so high that they discouraged consumption. The ICA's quota system ended the period of rapid growth in African coffee; through the 1960s, coffee production in most African countries remained high but stable.[35]

In most former colonies, decolonization did not disrupt coffee research programs. The Institut Français du Café et du Cacao (IFCC) had been formally established in the late 1950s, with its head office in France but most of its research staff in the Ivory Coast. The IFCC took over the operations of the colonial botanical garden at Bingerville and several other specialized laboratories and research stations. The IFCC continued to operate after independence, jointly funded by the governments of France and the Ivory Coast.[36] Likewise, the colonial coffee research center in Kenya continued operations after independence as the Coffee Research Foundation. The scientific staff of these stations changed little, at least over the short term. The main institutional casualty of decolonization—as far as coffee research is concerned—was the INEAC in the Belgian Congo. It ceased operations in 1961, in the wake of the violent and chaotic independence movement that gave birth to the Democratic Republic of the Congo.[37] Taken as whole, though, the community of coffee researchers in Africa remained small. In 1967, only eight countries or territories in Africa had "well-developed" research and extension services; even the largest of these had fewer than twenty scientific staff.[38]

The anticolonial struggles presented challenges to the CIFC. It depended on continuing collaboration and exchanges with coffee-producing countries around the world. During the early years of decolonization, these exchanges continued unabated. But in the mid-1960s, Portugal became embroiled in brutal colonial wars in Angola and Mozambique. In response, Portugal was expelled from some multilateral organizations, such as the Commission for Technical Cooperation in Africa South of the Sahara.[39] Many countries broke off diplomatic relationships—including scientific exchanges—with Portugal. For example, the CIFC could no longer directly exchange material with India, an important source for genetic diversity of arabica coffee. It is a testament to the CIFC's growing importance, however, that collaborations continued in spite of the blockade. D'Oliveira arranged to route exchanges indirectly, through the FAO in Rome.[40] This situation continued until 1974, when the Portuguese Estado Novo regime was overthrown. Angola, Mozambique, and Guinea became independent the following year, after which Portugal resumed normal diplomatic relationships. Decolonization presented the CIFC with some new problems because its operations had historically been funded by revenues from Portuguese colonies. After 1975, it had to seek new sources of funding.[41]

Coffee research programs in postcolonial Africa gradually shifted to reflect the changing political and economic conditions. During the 1960s, scientists at the IFCC produced an artificial hybrid between arabica and robusta, which they baptized "arabusta." Unlike the Timor hybrid, which breeders used to make an improved arabica, the arabusta was meant to be an improved robusta. Improving the cupping quality of robusta was a way of increasing revenues while staying within the export quota. While the Timor hybrid originated as a spontaneous hybrid, arabusta was an artificial hybrid. Since the 1940s, plant breeders had been using a plant-based alkaloid called colchicine to double the chromosomes in plant cells, which they then used in breeding programs. Breeders at the IFCC used colchicine to produce a tetraploid robusta, which they crossed with arabicas. These, in turn, produced fertile tetraploid offspring. Like the Timor hybrid, the arabusta coffees were resistant to the rust; they also had good cupping quality. But they faced other problems, such as comparatively low yields, so they were never cultivated on a large scale. Farmers have preferred to stick with robusta and other varieties of *C. canephora*.[42]

Coffee breeders also collected wild arabica germplasm—to use in breeding programs to expand the genetic diversity of the world's cultivated arabica. In 1964, the FAO sponsored a coffee mission to Ethiopia to study arabica coffee at its wild origin and to collect and distribute Ethiopian coffee seed. The team included a botanist, breeder, geneticist, and entomologist and also represented seven countries: Kenya, Tanzania, Uganda, Brazil, the United States, India, and Ethiopia. The mission's report described the collection of coffee germplasm as "a matter of some urgency to recover valuable information now before the advance of the axe and bulldozer made further ruinous inroads in the most important areas." Several of the mission's objectives touched on the coffee rust and its control. The mission sent a complete set of its seed collections to the CIFC for screening, along with fifty samples of the fungus collected in the field. The seed collections promised to add badly needed genetic diversity to arabica breeding programs. "The highest producing and at the same time fully rust susceptible coffee plants in Brazil," the report noted, "are products of a relatively depauperate genetic stock. Available germ plasm reserves for combatting coffee leaf rust are wholly inadequate." The mission sent collections of Ethiopian arabica seed to coffee research centers in India, Tanzania, Costa Rica, and Peru. The seeds were sown and now form live collections of Ethiopian germplasm, some of which have since been used in arabica breeding programs.[43]

In the midst of this political and economic tumult, the coffee rust was finally detected in Angola in 1966. The largest surprise was that it had taken so long to appear. It may well have been present on the many wild coffee species that inhabited Angola's forests. The rust expert Albertus Eskes later suggested that the fungus had escaped detection because the local races of *H. vastatrix* were not well adapted to arabica coffee.[44] The significant expansion of coffee cultivation in the late 1950s and early 1960s—especially coffee estate production—helped create ideal conditions for the rust to reproduce on a large scale. The government had promoted arabica cultivation; although these initiatives were a commercial failure, the arabica plants may have helped the rust propagate and spread. The anticolonial struggle may have also contributed. In 1961, nationalist guerrillas invaded northern Angola from the southern Democratic Republic of the Congo (DRC). Over the following years, thousands of guerrillas—and tens of thousands of refugees—moved back and forth across the border between northern Angola (which included many coffee estates) and the DRC (where coffee rust had been present for some time). It is certainly possible that such large-scale movement of people may have hastened the dissemination of the coffee rust to northern Angola, assuming it was not previously present.

BY THE mid-1960s, the rust had reached virtually every corner of Africa. The postwar spread of the rust through Central Africa and West Africa did not disrupt coffee production as it had elsewhere simply because most coffee farmers were already cultivating rust-resistant varieties of coffee. The robusta boom in Central and West Africa helped refashion the global coffee trade. It expanded the space for low-quality robustas that the Dutch had created thirty years before and fueled the growing markets for instant coffee. Ecologically, this episode shows the power of resistant hosts; even when the pathogen is present in such a population, it causes little or no harm and requires no special control measures. But even so, farmers elsewhere were not keen to follow the West African model since the resistant varieties in question—especially the robusta coffees—were of lower quality than the prized arabica coffees and therefore fetched lower prices. Scientists began working systematically to develop rust-resistant coffees that retained arabica's quality. International scientific cooperation on rust research became more deliberate and formal, as embodied in the CIFC. This kind of global cooperation led to new scientific insights about the nature of the rust fungus itself and rust resistance in the coffee plant. And as the fungus moved westward, observers became increasingly concerned about the growing risk that it would spread to the Americas. In 1960, the British rust expert R. W. Rayner predicted that "the disease would certainly sweep through many areas [of the Americas] like a fire," and that when it did, "there would be a disaster of the first order."[45]

CHAPTER 8

A Plague Foretold

Latin America

IN THE 1981 novella *Chronicle of a Death Foretold*, the Colombian novelist Gabriel García Márquez tells a story of how a young man, Santiago
Nasar, was murdered on his doorstep—even though most of the village
knew beforehand that the murderers were after him. For a variety of reasons, deliberate and accidental, the people who knew about the intended
murder did nothing to prevent it. Similarly, the coffee rust was a plague
foretold. Since the early 1950s, Frederick Wellman and others had warned
that the rust would soon find its way to the Americas. Some coffee growers,
and even apparently some leading scientists, countered that the conditions
in Brazil would be too dry for the rust; Wellman countered that "its rapid
spread and vigorous development in such dry countries as parts of Kenya,
Tanganyika, India, and the Sudan, show nothing upon which Brazil can
base any great confidence." Wellman also expressed concern about the
rust's arrival in West Africa during the 1950s, which brought large-scale
rust infections closer to the New World than ever before. The South Atlantic

still presented a formidable barrier, but one that could be overcome. "For the first time," worried Wellman, "rust areas are in the direct path of winds and storms reaching from rust-diseased coffee of Africa to coffee plantings in the Americas."[1] Over the 1950s and 1960s, at least ten articles predicted that the rust would eventually reach the Americas.[2] But coffee organizations and coffee farmers of the Americas did little to prepare for the rust's arrival.

Coffee research in Latin America had expanded and consolidated since World War II. This reflected the greater institutionalization of the coffee industry as a whole. Since the 1930s, most Latin American governments became directly involved in managing the cultivation, processing, and marketing of coffee—in contrast to the general laissez-faire that had prevailed before the war. In most Latin American countries, the coffee industry was overseen by public agencies, usually coffee institutes. The most powerful of these was the Brazilian Coffee Institute (IBC); Mexico and Costa Rica also had powerful coffee institutes of their own.[3] The coffee industries of Colombia and Guatemala were overseen by semipublic growers' associations: FEDECAFÉ and ANACAFÉ, respectively. National research institutes, such as the Instituto Agronômico de Campinas (IAC) in Brazil and CENICAFÉ in Colombia, likewise played an important role in this network. These national institutions were supported by a network of international research institutions, including the IICA in Costa Rica and the CIFC in Portugal. During the years of the International Coffee Agreement, which lasted until 1989, these institutions played an unprecedented role in shaping coffee cultivation in Latin America. They supported basic and applied research into coffee cultivation, they operated large-scale extension networks, and, in many cases, they shaped *how* farmers cultivated coffee.

In the 1950s and 1960s, this network of coffee institutes and research centers was principally concerned with maintenance research—sustaining and (ideally) increasing coffee production in areas where coffee had been produced for a long time. They worked on coffee breeding, on the introduction of agricultural chemicals (fertilizers and pesticides to help sustain and increase productivity on long-established coffee lands), and on planting systems more generally (soil management and conservation, shading, etc.).[4] These problems were more pressing than the coffee rust, which—in spite of the warnings—still seemed like a distant threat. Still, the IAC, CENICAFÉ, and IICA all did some research on breeding rust-resistant coffees. In the 1950s and 1960s, they received potentially rust-resistant coffee seeds collected in Africa and Asia by Wellman and Cowgill's coffee rust survey, and seeds collected in Ethiopia by the FAO coffee mission. They also received selections of the rust-resistant Timor hybrids from the CIFC. Breeders at the IAC also developed their own hybrid of arabica and robusta—the Icatú—using a tetraploid robusta that researchers there had produced in 1947. Like the Timor hybrids and the arabusta coffees, the Icatú plants showed good rust resistance but required further crosses to produce a coffee that could match the productivity and quality of the prevailing arabica cultivars. But even these breeding initiatives remained desultory before 1970. None of the coffee regions of the Americas were as well prepared for the epidemic as they could have been (fig. 8.1).[5]

Containing the Rust in Brazil

The rust was first detected in Brazil in an unlikely location: a small stand of coffee on the edge of a cacao farm in Ubaitaba, about 80 kilometers northwest of the port city of Ilhéus in the state of Bahia (see map 8.1). Coffee there was grown on a comparatively small scale; Bahia was not one of Brazil's major coffee-growing regions. An agronomist named Arnaldo

Figure 8.1. "I got rusted!" (Drawing by Hugo Díaz Jiménez. In Ministerio de Agricultura y Ganadería, *Manual del caficultor*, 10. Courtesy of Rosa Ma. Fernández.)

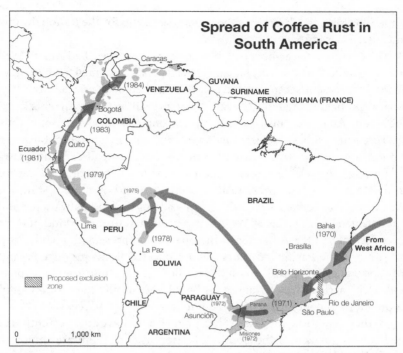

Map 8.1. Spread of *H. vastatrix* in South America. (Map by Marie Puddister)

Medeiros, who specialized in cacao diseases, was the first person to spot the rust. While conducting a field study, he noticed some infected leaves on coffee plants growing at the margins of a cacao plantation.[6] He was familiar with the rust because he had seen it while on a research trip to Angola in 1967.[7]

The discovery triggered a swift and unprecedented institutional response. When the rust had broken out in Ceylon almost a century before, the British government had sent a lone scientist to study it. In 1970, reports of the rust mobilized a global network of government agencies, coffee institutes, coffee associations, universities, and international scientific organizations. Brazilian researchers sent samples of the infected leaves to the IAC and the CIFC, which confirmed that it was indeed the rust. Within weeks, international experts joined Brazilian researchers to study the disease in the field. The group included Fredrick Wellman (then at North Carolina State University), Russell Desrosiers (from the US Agency for International Development), and Eugenio Schieber, then at Guatemala's Instituto Agrario Nacional. These visitors accompanied José Maria

Jorge Sebastião, the director of the Executive Group for the Rationalization of Coffee Farming.[8]

It remains unclear how or when the coffee rust reached Brazil. Wellman concluded that the rust had likely been present in Brazil for at least two years. Some scientists speculated that the rust had been carried from West Africa (probably Angola) to Brazil by the prevailing wind currents across the South Atlantic. And certainly, the chronology makes sense, because the rust had first been detected in Angola in 1966. In a paper published in *Nature*, a group of British scientists at the Rothamstead experiment station argued that viable spores could have made the transatlantic journey in five to seven days.[9] These insights were modeled on similar studies of the dispersal of cereal rusts (although the analogy was not always perfect). The infected coffee farms of West Africa presented the same kind of threat to coffeelands in the Americas as the one Ceylon presented to coffeelands in Asia and the Pacific a century before: infected farms produced countless spores, some of which could have floated high into the atmosphere and been carried great distances. In Brazil, they would have found ample populations of coffee plants on which to feed and reproduce.

Other scientists suggested that people may have inadvertently carried the spores across the South Atlantic.[10] Again, there are important parallels with the long-distance dispersal of the rust a century before. New transportation technologies—in this case, jet transportation—may have hastened the fungus's travel. The Guatemalan agronomist Francisco Menchú noted that "currently, a jet flies the distance from Natal to Fernando Po, Dahomey, etc., in just a few hours."[11] The British coffee expert James Waller agreed that the rust could have been carried by the wind, but suggested it was more likely that rust spores had been "accidentally carried across on plant material, baggage, or clothing."[12] For that matter, coffee agronomists themselves could have been a vector; they had been moving between Brazil and Angola in the late 1960s. Both natural and anthropogenic forces carried the spores across the South Atlantic. There were likely *many* acts of dispersal, and it is hard to see how Brazil could have escaped infection.

The IBC created the Executive Committee on the Eradication of Coffee Rust (CEFCA) to oversee the eradication projects. They initially planned to establish an internal quarantine of all infected areas and then eradicate all infected coffee trees within those areas. This involved stumping the trees to a height of about 50 centimeters (a process known as *recepa* in both Spanish and Portuguese) and then spraying the plant and surrounding areas with fungicides. Researchers organized survey teams to map the extent of the outbreak. To their dismay, they found that the rust was much more widespread than they had originally anticipated. By May 1970, just three months after the rust had first been detected, the surveys found that it had spread over much of the states of Bahia, Espirito Santo, and eastern Minas Gerais, an area about the size of Central America.[13] Small coffee farms could be found "haphazardly in the countryside and towns," wrote Wellman. This coffee was "seldom gathered," which helps explain why the disease escaped detection for so long.[14]

For the time, the major coffee-growing regions of São Paulo and Paraná remained free of the disease. The CEFCA proposed creating a "sanitary barrier" to protect the rust-free coffee states from the infected ones. The proposed barrier—some 385 kilometers long and 50 kilometers wide— would run along the 44th meridian from near Rio de Janeiro northward to Belo Horizonte, in the state of Minas Gerais. Within this zone, all coffee cultivation was to be completely eradicated, and the movement of all coffee plants and seeds through the zone was to be prohibited.[15] This ambitious plan by the IBC was very much in keeping with the large-scale pharaonic projects of Brazil's military dictatorship. The Brazilian state viewed the threat of the rust seriously; the coffee industry provided the state with the hard currency to fuel its modernization and industrialization projects.

Although Brazilian scientists had missed the initial arrival of rust, the IBC quickly developed and implemented a nationwide campaign to engage coffee farmers in rust-control efforts. They launched large-scale publicity campaigns—slide shows, short films, murals, radio programs, and photo leaflets—to show farmers how to identify the rust and how to treat it if it appeared on their farms. For example, during 1971 the IBC distributed some one hundred thousand photo leaflets on rust surveillance. Farmers would play an essential role in tracking the rust's spread through Brazil. The IBC also created films showing farmers how to stump and spray coffee trees, and it published other materials (including some 120,000 flyers) on the renovation of coffee farms.[16] Early detection would be essential in mitigating the disease's impact.

The CEFCA soon abandoned ambitious plans for the security belt, as it became apparent that the rust would be impossible to contain. The prevailing winds in Brazil blew southwest, carrying spores from the infected zones southward into the major coffee areas, passing easily over the proposed containment zone. The IBC, in collaboration with the Biological Institute of São Paulo and the Escola Superior de Lavras, used airplanes to track how the rust spores were spreading. Scientists flew airplanes at predetermined altitudes over São Paulo and Paraná and dangled glass slides covered in a sticky medium that trapped spores. The slides were then taken to a laboratory and examined under a microscope to determine the population of spores at various altitudes. The news was discouraging; the flights found airborne rust spores 150 kilometers from the nearest focus of infection in São Paulo. They found viable spores as high as 1,000 meters above ground. To nobody's surprise, the rust appeared in Paraná in October 1971, just a year and a half after it had first been detected in Bahia. The speed of this dispersal reflects the prevailing wind patterns and the massive scale of coffee production in Brazil, where billions of trees produced unprecedented quantities of spores, which found congenial hosts on which to reproduce downwind. The researchers demonstrated that any attempt to contain or eradicate the rust would be both expensive and futile. Official plans for eradication and containment were quietly abandoned after 1971, and within Brazil the researchers and policymakers shifted their focus to finding strategies for coexisting with the rust.[17]

Rust and "Rationalization" in Brazil

As it became apparent that the rust could not be eradicated or contained, the IBC and its partner institutions quickly began promoting the full-blown "rationalization" of coffee farming in Brazil, overseen by the Executive Group on the Rationalization of the Coffee Industry. Controlling the rust was, for the Brazilians, an "agroecological imperative," not to mention an economic and political one.[18] Farmers, and the state, had to address the outbreak as quickly as possible, using the tools that they had available. The agency had been promoting the whole renovation of coffee farming in Brazil for more than a decade. The rust gave the renovation programs a new urgency (and new resources and political support). As a Guatemalan observer described it, the "efforts to contain the advance of the rust were unsuccessful, and resources and energies were shifted to achieve the technification of Brazilian coffee farming at an accelerated pace."[19]

In this view, rust control required a complete restructuring of coffee farms and a reorganization of coffee production. These renovation projects were governed by a series of national programs for the renovation of coffee farming, the first of which was approved in August 1970, just months after the rust had first been detected. The programs provided funds for propagating new high-yielding coffee varieties such as the Mundo Novo (none of which were yet rust resistant), replanting coffee farms according to "rational" principles (i.e., high-yield, intensive cultivation), and helping farmers acquire fertilizers, fungicides, and insecticides. Between 1969–70 and 1973–74, some 730 million coffee plants were sown under these rationalization programs, mostly in Minas Gerais and São Paulo, and to a lesser extent in Paraná and other states.[20]

The Brazilians also adopted chemical control on a large scale. Most of Brazil's coffee farms were in landscapes where chemical control was—in principle—a viable option. Rust infections were not as severe as they had been in the humid lowlands of Africa, Asia, and the Pacific. Most of Brazil's coffeelands had distinct dry and rainy seasons, which helped keep the levels of inoculum manageable. Brazilian researchers could also build on decades of research on the chemical control of rust elsewhere, especially India and Kenya. Still, many aspects of the control program had to be adapted to the economic and ecological conditions of Brazilian farms. This did not happen quickly: a 1972 leaflet published by the State of São Paulo's extension service told farmers that the rust had "found the spraying industry unable to attend satisfactorily to the needs of Brazilian farmers."[21] Brazil's rainy seasons were longer than Kenya's, and for each region, scientists had to conduct local studies to determine when, how often, and how much to spray.

Sprays and spraying technologies had evolved since World War II. Commercial copper oxychloride sprays gradually supplanted the more traditional Bordeaux mixture, which had been used since the late nineteenth century.[22] But the basic principle remained the same; all copper sprays acted as preventives, which stopped the germinating rust from penetrating the plant tissue. Even over the short term, copper sprays proved to be highly effective in managing the rust in Brazil. One study showed that spraying could reduce rust infections from 65 percent to 10 percent. Furthermore, copper sprays could even *increase* yields over what they had been before the rust outbreak. In one place coffee yields increased from 1,415 kilograms per hectare to 1,807 kilograms per hectare. This was a known tonic effect of copper sprays; copper helped increase the foliar density of coffee trees. In 1972, Brazil imported more than 15,000 tons of copper sprays for rust control.[23]

Brazilian agronomists also experimented with a new class of fungicide: the systemics. Chemical companies had begun to develop these after World War II. While copper fungicides were preventive, the systemics were both preventive *and* curative. Systemic fungicides were taken up into the leaf tissue, so they could kill the fungus even after it germinated and penetrated the leaf. Systemics could, therefore, be particularly useful in controlling outbreaks on farms where farmers had not applied preventive sprays.[24] While systemic fungicides did offer an important new tool in controlling rust, it seems that they were not widely used through the 1970s and early 1980s. In 1982, Waller wrote that in field experiments, "systemic fungicides have shown consistently less efficient control than have copper fungicides," which were more effective because of their "greater persistence in the field."[25]

Still, spraying was not a panacea in Brazil, and coffee farmers wishing to begin spraying programs faced many challenges. Wellman warned that "spraying equipment, chemicals, and containers brought in from the [temperate] zone deteriorate rapidly in the tropics."[26] Beyond this, most spraying equipment was designed around the assumption that farmers had ready access to large quantities of water. Chemicals were usually sold as powder and then mixed with water on the farm. But access to water was a problem in many parts of Brazil. At first, then, Brazilian agronomists worked to adapt imported technologies to Brazilian conditions. Over the 1970s, they developed a range of low-volume spraying technologies that required considerably less water than imported equipment. The technologies also had to be adapted to the size of the farm. Smaller farms could be sprayed using knapsack mist blowers, while larger farms could use tractor-drawn sprayers that could cover several rows at a time.

Spraying was also expensive; this was another reason it had not been widely adopted in other parts of the world. Shipping costs could be "colossal," sometimes even exceeding the cost of the equipment itself.[27] In 1977, Lourival Monaco of the IAC estimated that Brazil would need to import 50,000 tons of fungicide annually to combat the rust. The chemicals alone would cost "more than 200 million dollars of capital investment, plus the cost of labor."[28] Estimates from the early 1970s suggest that chemical control could increase the cost of production by 10–20 percent. It would be cost-effective if farms produced enough coffee to offset those costs. Ironically, rust control in Brazil became more cost-effective after another ecological catastrophe—the Black Frost of 1975—killed or damaged billions of coffee trees in Brazil. The sudden decline in Brazilian coffee production caused a sharp rise in global coffee prices. Before the Black Frost, a 1972 estimate set the threshold at which chemical control would be cost-effective at around 600–900 kilograms per hectare; an estimate after the frost set the threshold at about 300–400 kilograms per hectare.[29]

Still, given the many challenges of spraying, Brazilian scientists continued to pursue the holy grail of rust-resistant coffees. Coffee breeders were inspired by the "spectacular success of breeding for resistance in cereals," although coffee differed from cereals in several key respects.[30] In particular, cereals were annuals, which could be bred and distributed quickly, while coffee was a slow-maturing perennial crop. As with many other slow-growing tropical perennials, the development of resistant coffee varieties could take years.[31] The rust fungus, in contrast, could evolve much more quickly than the coffee plant, especially when large-scale monocultures such as Brazil's produced such large quantities of the fungus.

In the early 1970s, breeders at the IAC tried to develop rust-resistant arabicas. Their breeding programs were based on wild arabica germplasm collected in Africa by Wellman and Cowgill in the 1950s and in Ethiopia by the FAO mission. An Ethiopian variety known as Geisha (which a few decades later would be celebrated as a boutique specialty coffee) seemed to be resistant to Race II of the rust, the most widely distributed race of rust in Brazil (and globally). But the Geisha and the other wild arabicas had agronomic problems of their own. Lourival Monaco noted that they produced significantly less coffee than established cultivars and showed great variability in "vegetative growth, branching pattern, plant height, fruit shape and size, and maturation period."[32] Still, as early as 1972, the IAC was conducting adaptation trials in parts of Minas Gerais, Espirito Santo, and Bahia to see whether one of these wild coffees could address these problems.[33]

But new races, seemingly mutations of the original Race II, began to appear in Brazil. Monaco pointed out that, troublingly, "the new races occurred in the absence of any selection pressure." They were "detected in the same uniformly susceptible host, although in a low frequency."[34] When coffee plants were "selected for simple resistance to one race or a certain group of them, coffees [would] eventually become diseased by attack from a physiologically different rust race."[35] In light of these new races, the researchers abandoned breeding programs based exclusively on resistance genes from arabica, concluding that genes from arabica did "not provide effective resistance for more than a few years."[36]

Over the longer term, then, Brazilian breeders shifted their focus from resistant arabicas to hybrids, especially the Timor hybrid and Icatú coffees, both of which contained resistance genes from robusta. This research involved more than just breeding for resistance. A commercially viable plant also had to be at least as productive as established cultivars and adapted to local growing conditions. Breeders therefore crossed the Timor hybrid and Icatú coffees with the most successful Brazilian arabica cultivars (including Mundo Novo and Cautaí), to introduce more genetic variability into the plants, which could then be used as a basis for selection programs.[37]

It was difficult to produce a rust-resistant coffee that met the growers' various requirements. In 1977, Monaco wrote that "the yield of the new selections is usually no better than the best susceptible varieties" and that "their strong preference for certain ecological niches is also a problem."[38] In Brazil, as elsewhere, farmers were reluctant to adopt new coffees without proof that they offered a decisive advantage. Monaco and his colleagues found that it was "very difficult to convince the farmer to pull out the producing plants and replace them with the new cultivars."[39] While resistant cultivars thus remained experimental, coffee farmers had to either control the rust with chemical sprays or absorb the losses from the rust.

Containing Rust along the Cordillera

Coffee producers and researchers elsewhere in Latin America responded quickly to the events in Brazil. Over the 1970s and 1980s, their responses to the rust epidemic would build on the lessons learned in Brazil. They framed the coffee rust as a collective, transnational problem that would require coordinated responses. National, regional, and multilateral institutions cooperated in the campaigns to manage the epidemic. In March 1970, just two months after the rust had been discovered in Brazil, the CIRSA (the international agricultural health agency for Central America and the Caribbean), convened a meeting to discuss the rust. The agency charged the IICA in Costa Rica with studying the rust and helping countries manage the epidemic. The director of the IICA called for a "continental response" to the epidemic, focusing on quarantines, disease control, and the search for resistant varieties. In addition to these international scientific efforts, national campaigns against the rust also sought to enlist the aid of *everyone* in the coffee zones.[40]

In the broader context of the Cold War, the coffee rust outbreak in Latin America also presented a potential social and political problem. Some commentators feared that the epidemic might produce unrest among small-scale coffee producers, raising the specter of revolution. Some of the region's leading coffee-producing nations—Colombia, El Salvador, Guatemala, and Nicaragua—were already suffering from internal conflicts.

Economists made grim predictions of the rust's potential economic and political impacts. The Salvadoran economist M. Muyshondt warned that "it has to be understood, that the importance of an economic loss caused by the rust, directly on coffee industry activity, would also [effect] profoundly a depression in the activities of the banking system, industry, commerce, and service institutions; consequently indirectly affecting the working class." He calculated that if the rust caused a 5 percent decline in production in the area including Panama, Central America, and Mexico, then it would cause $22 million in losses and 7,750,000 lost days of labor. In the worst-case scenario, a 30 percent decline in production would cause $132 million in losses and 46,500,000 lost days of labor. He concluded that "even a 5% loss due to the rust would have a true negative impact on the economic and social development of these countries, carrying great disturbances in the internal political order in each of these countries."[41] Such fears of revolution were seldom expressed explicitly, but they shaped development programs across the Americas.

The coffee experts in Central America and Mexico benefited from the lessons learned in other parts of the world. They regularly visited other coffee-producing regions—especially Brazil—to study how they had coped with the rust. In 1970, the Guatemalan coffee expert Eugenio Schieber traveled to Kenya and Brazil, sponsored by OIRSA (a transnational organization for agricultural health in Mexico and Central America) and the Guatemalan Ministry of Agriculture.[42] In 1971, an international delegation of OIRSA scientists traveled to visit coffee research institutions in Colombia and Brazil and to study the rust in the field. The delegation included coffee researchers from Mexico, Guatemala, El Salvador, Honduras, and Costa Rica. In Brazil, they looked at a range of technical issues, particularly the development of the rust, and strategies for eradicating or controlling the disease. As early as 1971, the Brazilians advised their Central American counterparts that eradication was impossible and that they would have to learn to coexist with the rust. Brazilian technicians also told them that "only farms with a productivity of greater than 10 bags of coffee per 1000 trees would be sufficient to cover the costs of disease control."[43] These visits mattered: the national and regional rust strategies in Central America were strongly informed by the Brazilian experience. In the following years, Central American coffee experts continued to visit Brazil, and Brazilian experts likewise visited Central America.

Countries along the coffee-producing zones of the American Cordillera (Colombia, Central America, and Mexico) established regional and national

quarantines to exclude the rust for as long as they could. They sought funding from the United Nations Development Programme, in cooperation with
the FAO and OIRSA. While the quarantines held, the national coffee institutes trained their scientific and technical staff to prepare for the rust. As in
Brazil, they rolled out publicity campaigns to teach farmers how to recognize the disease and developed action plans for when the rust appeared.[44] In
Colombia, the Federation of Coffee Growers and the Instituto Colombiano
Agropecuario launched national press, radio, and television campaigns and
also sent extension agents to the communities "to train coffee farmers so that
they can recognize the disease with all of its symptoms and details, so that
they learn how to inspect and actually do inspect their crops and thereby
can alert people when the first foci of infection appear."[45] Even if these campaigns could not contain the rust's spread through the Cordillera, they still
mattered. In many of these countries, the initial outbreaks were reported by
farmers who had learned to recognize the disease through the campaigns
and who knew what to do (and who to notify) once the disease was detected.
This early detection allowed countries to deploy containment and control
campaigns, mitigating the initial impacts of the rust.

Publicity campaigns continued through the 1970s and into the early
1980s; extension agents met with coffee farmers in schools, town halls, and
churches, where they gave talks, showed films, and distributed literature.
In Colombia, participation "exceeded expectations." If the numbers are
to be believed, during a single season more than fifteen thousand people
participated in campaign events in the Colombian department of Norte
de Santander alone. As in Brazil, the sermons about rust control evolved
into broader discourses about technification. By their own account, the
technicians on the campaign "vehemently insisted to the farmers on the
urgent need to renew the old coffee farms of the Norte de Santander, with
technified crops that can . . . allow for the control of diseases and pests and
also have greater economic productivity, which gives coffee farmers the
resources to cover the costs of treatment."[46]

In 1976, the rust jumped more than 5,000 kilometers, from Brazil
to Nicaragua. Nobody knew for sure just how this happened, although
it was probably introduced anthropogenically. The outbreak was initially
restricted to a small focus in Carazo, Nicaragua—thousands of miles
away from the nearest infected zones in Brazil. One newspaper speculated
that the rust had been accidentally introduced by a Nicaraguan studying agronomy in Brazil who "sent to his father, as a curious experiment,
a coffee leaf infected with the fungus" so that his father would recognize

it.[47] This scenario is certainly plausible: progressive coffee cultivators in Central America had a long history of adopting innovations from Brazil. Over the years, organizations and individuals in Central America regularly imported new coffee cultivars, such as the dwarf Caturra coffee, from Brazil. Although many innovations were disseminated through public and private institutions, individual farmers also continued to innovate. These private transfers did not always pass through the same sanitary inspection as the official transfers did.[48] It is unlikely we will ever know for sure how the disease reached Nicaragua, but as in Ceylon, the pattern strongly suggests an anthropogenic introduction: it appeared at a single focal point, a long way from any other infected region.

The rust was detected much more quickly in Nicaragua than in Brazil because there were trained observers on the ground. The rust in Nicaragua was first detected when two agronomists were visiting a coffee farm in Carazo. One of them pointed out some defoliated coffee plants to his companion, engineer Jaime Solorzano, the head of Nicaragua's coffee program. Solorzano was familiar with the rust symptoms because he had participated in an OIRSA mission to Brazil in 1974. The very day after discovering the defoliated plants, he flew to Brazil to take the leaves to Monaco at the IAC. Monaco confirmed that it was indeed the rust, and shortly afterward, the Nicaraguan government confirmed that the rust had appeared.[49] People, samples, and information traveled through international scientific networks much more quickly than a century before. In 1869, it had taken six months for the infected leaves collected in Ceylon to be analyzed by a scientist. A century later, a similar transnational process took a matter of days.

Once the disease was confirmed, the Nicaraguan government began a campaign to eradicate it. The government argued that this outbreak was a regional problem requiring a regional response. The member countries of OIRSA likewise understood the issues of control and containment as a regional problem. If the outbreak in Nicaragua could not be contained, then all Central American coffee producers were at risk. Each country contributed funds to the Central American Bank for Economic Integration, which then channeled resources to Nicaragua for use in the campaign. The campaign also received technical and financial assistance from regional agencies, such as OIRSA, and the German Technical Cooperation Agency, the West German international development agency.[50]

During its first year, the eradication campaign reduced the number of rust focuses from 2,068 down to some 15. The containment efforts involved the recepa (stumping) method, which had also been used to contain rust focuses in Brazil. Infected coffee plants were cut down to a stump about 50 centimeters tall, eliminating all branches and leaves. Then, an area 30 meters around each infected plant was sprayed with protective (copper) and curative (systemic) fungicides. The recepa was expensive; in the first year, it involved some 1,600 people, and in later years involved as many as 3,000.[51] In the years to follow, the OIRSA, in collaboration with regional coffee institutes, completed annual reviews of Nicaragua's quarantine and eradication programs. Rust levels remained low from 1977 to 1979, but the rust proved impossible to eliminate entirely.[52]

According to James Waller, the eradication zones around infected trees were not always fully enforced, because of "political and economic considerations"—in short, because many of the coffee farms in the area were owned by allies of the Somoza dictatorship. By 1979, the rust campaign had cost more than $20 million.[53] At the start of 1979, the OIRSA proposed a dramatic solution: the complete renovation of 10,000 hectares of coffee in the infected region. It proposed that all coffee farms in the infected area be eliminated for at least an entire season. Without the host plant, according to the plan, the rust would not be able to reproduce. Additionally, all the plants and soils would be sprayed with fungicides to eliminate any remaining spores.[54]

The Nicaraguan containment programs were disrupted by the Sandinista revolution of 1979. During the fighting, rust control and inspection offices were badly damaged or destroyed altogether; according to one count, some 90 percent of the spraying equipment was destroyed. As the containment effort broke down, the rust began to spread once again.[55] In 1980, the new Sandinista government requested OIRSA funding to begin its own struggle against the rust. It initiated an aggressive program to renovate coffee farms in the infected area, but by that point the epidemic had spread beyond its initial focus. The Sandinista government, under commander Sebastián González, did what Somoza's government would not—it stumped the coffee trees on every farm in Carazo. The Sandinistas wanted to use the rust-control plans to launch a full technification of coffee farming, but the renovation plan was expensive, and circumstances had changed. The Sandinistas did not enjoy the same regional and international support as Somoza's government. And the rust had at last spread beyond Nicaragua's borders. Nicaragua's neighbors had been willing to fund its efforts to contain the rust because these programs were also in their interest. The countries of Central America "had promised all the help necessary to eradicate it [the rust]," complained González, "but all that changed only days after El Salvador announced that the fungus had appeared in its plantations."[56]

Between 1979 and 1982, the rust spread northward through El Salvador, Guatemala, and Honduras, and finally into Mexico (see map 8.2). Scientists argued that the rust spread because of "intensification of movement [of people] in this region, above all intensification caused by political factors."[57] For reasons still unknown, the coffee zones in northern Nicaragua initially avoided infection. In December 1979, the epidemic bypassed northern Nicaragua and made its way to the department of Usulután in eastern El Salvador. The outbreak in El Salvador did not start at a single focus—which would have made it easier to contain—but rather encompassed over 10,000 hectares. In El Salvador, the rust broke out two months after a coup d'état in October 1979; the coup triggered political unrest and a civil war that lasted more than a decade. By December 1980, despite border control and inspection programs, the rust had crossed from El Salvador into Guatemala (also embroiled in a civil war) and Honduras. From Guatemala, the disease reached the Mexican province of Chiapas in 1981, and Soconusco the following year. The rust would have spread through Central America regardless of the political situation, but the political instability made it difficult to mount effective control or containment programs and help farmers buy additional time.

Costa Rica, immediately to the south of Nicaragua, offers a counterpoint to the experience in the rest of Central America. Costa Rica kept the rust out until December 1983, through a combination of strict quarantine and control measures at the border with Nicaragua and at the international airport and a certain amount of luck. From the first outbreak in Nicaragua, though, Costa Rican officials worried that the disease might be transmitted by migrant coffee pickers from Nicaragua. And indeed, the rust was first found on a farm in northern Costa Rica, in the coffee zones closest to Nicaragua. Costa Rica had a large coffee harvest that year, so coffee farmers hired migrant laborers from Nicaragua to help. By the time the disease had been detected in northern Costa Rica, however, the pickers had moved on to the harvest in the Central Valley; they may well have spread the disease there too.[58]

The rust spread through the Andean countries at about the same time it was making its way through Central America. It first reached the minor coffee districts of Paraguay and Argentina in 1972, likely carried by the wind. In principle, the rust should have been contained in Brazil by a

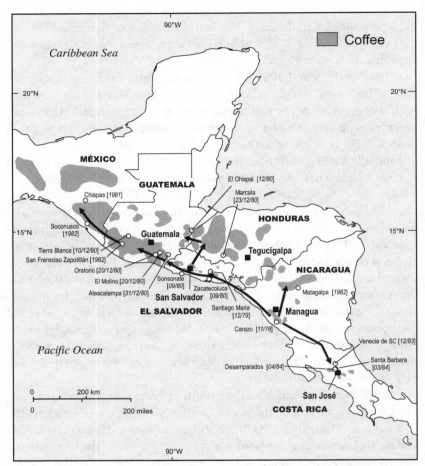

Map 8.2. Spread of *H. vastatrix* in Central America. (Map by Marie Puddister. Reprinted from McCook, "La roya del café en Costa Rica," 107.)

set of massive geographical barriers: the Andes, the vast *cerrado*, and the Amazon basin. But since the 1960s, Brazilian governments—both civilian and military—had been building highways into the interior, to connect Amazonia with the rest of the country. By the 1970s, BR-364 connected the state of São Paulo with the Amazonian state of Acre. In 1975, the rust appeared on small coffee farms in Acre. The rust then broke out in Bolivia in 1978, possibly on infected seedlings imported from Acre. From Bolivia, the fungus worked its way northward along the Andean Cordillera, carried in coffee seedlings and by the wind. The infections also spread along the region's highways. In 1979, the members of the Andean Pact (Bolivia, Ecuador, Colombia, and Peru) established the Andean Program against the Coffee Rust. Its goal was to quarantine the infected zones of Bolivia and Peru and prevent the rust from spreading northward into Ecuador and Colombia. These efforts also included publicity campaigns that "intended to create a spirit of struggle against the disease on the part of the public, emphasizing the recognition of any focus of the disease and its eradication or control."[59] Despite these efforts, quarantine proved futile. The rust reached Peru in 1979, and Ecuador in 1981.[60]

Colombia, then the world's second-largest coffee producer, managed to escape the rust until 1983. It benefited from relative geographic isolation from the infected regions of Brazil and Central America. Government agencies and the FEDECAFÉ also maintained a strict regime of inspections and quarantine at the airports and major border crossings to prevent infected planting material from arriving in the country. The rust was finally detected in the middle of Caldas Department during 1983. It first appeared on a coffee farm that belonged to the president of the Comité de Cafeteros de Caldas, one Jaime Restrepo Mejía. It seems likely that the disease was introduced anthropogenically, as it had been in Nicaragua. Caldas is in the middle of the country, and roughly 900 kilometers from the nearest infected coffee zone, Ecuador's Carchi province. Had the disease spread naturally, from one infected region to its nearest neighbor, it should have appeared in Colombia's southern coffee zones first. The discovery triggered a series of quarantines and plans for chemical control, but as elsewhere, the rust could not be contained.[61]

The rust epidemic also left a curious linguistic legacy in Colombia. The expression *caer la roya* ("to be rust-stricken") became a slang term meaning to suffer a sudden misfortune, and in some contexts to be unlucky in love.[62] It was used frequently when a major national or international public figure—for example the Italian president Silvio Berlusconi—endured a disgrace.[63] It is commonly used when a sports team is plagued by injuries or penalties, as happened to Colombia's soccer team (appropriately nicknamed *Los Cafeteros*, "The Coffee Growers") in the 2014 World Cup.[64] The expression could also be found in music: it's the first line in the bouncy 2000 hit "Luz Azul" by the Colombian band Los Aterciopelados. The song goes on to list other misfortunes, before reminding listeners that life is rosy after all.[65] The expression has since come full circle: it is often used both metaphorically and literally to describe the misfortunes—including the rust itself—that afflict Colombia's coffee farmers.[66]

Between 1976 and 1983, the coffee rust had reached every corner of the Americas. In some senses, this represented a failure. The quarantines and eradication programs could not contain the rust; it became a permanent problem everywhere coffee was cultivated. The microscopic rust spores could travel in too many ways, moving inexorably along trails, highways, and flight paths, not to mention floating on the wind. The rust's spread was hastened by the growing formal and informal integration of Latin America's regions. No quarantine could contain it indefinitely. But they could slow it down, buying some areas another few years of disease-free production. As the rust spread, the focus of research and policy shifted from excluding or eradicating it to finding the best strategies for coexisting with it.

Technification along the Cordillera

In the volatile economic and political context of the 1980s, it was difficult to determine how best to coexist with the rust. The debt crisis struck many Latin American countries early in the decade; the easy credit on which governments had depended in the 1960s and 1970s dried up. Some responded by devaluing their currencies, which effectively increased the costs of imports. Inflation and recession were rampant. By 1983, the so-called Brazilian economic miracle of the 1970s had ground to a halt. Latin American governments began to reduce the power of state institutions, driven both by international forces (especially international financial institutions) and by domestic forces. At the same time, tumultuous political struggles engulfed many of Latin America's most important coffee-producing countries. Guatemala, El Salvador, and Honduras were all embroiled in civil wars. In Brazil, the military government slowly lost its grip on power, and a civilian won the 1984 presidential elections.[67] Publications on coffee cultivation and coffee rust from these years are almost pathologically silent about these larger political and economic processes. But nonetheless, these processes shaped how farmers and institutions responded to the rust.

Responses to the rust were also shaped by the ecological and economic changes in the coffee industry. The International Coffee Agreement had helped stabilize global coffee prices since the early 1960s. But while the agreement could help manage the global coffee trade, it struggled to respond to catastrophic ecological events. When the Black Frost in southern Brazil killed or damaged billions of coffee trees in August 1975, it caused a significant shortfall in the global coffee supply, which lasted several years.

Coffee prices soared in 1976 and 1977 and remained comparatively high for the rest of the decade. High prices gave a strong incentive for farmers in Brazil and elsewhere in Latin America to expand coffee production. The IBC encouraged farmers in the frost-damaged regions of Paraná to switch from coffee to soybeans or cattle ranching. At the same time, it encouraged farmers to expand coffee cultivation in the state of Minas Gerais, which was closer to the equator and less susceptible to frosts than Paraná. By the early 1980s, as the coffee farms of Minas Gerais began producing, prices slackened once again before they resumed climbing in the mid-1980s, after a drought struck São Paulo.[68]

In Colombia and Central America, some groups saw the rust as an opportunity. "The threat of rust is the basis for technifying our coffee cultivation," said Rafael Quirós Guardia, Costa Rica's minister of agriculture.[69] At a regional meeting on the rust in San José in 1977, the IICA promoted the "constitution of a regional program for the modernization of coffee cultivation with contributions from the IICA, CATIE . . . and coffee-growing countries of the Central American isthmus, Panama, and México." This program was duly created, under the name of the Regional Cooperative Program for the Technological Development and Modernization of Coffee Cultivation (PROMECAFÉ) in Central America. It received financial support from national governments, bilateral development agencies (USAID), the US Regional Office for Central American Programs (ROCAP), and research organizations including IICA, CATIE, and OIRSA, and later the French Institute of Coffee and Cacao. PROMECAFÉ facilitated collaborative activities in research, training, and extension. It coordinated research projects with national coffee institutes in Central America. Researchers at PROMECAFÉ conducted studies on breeding rust-resistant coffees and on chemical control. The organization also helped develop regional and global networks of exchange; it organized visits from eminent coffee researchers from CENICAFÉ in Colombia, from CIFC in Portugal, and from the leading research institutions in Brazil. Bettencourt, of the CIFC, "visited the member countries on four occasions, suggesting work methodologies, criteria for selection, and, most importantly, helping with the training of personnel in charge of activities in member countries."[70]

Although there were many ways to technify coffee cultivation, most agencies presented technification as a package. This included, according to a USDA report, "a combination of measures, including scientific pruning, shading, application of fertilizer, insecticides, and fungicides as soon as they become available, and increasing the number of plants per manzana [roughly 0.7 hectares]."[71] In theory, a broad-based program of technification promised to increase production, sometimes by as much as 300 percent. This increased production was supposed to offset the cost of renovating the coffee farm and cover the ongoing costs of fertilizers and fungicides. Technification was a much larger change for coffee farmers in northern Latin America than it had been for producers in Brazil. Coffee in Central America had often been cultivated under shade, either under the forest canopy or under cultivated shade trees. Technification programs recommended that farmers reduce this shade or eliminate it altogether since the high-yielding dwarf coffees would be more productive under full sun. Eliminating the shade trees would reduce the incidence of rust by reducing water on the coffee plants. The simplified agricultural ecosystem would also make it easier for farmers to apply the chemical fertilizers necessary to sustain high levels of productivity, the herbicides to keep weeds in check, and the fungicides to manage the rust and other diseases. Costa Rica's Ministry of Agriculture published a manual in 1985, shortly after the rust had appeared, depicting these best practices for rust control. The ministry commissioned the eminent Costa Rican cartoonist Hugo Díaz Jiménez to depict some of these best practices (figs. 8.2 to 8.4; see also figs. 8.1 and 8.5); his graceful and funny drawings illustrate the ideas and practices at the heart of technification. The rust is portrayed as a long-tailed devil.

At the heart of the technified system were new, high-yielding coffee cultivars, mostly developed in Brazil and then adapted to local conditions. In Brazil, technification programs were initially based on the Mundo Novo cultivar, a high-yielding tall arabica developed by the IAC. Breeders at the IAC also developed a dwarf arabica cultivar that they named Caturra. The original Caturra plants were a spontaneous mutation of the traditional Bourbon cultivar, discovered in the field in Espirito Santo during the 1930s. Carvalho and his colleagues found that Caturra had economic promise; its short stature allowed denser planting and therefore improved yield and facilitated harvesting. Caturra did not do well in Brazil, but it did prosper in the wetter environments along the Cordillera, where it became the basis for technified coffee production. It could be cultivated up to three times more densely than the traditional tall arabicas. Since the Caturras were a mutation of the Bourbon variety, they retained its cupping quality, a feature that was important to the producers of high-quality mild coffees preferred by farmers in Colombia and Central America.[72] Although these dwarf cultivars were highly productive, they were still based on pure arabicas, so they remained susceptible to the coffee rust.

Figure 8.2. Structure of a technified farm. "How do you feel at this distance, neighbor?" "Cool!" "I feel super well ventilated and lighted, neighbor, and safer against the rust." (Drawing by Hugo Díaz Jiménez. In Ministerio de Agricultura y Ganadería, *Manual del* caficultor, 14. Courtesy of Rosa Ma. Fernández.)

Figure 8.3. Practice good pruning. "Dear coffee farmer: when you prune your coffee farm, you cut the rust's tail." (Drawing by Hugo Díaz Jiménez. In Ministerio de Agricultura y Ganadería, *Manual del caficultor*, 21. Courtesy of Rosa Ma. Fernández.)

On technified farms, rust would therefore be managed primarily by chemical sprays (fig. 8.5). Coffee farmers already had some experience with chemical control. Since the 1960s, they had used copper sprays to control another fungal disease, *ojo de gallo* (rooster's eye), caused by the fungus *Mycena citricolor*. The ojo de gallo, which is endemic to the Americas,

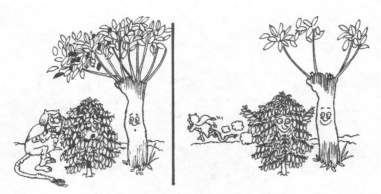

Figure 8.4. Manage shade. Experts encouraged farmers to reduce shade, to expose the coffee plants to more sunlight and (in principle) reduce the rust. (Drawing by Hugo Díaz Jiménez. In Ministerio de Agricultura y Ganadería, *Manual del caficultor*, 21. Courtesy of Rosa Ma. Fernández.)

could cause losses of 20–70 percent.[73] So once the rust appeared, farmers used these sprays on a larger scale. As in Brazil, farmers also started using the newer systemic fungicides, which could be curative as well as preventive. Access to water could be a major problem, as rainwater was quickly absorbed into mountain soils in some places. Topography was also an issue; spraying could be much more difficult on the steep mountainsides of the Cordillera than on the rolling hills of São Paulo or Minas Gerais. In most of the Cordillera, tractor-drawn sprayers were out of the question. Spraying had to be done by handheld knapsack sprayers.[74]

While chemical sprays could effectively control the rust—if they were applied appropriately—their cost remained a chronic problem, just as it had been everywhere else. In the early days of the outbreak in Brazil, the French coffee expert Raoul Muller argued that chemical control might be necessary over the short term. But he worried that the regular use of fungicides presented a "permanent and expensive burden" on coffee growers. On smaller coffee farms, "the productivity [of coffee] might not be enough to cover the cost of these interventions."[75] In the years that followed, other experts made similar arguments. In the early 1980s, Waller argued that "most of the fundamental knowledge of pathogen biology necessary for a rational control strategy is now available."[76] The chief problems were economic and technical.

Technology was also a significant obstacle in Colombia and Central America, perhaps even more so than in Brazil. The steep hillsides, dense

Figure 8.5. Chemical control: copper fungicides beat the rust. "Goooooooal!" (Drawing by Hugo Díaz Jiménez. In Ministerio de Agricultura y Ganadería, *Manual del caficultor*, 27. Courtesy of Rosa Ma. Fernández.)

planting, and shade all presented physical challenges. Waller also worried that many countries did not have the expertise necessary to maintain the spraying equipment. He called for researchers to focus on developing a "cheap, simple, reliable system with adequate biological efficiency that can be rapidly adopted and used by local farmers in isolated areas and on steep land."[77] In Costa Rica, the West German Technical Cooperation Agency helped farmers address this problem by offering them low-interest credit to buy spraying equipment, training them on how to use the equipment, and selling them the sprays at cost.[78] Two of the chemicals most widely used in rust control, Bayleton and Sicarol, were manufactured by the West German companies Bayer and Hoechst AG, respectively.

Given the economic burdens of spraying, scientists continued to work on breeding rust-resistant coffees. During the 1970s, researchers at the CIFC crossed Timor hybrid coffees with the major commercial arabica cultivars cultivated in the Americas.[79] One of these cultivars, a cross between a Timor hybrid and Caturra, showed considerable commercial promise. The CIFC released this variety, known as the Catimor, to partner institutions in the Americas. Researchers at these institutions—especially the IAC and the Federal University of Viçosa in Brazil and CENICAFÉ in Colombia—crossed the Catimors with local arabica varieties. In Central America, the PROMECAFÉ program strengthened and accelerated the exchange and improvement of coffee varietals in the Americas. According to a Guatemalan researcher, "the introduction and distribution [of coffee varietals] through Central America can be divided into two periods: before and after PROMECAFÉ." He praised PROMECAFÉ for developing "regional experiments with the best materials from the germplasm bank" and for systematically acquiring new cultivars from Portugal, Angola, Colombia, and Brazil.[80]

Almost everywhere, breeders focused primarily on rust resistance and productivity. Some Catimor selections performed better than others. In Mexico, for example, early Catimors showed "uneven production, inconsistent heights, and 'bad fruit.' "[81] Carvalho, at the IAC, praised Catimors for their rust resistance but worried that their productivity was "not encouraging."[82] Others expressed concern with Catimor's cupping quality and its resistance to other diseases and pests. Still, as the rust spread through Central America in the early 1980s, Catimor offered coffee growers a measure of hope for the longer term. The Guatemalan agronomist Jorge Echeverri argued that the Catimor had "solved" the problem of the rust and that the main task of breeders was "to select the plants that are the most productive and best adapted to [Central] American ecology."[83] But this solution was, in the early 1980s, still a solution in principle only, not yet in practice. Coffee breeders shifted their focus from arabicas to Catimors and other local Timor hybrid crosses (Sarchimor, Cavimor). PROMECAFÉ breeders conducted a range of regional experiments before releasing promising Catimor progenies to national research programs.[84]

Colombia was the first country to release a Catimor on a large scale. Researchers at CENICAFÉ, the research center for Colombia's Federation of Coffee Growers, had begun breeding programs in the late 1960s. In 1981, after a decade of backcrossing Timor hybrid selections with Caturra over five generations, CENICAFÉ researchers had developed that selections that met the requisite criteria.[85] The Colombian scientists Germán Moreno and Jaime Castillo Zapata pursued a multiline breeding strategy, a technique initially developed to control grain diseases, especially the stem rust of wheat.[86] Multiline breeding, "one of the truly new concepts of the century in breeding self-pollinated crops," had become popular among crop breeders globally during the 1960s and 1970s.[87]

Rather than seeking a single pure line of coffee that was resistant to the prevailing races of rust, the multiline strategy involved mixing different lines of Catimor. The lines purposefully had similar agronomic characteristics (phenotypes) but different combinations of rust-resistance genes. These composite, multiline varieties sought to address the possible rapid breakdown of resistance in genetically homogeneous coffee cultivars, as had happened in India and the Dutch East Indies. In principle, coffee farms with a mix of resistance genes would reduce the selection pressure that accelerated the development of new virulent races. These selections were released as the composite, multiline Colombia variety. Like its Caturra parent, the Colombia variety was a dwarf coffee meant to be cultivated in full sun on technified coffee farms. It contained five rust-resistance genes from its HdT progenitor, in various combinations.[88] By the early 1990s, about a third of Colombia's coffee farmers had switched from traditional arabicas to the Colombia variety.[89]

While technification had many advocates, it was unevenly adopted across Latin America. Technification in Central America "happened at variable speeds," writes the historian Mario Samper Kutschbach, "with much more creative combinations and adaptations than one might expect from reading official manuals and technical recommendations."[90] According to one estimate, by 1990 about "half the area in coffee production in northern Latin America had been converted." But the conversion was not evenly distributed. Colombia had fully technified some 69 percent of its coffee farms, Costa Rica had technified 40 percent, Honduras 35 percent, Nicaragua 29 percent, and Guatemala 20 percent. Farmers in Mexico only technified 17 percent of their coffee farms, in spite of an intensive campaign by INMECAFÉ, the Mexican Coffee Institute. Farmers in war-torn El Salvador only technified 8 percent of their farms.[91]

Other farmers selectively adopted pieces of the technological package. They might, for example, eliminate shade but leave the rest of the system intact, or plant dwarf cultivars without fertilizing them.[92] The particular configuration of each farm in this category, called semitechnified farms, depended on a host of factors. The degree of technification in each country depended heavily on the available institutional support. In some places, farmers received support from national coffee institutes, ministries of agriculture, and development agencies. These organizations offered farmers a range of services: technical support, improved coffee seed, and subsidies on the cost of equipment and supplies. Some even offered long-term loans at favorable rates to help farmers renovate. But the level of institutional support varied considerably between countries, and even within them.

Some observers attributed the reluctance to technify as conservatism or ignorance on the part of some farmers. But this reluctance was more likely the product of (well-founded) risk aversion. Many coffee planters simply decided that full technification was not worth the risk, or the cost. Even with credits and other support, technifying a coffee farm could be expensive. Gabriel Cadena, head of Colombia's coffee research center (CENICAFÉ), noted that "not all peasants can wait the sixteen months necessary for the Colombia variety to begin producing."[93] By the mid-1990s, a plurality of coffee farms in Costa Rica (50 percent), Honduras (50 percent), and Mexico (73 percent) were partially technified.[94]

Other farmers along the Cordillera resisted technification because they worried that the new varieties and hybrids produced coffee of an inferior cupping quality. Under the International Coffee Agreement, the world's coffee producers had been divided into four groups, approximately by quality. Colombian Milds ranked the highest, followed by "Other Milds," which included those from Central America and Mexico. These countries exported high-quality washed arabicas, which helped secure these countries a place in the global market by distinguishing their product from the unwashed Brazilian arabicas. For example, the Guatemalan Association of Coffee Growers (ANACAFÉ) found that, for coffee grown at altitudes higher than 1,200 meters, the traditional Bourbon variety of arabica produced beans with a better cup quality than those of the Catimor hybrid. This difference in taste was significant because the high-quality coffees often fetched higher prices on the international markets. In parts of Guatemala and elsewhere, technification programs were also hampered by a lack of cheap labor, which was essential for planting, maintaining, and spraying the farms.[95] Full technification was not the panacea that its advocates had hoped it would be.

Coexistence, at a Cost

In spite of the all the apocalyptic predictions, the rust epidemic did not devastate coffee production in Latin America. From Mexico to Brazil, and everywhere in between, the epidemic had no appreciable impact on total coffee production. The doomsday scenario that many observers had foreseen did not come to pass. So it is worth asking, Why did the epidemic not cause wholesale catastrophe in Latin America as it had done in Asia and the Pacific?

The disease triangle offers us a helpful way of thinking through this. To recap: an epidemic requires a susceptible host, a virulent pathogen, and the proper environmental conditions. The hosts—the arabicas cultivated across the Americas—were all highly susceptible to the rust. Genetically, they were not significantly different from the arabicas cultivated in Ceylon and Java. The pathogen—the rust—was the same as the one that had devastated coffee farms in the Old World. Small field studies in Brazil, Colombia, and Central America showed that the rust, if left untreated, could cause significant losses in production, at least locally. In Brazil, agronomists found that unsprayed coffee plants yielded 38–85 percent less coffee than plants treated with a fungicide. In Colombia, similar experiments showed a decline of about 23 percent over four harvests. In Central America, experiments found losses of 40 percent on untreated plants in Honduras and 21 percent in Guatemala.[96] Although these studies are just snapshots, collectively they show that rust *could* cause significant losses. But at the aggregate level, no country saw losses on the scale suggested by these experiments. What happened?

Since we can discard the host and the pathogen as explanations, we turn our attention to the third apex of the disease triangle, the environmental conditions. Here, we can consider environmental conditions at two scales: the broad geographical conditions, and local cropping practices. In parts of Latin America, the geography of coffee production helped keep the rust in check. Farmers had not, as their counterparts in Asia had done, pushed the coffee frontier into the hot and humid lowlands where the rust flourished. Much of Latin America's coffee was, in fact, cultivated at higher altitudes, where cooler temperatures inhibited germination of the rust. At the time, control measures were not usually necessary for farms at altitudes higher than 1,200 meters above sea level in Brazil, 1,600 meters in Colombia, and about 1,000 meters in Central America. Control measures were only necessary at the middle and lower altitudes. In places, the prevailing patterns of rainfall also limited the rust epidemic; in places with longer dry seasons, the rust spores had fewer opportunities to germinate.[97]

At the national and local scale, cropping practices also played a critical role in limiting the rust's impact. One strategy, which did not receive much attention from scientists and bureaucrats, was to continue farming coffee traditionally as part of a shaded agroforestry system. These farms typically used few external inputs, if any. Traditional coffee farms persisted across the Americas; in the mid-1990s they accounted for as few as 10 percent of coffee farms in Costa Rica to as many as almost 90 percent in El Salvador, where production was sharply bifurcated between a few highly technified farmers and many traditional farms.[98] The literature on rust control from the 1970s and 1980s usually presented traditional farms as unproductive spaces that needed to be modernized. But more recent work by ecologists has offered a new way of thinking about how traditional farmers managed the rust. The ecologists John Vandermeer, Doug Jackson, and Ivette Perfecto argue that "the complexity of the coffee ecosystem, especially in its more traditional form, may have previously acted as a buffer against epidemics of the disease."[99] They found that a traditional farm ecosystem in Mexico could sustain populations of the fungus *Lecanicillium lecanii*, a fungal parasite of *H. vastatrix* that could limit the disease's impact. Other aspects of the traditional coffee landscape likely also helped keep the rust in check by blocking the wind currents that circulated the rust spores and limiting the amount of rainfall on coffee, depriving the fungus of the water it needed to germinate.[100] These features had limited the rust in Ethiopia's forests. This ecological resilience came at a cost, however, as traditional farms produced significantly less coffee per hectare than technified ones.

Full technification was most common in Brazil, Colombia, and parts of Central America. These farms did see large boosts in productivity over the short term, but they required heavy doses of fertilizers and fungicides to stay productive. On technified or semitechnified farms at the middle altitudes, where susceptible cultivars were grown under little or no shade, farmers depended on chemical control to manage the rust.[101] Coffee breeders continued to do the painstaking work of developing high-yielding, rust-resistant cultivars based on the Timor hybrid. By the 1980s their efforts were finally bearing fruit (literally). But these cultivars were only widely adopted in Colombia, where farmers at lower altitudes planted the newly released Colombia variety. Elsewhere in Latin America, resistant cultivars also showed promise, but as Costa Rica's official coffee manual proclaimed in all caps, "ALL OF THESE MATERIALS ARE STILL IN THE EXPERIMENTAL PHASE SO IT IS NOT RECOMMENDED TO CULTIVATE THEM AT A COMMERCIAL SCALE." The emphasis on this warning suggests that some farmers were planting these varieties anyway.[102]

Coffee farmers in Latin America could also draw on robust scientific and bureaucratic infrastructures that helped coordinate collective responses to the rust. Their situation was a world apart from the experience of Ceylon's farmers in the 1880s. They benefited from a century's worth of global research on the rust, which gave farmers and institutions alike some sense of how to respond to the epidemic. In the major coffee-producing countries—Brazil, Colombia, and Cost Rica—the epidemic was framed as a collective problem that required a collective solution. They had the support of transnational research centers and development agencies. New innovations—ideas, cultivars, tools, and technologies—were diffused quickly through institutional networks. Latin American coffee researchers were in constant contact with each other and with experts around the world. The rust became, as some officials had hoped, a lever of technifying coffee production. Public agencies across the Americas promoted technification as the official solution to the rust. Many farmers did adopt the full technical package; others chose to follow only some of the official recommendations, while still others continued to farm coffee as they had always done. Technification could work for farmers who had the necessary resources to carry out the program, but it was not well adapted to farmers with fewer resources. Nor was it well adapted to traditional farmers, who were not seeking to maximize production.

BY THE 1990s, the rust had become part of the landscape—just another disease—an irritant but no longer, seemingly, a serious problem. It was sometimes difficult for coffee farmers to see how rust affected their coffee production. For example, in Brazil, coffee yields were highly variable even in normal years. It was difficult for farmers to isolate the effects of the rust from the effects of other variables. In years of heavy production, "when the crop was lucrative even with the rust, farmers stopped spraying as regularly as they should, and when they should," allowing the rust infections to develop.[103] In Colombia, "planters have been lulled into a false sense of security after months of living with the disease on their farms," wrote Peter Nares of the *Tea and Coffee Trade Journal*. Since "rust does not cause an immediate fall-off in output," he continued, "numerous planters have decided to ignore the disease as harmless."[104] Scientific and technical reports from the 1980s and 1990s chastise coffee farmers for their supposed complacency about the rust, for their failure to understand the disease, and for their failure to control it "rationally."

But complacency was not the main problem. "Growers who turn a blind eye to plantation diseases," wrote Nares, "do so out of economic necessity and not out of ignorance or apathy."[105] Technification—even partial technification—had come at a significant economic and ecological cost. The technification programs in Latin America were built on a set of assumptions about the price of coffee and the cost of inputs that, in retrospect, proved to be fragile. During the 1970s, technification programs did seem to be cost-effective; the increased yields offset the added costs of production. During the early 1980s, coffee farmers were caught in a price-cost squeeze, as the global price of coffee started to fall at the same moment that the costs of inputs—labor and chemicals—started to rise. In 1976, it cost farmers the equivalent of one 60-kilogram sack of coffee to spray a hectare of coffee; by 1982 it cost them four.[106] Spraying could, then, be cost-effective in one year and prohibitively expensive in the next.

In Brazil, spraying "depended upon the economic conditions each year (price of coffee, price of fungicides, etc.)." As coffee prices declined in the early 1980s, many farmers reduced or abandoned spraying "in function of the increasing costs and other conjunctural difficulties." The IBC reported that just 30 percent of farmers were spraying "rationally"—that is, applying the requisite number of doses.[107] By the late 1980s, similar problems could be found even in Colombia's comparatively well-organized coffee industry. "Fumigation against *roya* and other diseases can call for so large an outlay," wrote Nares, "that some growers do not even adopt preventive or curative measures." Instead, "they let plantation diseases run their course and take their toll" and then "pick what remains of their diseased and depleted harvest, and understandably their returns are less than perfect."[108]

In 1999, a group of French coffee experts worried that while rust "has ceased to be a mobilizing topic [in Central America] . . . it has *not* ceased to be a problematic topic."[109] The lasting impacts of the rust in the Americas differed sharply from those in Asia and the Pacific a century before. There, especially in Ceylon, Java, and the Philippines, the legacy of the coffee rust was one of destruction and (in some places) a resurrection based on robusta. In the Americas, the rust's legacy was transformation rather than destruction. Between 1970 and 1985, the rust epidemic precipitated an unprecedented and swift institutional response, which in turn produced widespread transformations in coffee farming across the Americas. Over the short term, chemical control prevented the sort of large-scale losses seen in other parts of the world.

Over the longer term, full and partial technification changed coffee farming across the Americas; coffee farming became more productive and less sustainable. In places, yields increased to unprecedented levels even as the area under coffee cultivation diminished. But these adaptations to the rust had other, more harmful, impacts, which were only partly visible at the end of the 1980s. The spraying and renovation programs left a legacy of contaminated and degraded soils and sharply reduced biological diversity. They also generated a growing economic stratification among coffee growers; smallholders in particular struggled to pay for the disease-control measures. But even larger coffee growers found that they were more vulnerable to economic and ecological shocks than they had been before.

CHAPTER 9

The Big Rust

IN THE early years of the twenty-first century, the fragile coexistence between coffee farmers and the rust collapsed. The coffeelands of Latin America were rocked by a series of rust outbreaks, known collectively as the Big Rust.[1] Unlike the regional pandemic of the 1970s and 1980s, the Big Rust happened with little advance warning and caused more significant damage. The first outbreak took place in Colombia. Between 2007 and 2011, it reduced Colombia's coffee production by a third.[2] Production only recovered after a national program of control and renovation. Starting in about 2012, a second cluster of outbreaks struck the coffeelands across a broad arc of the American Cordillera, from Peru to Mexico. In Central America alone, total coffee production declined by 16 percent. In some places, the Big Rust caused dramatic losses—far greater than when the rust reached Latin America a generation before. Production in Peru dropped by 39 percent, in Mexico by 46 percent, and El Salvador by 57 percent.

Coffee production in these places has not recovered as quickly as it did in Colombia.[3]

These cold production statistics only hint at the Big Rust's larger economic and social impacts. Over the previous two decades, coffee farmers had already been grappling with volatile coffee prices, hurricanes, droughts, and, in many places, chronic political instability.[4] During the worst years of the epidemic, farmers and laborers saw their already-meager incomes decline even further. They struggled to feed themselves and their families. Some tore up their coffee plants and switched to other crops, like coca, which had problems of their own. Others left the coffeelands altogether, adding to the flow of migrants seeking precarious living in the overcrowded cities or abroad. These shocks made it more difficult for coffee farms to respond to the Big Rust, both individually and collectively.

The Big Rust (see map 9.1) represents a new phase in the history of the disease. This outbreak was not triggered by the pathogen's dispersal to a new landscape; it was triggered by a breakdown in the relations between pathogen, host, and environment. The rust had been present in Latin America for a generation, and farmers had, in one way or another, found ways to coexist with it. But these adaptations were, as it turned out, more fragile than anyone recognized. The Big Rust was driven primarily by changes in the ecological conditions of production, both natural and anthropogenic.

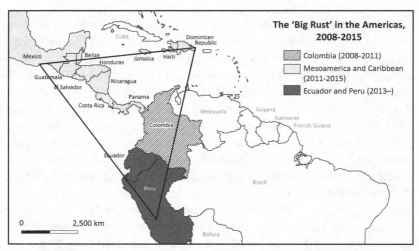

Map 9.1. The Big Rust in Latin America. (Map by Marie Puddister. Reprinted from McCook and Vandermeer, "The Big Rust and the Red Queen," 1165.)

Booms, Busts, and Vulnerable Landscapes

In the decades before the Big Rust, coffee cultivation across the Cordillera had also changed in ways that made the coffeelands vulnerable to the rust. A report by PROMECAFÉ, the regional coffee-modernization program, described the outbreaks as a "symptom of deeper problems of coffee cultivation in the region, such as inadequate crop management, neglected and ageing coffee farms, [and the continued planting of] susceptible varieties, among others."[5] This observation raises a series of important questions: *Why* were farmers not managing their crops adequately? *Why* were many coffee farms "neglected and ageing"? *Why* were farmers continuing to cultivate susceptible varieties? Perhaps these can be explained away as the products of complacency or indifference on the part of farmers, who had lost their fear of the rust. But complacency and indifference are only partial explanations that focus on individual farmers rather than on the broader structural conditions that shaped how they farmed. These maladaptive farming practices were adaptations to significant changes in global politics and the global coffee economy over the previous decades.[6]

The Big Rust was rooted in the post–Cold War economic and political order. Since the 1980s, leading multilateral lending institutions such as the World Bank had pushed for the deregulation of global trade and the reduction of state interventions in markets. The International Coffee Agreement's quota system was a victim of these broader forces. It broke down in 1989 when member states could not agree on new quotas. With the Cold War over and the prevailing economic philosophy opposed to market regulation, the United States under President Bush no longer had a geopolitical interest in the International Coffee Agreement. It withdrew in 1993, effectively ending the quota system.[7]

Since the end of the ICA, global coffee markets have entered a new cycle of booms and busts. Once the quota system ended, producers and traders flooded the market with coffee that they had stockpiled over the previous years. Ironically, the coffee-technification programs of the 1970s and 1980s did increase productivity but, in doing so, also contributed to global oversupply. Brazil and Vietnam both opened significant new coffee frontiers; from 1989 to 2009, Brazilian production tripled and Vietnamese production grew more than 1,800 percent. Vietnam surpassed Colombia as the world's second-largest coffee producer. Other countries also contributed to the global glut. In the face of increased supply and stagnant demand, coffee prices fell—at times even below the cost of production. "In the years 1999–2004," writes David Goodman, "international coffee prices in real terms plumbed depths not experienced for a century, throwing thousands of family producers and rural workers into desperate struggles to hold on to their way of life."[8] At the same time, coffee's political and economic weight in many producing countries had declined as they diversified their economies to reduce their dependence on export crops. So while individual coffee farmers were *more* vulnerable to market fluctuations than they had been during the years of the ICA, national economies were *less* vulnerable. These larger economic and political changes directly and indirectly shaped farming practices in the coffeelands and accidentally created conditions in which the rust could flourish.[9]

Farmers looked for ways to navigate their way out of the crisis. For the farmers who produced mild arabicas—mostly concentrated along the highlands of the American Cordillera, and also in eastern Africa— the growing markets for specialty and ethical coffees created new economic niches. Such coffees could fetch higher prices as long as they met the appropriate standards of quality and sustainability. Demand for high-quality arabicas was fueled by the rapid growth of Starbucks in the 1990s and "third wave" specialty roasters such as Stumptown and Intelligentsia in the 2000s. These new markets had repercussions on the farm; since specialty coffee buyers placed a premium on quality, farmers had a strong incentive to continue planting susceptible arabicas. The farms of the Cordillera had long focused on quality, and they produced the bulk of the world's mild arabicas, prized by coffee drinkers around the world. New industry associations, especially the Specialty Coffee Association of America (founded in 1982) and its offshoot the Coffee Quality Institute, developed standards for assessing and codifying coffee quality. Coffees that met or exceeded those standards could receive significant premiums over the standard New York "C" price for coffee. Quality was also an important consideration for fair trade and certified organic coffees because they also depended on consumers willing to pay a premium.[10]

This quality depended—at least in part—on the cultivar. Along the American Cordillera, the Caturra was the most widely grown of the traditional cultivars. A dwarf mutation of the Bourbon cultivar, it retained Bourbon's reputation for quality. As a dwarf plant, Caturra was also— unlike its Bourbon parent—well adapted to intensive production. It could be planted at significantly higher densities, up to six thousand plants per hectare. However, it also required more inputs and more labor than the traditional cultivars and had to be replanted more frequently. The traditional tall cultivars—Typica and Bourbon—were still widely grown wherever traditional agroforestry production predominated. They were not as productive as the Caturras or Catimors, but they also required fewer inputs and produced high-quality coffee. All of these cultivars were highly susceptible to the rust.[11]

The rust had made it difficult for farmers at lower altitudes (usually below 1,000 meters) to cultivate these older cultivars, so there they switched to the rust-resistant Catimors and Sarchimors. Over the years, breeders at the national coffee institutes had tried to develop cultivars that combined the rust resistance of the Timor hybrid with the cupping quality and productivity of the Caturra cultivar. Colombia's CENICAFÉ released the Colombia variety in the early 1980s. It had enjoyed some success, although it was not as widely adopted as the breeders had hoped.[12] In Central America, several national coffee institutes produced their own Catimor selections: IHCAFÉ 90 and Lempira in Honduras, ANACAFÉ 14 in Guatemala, and Costa Rica 95.

Buyers in the specialty coffee market remained skeptical about the cupping quality of these coffees, which contained genes of the much-maligned robusta plant. "Catimor and other Robusta hybrids, even with good disease resistances, often impart undesirable flavour to the cup," claimed a coffee manual published by Italy's Illycafè, a major buyer of high-quality arabicas. The manual warned farmers to "reconsider before planting a Catimor cultivar. It has poor cupping quality in most places where it has been grown. It has ruined the coffee industry in Colombia and has been banned from planting in Costa Rica."[13] In 2003, a buyer for Sweet Maria's Coffee—a leading specialty coffee roaster in the United States—described Costa Rica 95 as having an "unpolished, rough character" and stated that if it accounted for more than 10 percent of the coffee in a cup, "it can be foul."[14] Cup quality is strongly correlated with altitude, so the quality problems of these cultivars may well have had as much to do with *where* they were cultivated as with their genetics.[15] The Catimors also faced some agronomic challenges: at higher altitudes they could be susceptible to another common disease, the ojo de gallo (*Mycena citricolor*).[16]

The "neglected and ageing farms" and "inadequate crop management practices" that the PROMECAFÉ report criticized also reflected farmers' responses to the volatile post-ICA coffee market. Farmers responded to falling coffee prices or rising input costs by reducing expenditures. They might, for example, decide to delay renovating their coffee plants. Renovating a coffee farm, whether by stumping the coffee plants or planting new ones, meant additional costs and reduced revenue for several years until the plants had matured enough to produce a full crop. It was often easier just to leave aging plants in place. One way to gauge interest in renovation is to track demand for improved coffee seeds. In 1987, Costa Rica's national coffee institute ICAFÉ prepared almost 65 tons of selected seed to sell to farmers. By 1991, it produced 70 percent less improved seed, and farmers only bought three-quarters of that.[17] In difficult years, they would reduce their applications of fertilizers and fungicides, or stop altogether. Or, although this is more difficult to determine, they might have bought counterfeit chemicals of dubious efficacy. These responses to the economic crisis left coffee farms more vulnerable to the rust by weakening the host plants and removing essential controls that kept the rust in check.[18]

The problems with crop management also reflected waning institutional support for coffee farmers. Over the 1980s and 1990s, precisely when farmers were most vulnerable, governments in Latin America significantly reduced their economic and technical support for coffee farmers. In 1992, the Mexican government closed the Instituto Mexicano de Café, an organization that had driven the expansion and modernization of coffee farming in Mexico. Coffee farmers there suddenly lost the financial, technical, and other support on which the industry had been built.[19] Similar scenarios played out in other countries. Nongovernmental organizations (NGOs), cooperatives, and local coffee enterprises filled some of these gaps, but usually on a much smaller scale, with smaller groups of farmers. Even where farmers had access to credit, they often had trouble repaying their loans. Farmers in Costa Rica, for example, could borrow money from their cooperatives. But "when I go to receive payment for my crop," complained one farmer, "after the loan payments are deducted, there is no money to bring home."[20]

These economic stresses had already contributed to localized outbreaks of the rust in the 1990s and early 2000s, although none on the scale of the Big Rust. There were small outbreaks in Costa Rica (1989–90), Nicaragua and Honduras (1995–96), and El Salvador (2002–3). The outbreaks in Costa Rica and El Salvador coincided with historic lows in coffee prices and a corresponding degradation of disease-management practices. But local environmental and economic factors, such as unusually heavy rainfalls, also contributed. The low prices wreaked havoc across Latin America (and around the world), but the epidemics were not widespread. Significantly, Costa Rica and El Salvador were two of the most heavily technified producers in Central America, and their dense farms might have been particularly susceptible. The outbreak in Nicaragua followed a massive renovation program in which some 20,000 hectares of coffee were planted with susceptible varieties.[21] Still, these deteriorating agronomic conditions were not enough—on their own—to trigger outbreaks on a continental scale.

The immediate trigger of the Big Rust was climate change. A complex series of changes in regional weather patterns changed the rust's behavior. In particular, it allowed the fungus to reproduce more rapidly, and increased its severity at higher altitudes where it had not previously been a significant problem. The outbreak in Colombia seems to have been triggered by unusually heavy rainfall, while the epidemic in Central America may have been the result of irregular rainfall patterns and warming minimum temperatures.[22] This reduced diurnal temperature range—the difference between the daily maximum and minimum temperature—shortened the rust's latency period (the time between infection and the appearance of symptoms). The shortened latency period might help explain why the outbreak produced unusually high primary losses, and the changing temperature range might explain why the outbreaks began having larger impacts at higher altitudes.[23] The outbreaks may have been shaped by the intensification programs, which changed the traditional structure of coffee ecosystems in ways that gave the fungus more opportunities to reproduce and spread (much as they had done in Ceylon); the programs also eliminated control by natural enemies found in traditional ecosystems.[24] The shifting weather patterns provided an opportunity for the fungus to proliferate and spread, aggravating an already-serious productive and economic crisis.

The Big Rust disrupted the lives of people across the coffeelands from Peru to Mexico, and eastward to the West Indies. The disease's economic impact was compounded by a sharp fall in coffee prices. In just two years, the total export value of coffee from Central America dropped by half. Early in 2011, the indicator prices for Colombian and other milds briefly topped $3 a pound. By June 2013, the year the rust epidemic reached its peak intensity in Central and South America, prices had fallen below $1.50 a pound.[25] At the same time, production costs—especially labor and inputs—continued to rise. As an International Coffee Organization report observes, "the dramatic decline in world coffee prices observed between 2012 and 2013 has caused many producers to sell their product at a price which is not remunerative, falling below the costs of production in many countries."[26]

The crisis had repercussions across the local commodity chain. "Given how much the whole economy of the coffee lands revolves around coffee income," observed one NGO worker, "even those not directly involved in coffee are suffering."[27] Smallholders and laborers were particularly vulnerable. Smallholders produced 80 percent of the coffee in Central America; they derived most of their small incomes from coffee and thus suffered disproportionately from the rust. According to Catholic Relief Services, an NGO working in Guatemala, some small farms produced nothing at all "as a result of massive losses due to [the rust] and their decision to stump all their remaining trees."[28] Impoverished farmers tried to make up for lost income by working on neighboring coffee farms, but the epidemic had also reduced the demand for labor—and the wages that they received. Demand for day laborers (*jornaleros*) on coffee farms dropped by about 17 percent overall, although some areas were hit much harder. In parts of El Salvador, demand for wage labor dropped by 80 percent, and family wages had fallen from $40 a day to $5 a day.[29] According to an estimate by PROMECAFÉ, the epidemic displaced 373,585 laborers across Central America.[30]

Some farmers turned to "atypical, negative coping strategies" that addressed short-term problems but increased vulnerability over the longer term. They ate less, worked more, and sometimes resorted to selling part or all of their land.[31] In Central America, farmers faced extended "lean seasons" and food stress through 2013 and 2014. Droughts had sharply reduced the production of maize and beans, key staples through the region. Emergency food aid from the United Nations World Food Programme and other NGOs helped mitigate the worst of the food stress. People displaced by the rust migrated to the cities. Rolando Ortiz, a farmer from a rust-blighted coffee zone in western Honduras, said that "people without resources are leaving their towns and walking to the city looking [for] work. They're turning to crime doing bad—bad decisions." Others fled the poverty and violence of Central America's cities to work as undocumented immigrants in the United States. Between 2012 and 2014, the number of undocumented children from Central America arriving in the United States doubled.[32]

Still, not all coffee farmers were devastated by the Big Rust. In spite of the broader economic challenges, some still had the resources to apply fertilizer and fungicides, which minimized losses and kept the fungus in check. Others had previously renovated their farms with resistant coffees, so the rust passed them by. Still others cultivated coffee in diversified agricultural ecosystems, whose structure helped keep rust levels low and typically offered other sources of income or food. But the farmers most seriously affected—the ones I describe above—faced two challenges: containing the rust in the short term, and building resilient farms over the medium and longer term. These patterns of short-term response and long-term recovery took parallel yet distinct pathways in Colombia and in the rest of the Americas.

National Rust: Colombia since 2008

Colombia was better prepared to deal with the rust than most coffee-producing countries. Its coffee farmers were well organized. The National Federation of Coffee Growers (FNC), founded in 1927, included most of Colombia's coffee farmers, large and small alike. Among other things, the FNC operated Colombia's national coffee research center, CENICAFÉ, which had provided research and extension services since the 1930s. Since the early 1960s, breeders at the CENICAFÉ had been working to develop and improve rust-resistant coffees. They had also developed the Colombia cultivar, the first commercially viable rust-resistant Catimor. By 2000, slightly more than a quarter of Colombia's coffee farms had been converted to the Colombia variety. Colombian coffee farmers, unlike their counterparts in much of the rest of Latin America, also continued to receive considerable financial and political support from the state. Colombian farmers suffered during the years of catastrophically low prices, but they could still draw on a range of technical and financial support to help them weather crises.[33]

After 2008, however, the coexistence with the rust broke down. Disease patterns changed: the rust struck farms higher than 1,600 meters above sea level, in a region that had previously been exempt from significant losses. Serious rust outbreaks were recorded at altitudes above 2,000 meters, almost the upper limit of coffee cultivation. From 2008 to 2009, Colombian production dropped from 12 million bags to 8.6 million bags. Over the next few growing seasons, a team of researchers at CENICAFÉ tried to identify the trigger for the outbreaks. They found that there had been no widespread breakdown in the resistance of the resistant cultivars, although the Caturras were just as susceptible as always. They collected samples of the rust to see whether the outbreak might have been triggered by a new race of the rust. They sent the samples to the CIFC in Portugal for testing. The reports came back negative; most of the samples collected were of Race II, the race that had originally reached Colombia in the early 1980s. They compared samples of the fungus collected before and after 2008 and found that the newer samples were not more aggressive. So they concluded that the outbreaks had not been caused by changes to the plants or the pathogen.

The Colombian scientists did identify some significant changes in the environmental conditions of coffee cultivation, many of which favored the development of the rust. Rainfall had been considerably higher than usual, associated with a La Niña event. The amount of sunshine was lower than usual because of increased cloudiness. And the range between the daily maximum and minimum temperatures had also increased. All of these environmental changes, in conjunction with problems in the agricultural conditions, made the outbreak possible.[34]

The FNC encouraged coffee farmers to renovate their farms, particularly with the newly developed Castillo variety. CENICAFÉ had produced the Castillo cultivar as a replacement for the aging Colombia cultivar. Like the Colombia variety, Castillo coffee was based on the Timor hybrids, and it was also a composite variety. Since the 1980s, breeders at CENICAFÉ had continued long-term pedigree-selection programs, using Timor hybrid selections developed by the CIFC. These selections, based on CIFC 832/2 and CIFC 1343, had different resistance genes from the earlier generation of Timor hybrid selections that breeders had used to develop the Colombia variety. By the fifth and sixth generations (F_5 and F_6), breeders had produced high-yielding dwarf plants that were resistant to the prevailing strains of rust and produced large beans with a cup quality that, they argued, matched that of Caturra. These features, breeders hoped, meant that Castillo could be a viable replacement for Caturra and other dwarf arabicas. In 2005, CENICAFÉ released eight variants of the Castillo variety, each localized to one of Colombia's coffee-growing regions.[35]

Critically, the government of Juan Manuel Santos also provided farmers with credits that made renovation financially possible. Under the Permanence, Sustainability, and Future plan, the government offered loans to farmers with traditional coffee farms (those that had not fully technified) smaller than 5 hectares. Because farm sizes had fragmented over the previous decades, this accounted for more than 80 percent of Colombia's coffee farms. The structure of the loans reflected the renovation process; the government covered 40 percent of each loan, so a farmer only had to repay 60 percent. The loans were given for seven years, with a two-year grace period at the beginning. The grace period was significant, since new plants did not start producing significant amounts of coffee until the third year. Farmers were only eligible for this loan if they renovated their farms with Castillo coffee. Most chose to do this because of the cultivar's resistance to the rust and its high productivity—and of course because of the financial support. By 2017, almost 83 percent of Colombia's coffee farms had been renovated, with resistant coffees accounting for 74 percent of the total, up from 35 percent in 2010.[36]

The specialty coffee community remained skeptical that Castillo's cup quality could match Caturra's. The American coffee expert George Howell criticized Castillo for its aftertaste, which he described as "harsh, with bitterish green notes," or more poetically as "the tail of the devil." Opinions like this limited Castillo's potential in the specialty coffee market, perhaps unfairly. In 2014 the Catholic Relief Services, which had been working with coffee farmers in the southern department of Nariño, invited leading members of the Specialty Coffee Association to the Colombia Sensory Trial. The trial showed that while coffees made from Castillo and Caturra tasted different, there were no significant differences in cupping scores. According to specialized tasters from Kansas State University, "good Castillo tastes fruity but not citrusy, with notes of dark chocolate and roasted nuts. Good Caturra tastes floral with notes of coca and caramel."[37] In this competition, several Castillos scored quite badly, receiving just 52 out of a possible 100 points. But others scored above 80, the threshold to be considered specialty coffee, and two Castillos scored above 90 ("outstanding," according to the Specialty Coffee Association's quality classification). Cuppers praised them for their "sparkling acidity" and "elegant flavor." This small competition showed that Castillo *could* be competitive in specialty markets, although buyers have remained slow to accept it.[38]

Despite the FNC's strong renovation campaigns, more than a third of Colombia's farmers have continued to grow traditional cultivars. Partly, they have balked at the costs associated with intensive production. Small family farmers in Colombia, as in other places, have responded to the crisis by technifying only partially, cultivating under intense shade, and reducing inputs. They have sometimes combined coffee cultivation with other food or cash crops and with raising livestock. Farming this way can offer them more sustainable livelihoods than they could obtain by technifying. Early in the 2000s, CENICAFÉ released a hybrid coffee, baptized Tabi, that was designed to be suitable for agroforestry systems like this. Tabi is a tall coffee, like the traditional Bourbon and Typica coffees rather than the Colombia and Castillo varieties. But farmers have not adopted Tabi on a large scale, preferring to continue with the traditional cultivars.[39]

Colombia's specialty coffee producers also rely heavily on traditional cultivars. Since the 1990s, Colombian farmers have produced coffee for the specialty, certified organic, and fair trade markets, building on Colombia's historical focus on quality. By 2011, these value-added coffees accounted for almost a third of Colombia's coffee exports. Between 2008 and 2013—at the height of the rust epidemic—the number of farmers growing certified coffees grew from 68,000 to 163,000. Growth was strongest in the southern departments of Huila, Cauca, and Nariño.[40] According to a survey conducted by Catholic Relief Services in Nariño, about 16 percent of farmers surveyed planned to stick with traditional varieties the next time they planted coffee, citing productivity and quality as their main reasons for doing so.[41] They preferred to control the rust using fungicides.[42]

In response, the FNC launched a national campaign to promote spraying called Colombia without Rust: A National Commitment. CENICAFÉ experts provided farmers with technical advice on the best practices for spraying and fertilizing their farms, including a careful consideration of the costs. Significantly, this support was only available to farmers "with farms between two and seven years old, planted with susceptible varieties." The FNC recommended that farmers with older plants renovate and spray their farms.

Since the 1990s, farmers have been using systemic chemicals to control the coffee leaf rust, often with the recommendation of coffee institutes. The major chemical companies—BASF, Syngenta, Bayer, and Adama—have all developed systemics for treating a wide range of fungal diseases, including the rust. Systemic fungicides are taken up into the leaf tissue, where they attack the fungal mycelia and prevent further spore production. They could, therefore, be both preventive (like the copper sprays) and curative, as long as the levels of infection were not too high. Systemics could be applied in much smaller quantities than copper sprays and required fewer applications: three per year in Colombia, instead of four for copper fungicides.[43] Still, they could be risky. If they were applied too late, they could do little to stop the rust from developing. They could also hasten the development of resistant strains of rust and interfere with potential natural controls.

New early warning systems helped farmers decide when to spray, or whether to spray. For example, starting in 2010, the FNC developed an early warning system for the coffee rust, the Coffee Information System (known by its Spanish-language acronym SICA). This and other early warning initiatives built on new strategies in disaster preparedness more generally. Early warning initiatives were meant to offer tools to predict emergent hazards, such as crop diseases. These allowed farmers (and other people in the industry) to prepare for outbreaks and apply preventive methods wherever possible. Every three months, inspectors measured levels of rust across Colombia. If the rust levels were low enough, no control measures were necessary. If they were higher, farmers could spray. The early warning system allowed Colombian coffee farmers to "activate, adjust, and conduct control measures against this fungal pathogen, interfering in its reproductive cycle, reducing the quantity of inoculum within and between epidemics, and thus mitigating its effect on coffee farms."[44] The campaign reached farmers both by traditional broadcast methods, such as radio and TV, and by new technologies, such as personalized emails and text messages directly to the farmers' cell phones.[45]

Although Colombia's coffee sector was as well equipped as any to deal with the rust, life for Colombia's coffee farmers has remained difficult. Over the short term, renovation programs aggravated losses in production as planters ripped out old plants and waited for the new ones to start producing. In the 2011–12 season, Colombian coffee exports reached a forty-year low of 7.6 million bags before slowly recovering as the renovated farms began producing anew. Over 2012 and 2013, an unusual rainy season disrupted the flowering of coffee plants across Colombia. Plunging coffee prices compounded the impact of these environmental challenges. From 2011 to 2013, producer prices for Colombian coffee dropped by more than half and labor costs rose 10–20 percent, as did the costs of water and electricity. These problems "have effectively squeezed margins to the point of unprofitability."[46] In late February and early March 2013, frustrated coffee farmers declared an industry-wide strike, demanding more financial support from the government. The government of Juan Manuel Santos reluctantly agreed to provide a one-time $400 million fund for the "protection of coffee farmer incomes."[47] Although Colombia weathered the Big Rust, the larger structural problems in the global coffee industry have remained.

Gradually, the national campaigns brought the rust under control. From 2010 to 2015, infection levels dropped from 33.4 percent to just 2.4 percent. This was well below the critical threshold of 5 percent infection. The area planted with resistant varieties had doubled, reaching 63 percent in 2014. From 2009 to 2014, the productivity of Colombian coffee farms increased by 50 percent, and by 2015 production finally recovered to pre-2008 levels.[48] Specialty coffee buyers have, it seems, started to warm up to Castillo, or at least accept it. James Hoffman, an author and leading specialty coffee roaster in the United Kingdom, wrote that "as global climate change has an increasing impact on the stability of Colombia's production, it is increasingly difficult to argue against varieties that ensure livelihoods for producers, even at the expense of losing some great cups of coffee."[49]

The development expert Michael Sheridan aptly described Colombia as being "better positioned than any other coffee growing country in the world to respond to the rust outbreak." He pointed to CENICAFÉ's "50-year-old breeding program," a "standing army of agronomists based in its vast network of field offices all over the coffeelands, ready to lead the charge against the rust." Furthermore, the Colombian government had both the political will and the public funds to subsidize the renovation and control campaigns.[50] But even with all those advantages, Colombia's struggle to recover from the Big Rust was still slow and contentious. Elsewhere, the struggle against the Big Rust was even more difficult.

Transnational Rust: Central and South America since 2012

Unlike the Colombian outbreaks, the outbreaks in Central and South America crossed national boundaries. This difference shaped almost every facet of the responses to it. In Colombia, the scientific, financial, and policy responses to the disease were addressed almost exclusively by Colombian institutions. Few countries in Central America or the Central Andes had the resources—or in some cases the political will—to respond to the rust in the same way. Generations of policy decisions and political struggles had produced distinctive coffee industries in each country, each with different capacities to respond to crises like the rust. In some cases, as with Honduras, coffee was a nationally important export, and the state worked closely with the national coffee institute (IHCAFÉ) and farmers' organizations. Elsewhere, such as in Mexico, El Salvador, and Nicaragua, connections between coffee farmers and the state were much weaker. In these places, the coffee industry's economic weight—and its *political* weight—was much smaller than it had been a generation before. Because of this, farmers also depended heavily on regional and multilateral organizations, NGOs, and the private sector for support.

Regional and international organizations mobilized people and resources to assess the extent of the rust and to develop plans for how best to respond. Early in 2013, a revitalized PROMECAFÉ developed an action plan for dealing with the rust. The plan had six goals, some of which were familiar from earlier epidemics, such as breeding resistant varieties with good quality. Other goals reflected the distinctive problems of coffee in the twenty-first century: developing "institutional and local capacities to manage and combat the coffee rust epidemic," a tacit recognition that these capacities had seriously eroded over the previous decades, and "large scale rehabilitation and/or renovation of old and unproductive coffee plantations," a recognition that farmers had not been able to do so previously. The other goals reflected a more holistic vision of the rust and how to respond to it; they spoke of "integrated coffee rust management" and of developing "regional strategies." Tellingly, the plan also explicitly addressed the social dimensions of the rust, calling for a "program to support vulnerable populations such as small farmers and laborers and their families."[51]

In April 2014, PROMECAFÉ hosted the first International Coffee Rust Summit. The list of participants and speakers at the summit reflects the evolving international engagement with the rust. The summit was sponsored by some familiar international actors—the USAID and the Interamerican Institute of Agricultural Sciences—and it was hosted by the Guatemalan coffee institute ANACAFÉ. But tellingly, it was also sponsored by several major players from the private sector: Starbucks, Green Mountain Coffee Roasters, RGC Coffee, ECOM, and Folgers. And along with PROMECAFÉ, the summit was organized by World Coffee Research, a new US-based research organization primarily funded by the specialty coffee industry. This strong private sector engagement in coffee production was unprecedented but perhaps not surprising. These private sponsors were deeply involved in the specialty coffee trade, and for them, the rust outbreaks represented a serious threat to their business.

National and international NGOs and other civil society organizations also got involved in the conversations about how to address the rust. Some of them, such as the American humanitarian agency Catholic Relief Services (CRS), had been operating in the coffeelands for some time and were well placed to see the rust's social and economic impacts on farming communities. At the summit, the CRS's Michael Sheridan emerged as a powerful and articulate voice in discussions about the socioeconomic dimensions of the rust. He and other members of the CRS also reached larger audiences through the *CRS Coffeelands* blog. New organizations, like the social investment fund Root Capital, explored new ways of offering financial assistance to small farmers. The summit provided an interdisciplinary, international assessment of the problems and offered a range of technical and policy solutions to the Big Rust, as well as sketching out a research agenda for scientists.[52]

Governments still mattered, but their responses could be tempered by the perceived severity of the outbreak, and the significance of coffee in the national economy. The national governments of Honduras, Costa Rica, Guatemala, and Peru quickly declared phytosanitary emergencies and launched rust-control campaigns. Elsewhere, governments responded to the rust more slowly or less effectively. Mexico's producer associations, for example, accused the Secretariat of Agriculture of underreporting the severity of the outbreak, dragging its feet in declaring a state of emergency, and not providing farmers with the kind of aid that they needed. Official responses in El Salvador were similarly slow; in early 2015, two years after the original outbreak, a USDA attaché described the government's official response as too "late and ill-designed to have any positive impact on the recovery of coffee producers."[53] Wherever coffee producers felt that government responses were slow or inadequate, they mobilized to pressure national governments, in the same way that Colombian farmers did during the coffee strike. They wanted effective technical and institutional support for disease-control and recovery programs that was accompanied by adequate financial support to carry them out. Few countries, however, were willing or able to offer their farmers the same level of support that Colombia had offered to its farmers.

Official programs encouraged farmers to spray their coffee in order to contain the current outbreak and forestall future ones. Cost, however, remained a perennial problem. One Nicaraguan farmer observed that "most farmers simply do not have the funds to apply a full course of treatments, so they cut corners, reduce applications, buy cheap products from dubious sources and so become hostages to fortune."[54] None of these countries developed control programs as comprehensive as Colombia without Rust. Guatemala's ANACAFÉ used state funds to buy fungicides to distribute to farmers whose farms had been afflicted. They purchased systemics: Opus (BASF) for the first round of treatment and Alto 10 (Syngenta) for the second and third rounds.[55] In January 2013, Mexico's national health service SENASICA and AMECAFÉ launched an unsuccessful campaign to spray along the border areas with Guatemala to prevent the rust from spreading northward.[56] In Nicaragua, the trading company Exportadora Atlantic (a subsidiary of ECOM) negotiated with chemical distributors to "facilitate better products at fair prices."[57]

Attitudes toward agricultural chemicals had also evolved over the previous decades. Farmers and consumers alike had become more concerned about the impact of agricultural chemicals (fig. 9.1) on human health and ecosystem health. Such concerns were relatively new in the coffee industry, or at least they have only been documented recently. This silence is somewhat surprising given the long history of concerns about fungicides and health in other facets of tropical agriculture—especially in the banana

Figure 9.1. Spraying for the coffee rust in Central America. (© World Coffee Research)

industry.[58] Perhaps this reflected the prevailing use of comparatively benign copper fungicides before the 1990s.

As systemic fungicides became more common, so too did concerns about their possible health impacts on landscapes and on people all along the commodity chain. In Veracruz, a group of farmers refused to accept systemic fungicides from the Secretariat of Agriculture. Cirilo Elotlán Díaz, an advisor with the Coatepec Regional Coffee Council, told a local newspaper that the farmers would not use "even a single litre of Alto 100, because not only will we poison the coffee, we will pollute the environment, we will exterminate all the species, and all of the producers who apply Alto 100 run the risk of becoming sterile."[59] Farmers who produced certified coffee had to work within national and international standards that set limits on the kinds and amounts of chemicals they could use. Consumer concerns about food safety drove environmental regulations in the major consuming regions. The European Union, the United States, and Japan all set maximum residue levels for green coffee; any coffee that exceeded those levels could be refused entry. Still, the chemicals could be so effective—if used properly—that many conventional coffee farmers continued to use them.

Agronomists also encouraged farmers to rehabilitate badly infected farms. Rehabilitation, in this context, meant heavily pruning or stumping older coffee plants. According to one estimate, about 20 percent of farms in Central America—"heavily defoliated with widespread dieback"—ought to be rehabilitated.[60] Rehabilitation had many advantages: Over the short term, it could help restrict outbreaks by depriving the fungus of the living leaf tissue it needed to reproduce and spread. According to a rust-control manual published by Costa Rica's CATIE, rehabilitation "keep[s] the branches and leaves actively growing, improve[s] the aeration within the farm and the spacing between plants, promotes conditions adverse to the rust like lower relative humidity and greater penetration of sunshine which limit the development of the disease, and increases the effectiveness of the products which are sprayed on the foliage."[61] The exact strategy depended on the intensity of the infection, the nature of the farm, and the resources available to the farmer. It could be quite expensive over the short term; it took several years for radically pruned or stumped plants to return to full production. In the short term, then, rehabilitation added to the losses caused directly by the rust and aggravated the economic problems faced by farmers and laborers. Furthermore, renovated arabica plants were still genetically susceptible to the rust, so they remained vulnerable to future outbreaks.

Most research institutions encouraged farmers to replant their farms with resistant coffees. This was broadly similar to the preferred strategy in Colombia. In both places, the resistant coffees were based on Catimors and Sarchimors, arabicas that had been crossed with the rust-resistant Timor hybrid. But CENICAFÉ and PROMECAFÉ pursued different breeding strategies. Colombia's CENICAFÉ developed composite varieties—first the Colombia variety and later the Castillo—each of which contained mixes of resistance genes. One of the disadvantages of the Colombian strategy was that it increased selection pressure on the rust population, favoring the development of strains that could overcome the resistance genes.

So breeders in Central America—at PROMECAFÉ and the national coffee institutes—worked to develop single varieties with strong rust resistance. Since the 1990s, most countries in Central America had developed local selections of these resistant coffees, most of which were based on crosses between traditional arabicas and the Timor hybrid selections CIFC 832-1 or CIFC 832-2. These included Costa Rica 95 (Costa Rica), Lempira and IHCAFÉ 90 (Honduras), Oro Azteca (Mexico), and ANA-CAFÉ 14 (Guatemala).[62] Before the Big Rust, these cultivars had been adopted only on a limited scale. First, they were all dwarf coffees, making them better suited to intensive farming than to the agroforestry that many farmers in Central America and the Central Andes still practiced. Second, like Colombia's Castillo, they did not produce coffee of the same quality potential as coffees of the traditional arabicas and Caturras. The issue of quality presented a particular challenge to farmers who hoped to sell their coffees for a premium in the specialty market.

Private sector organizations also developed their own research and extension programs, often in collaboration with national coffee institutes and development agencies. Since the early 1990s, ECOM Agroindustrial (a Swiss commodity-trading company) and CIRAD (the French Agricultural Research Centre for International Development) had collaborated in a breeding program to develop F_1 hybrid coffees. In 2013, coffee giant Starbucks established an experimental farm in Costa Rica, Hacienda Alsacia in Alajuela, to carry out research on the rust and sustainability over the longer term. By 2017, the center had released its first new coffee cultivar.[63]

Perhaps the largest new player in global coffee research is World Coffee Research (WCR), a not-for-profit organization based at Texas A&M University and funded by leading specialty coffee companies. In a few short years, WCR has become a global hub for research and collaboration, working with national coffee institutes, universities, and research organizations such as CIRAD and Kew Gardens. The WCR focuses on precompetitive research on coffee; sponsors share the research costs essential to keep the coffee industry viable. WCR recruited some leading coffee researchers who previously worked for public institutions, development agencies, and NGOs. Its goal, explicitly, is to "ensure the future of coffee in the face of threats like global climate change."[64] To date, all the coffees produced by these breeding efforts are open-source.

One of the biggest initiatives involved developing a new kind of hybrid coffee, known as F_1 coffees. Research on these hybrids had begun in Nicaragua during the 1990s, as a collaboration between CIRAD and the ECOM. With traditional pure-line breeding, such as for the Catimor coffees, it typically took five or six generations (F_5, F_6) to create a stable cultivar with a consistent phenotype. This could take twenty to thirty years. F_1 breeding reduced this time to about ten years and, in the process, created more productive and resilient coffees. Breeders crossed two distinct cultivars of arabica coffee using traditional methods of hybridization: dusting the pollen of one tree onto the flowers of another and then collecting, cultivating, and evaluating the resultant seeds. The offspring of this cross benefited from heterosis, or hybrid vigor, a phenomenon well known in plant breeding.

Like most previous coffee-breeding programs, the F_1 breeding programs continued to emphasize productivity and disease resistance. But the programs had additional goals that reflected the changing nature of the coffee economy and the coffee trade. They also focused on "ecologically intensive production" (production that was viable in both agroforestry systems and intensified systems) and on cupping quality.[65] The breeders crossed traditional Catimors with "wild" arabicas that had been brought to CATIE from Ethiopia and Sudan in the 1960s. These Ethiopian coffees included the Geisha variety, which had become wildly popular in the specialty coffee market during the early 2000s. The F_1 offspring of the Catimors and Ethiopians produced coffees with high cup-quality potential (making them viable for the specialty market) that also retained the rust resistance of the Catimors. The first F_1 coffees were tested in the field in the early 2000s; many showed considerable hybrid vigor and, in the best cases, yields as high as 58 percent greater than the traditional varieties. These coffees remained experimental until the Big Rust struck. Since then, World Coffee Research has gotten involved in supporting the breeding programs (fig. 9.2) and also publicizing and propagating the most successful coffees. In 2017, one of these hybrids, Centroamericano, received a score of 90.5 and ranked second overall in Nicaragua's Cup of Excellence competition.[66]

The main challenge with F_1 coffees was figuring out how to multiply them on a large scale, to mass-produce the seeds or seedlings that growers needed to renovate their farms. Multiplying traditional pure-line arabica varieties was straightforward because their seeds were identical to the mother plant. Traditionally, farmers selected and planted seeds from coffee plants on their farm. Later in the twentieth century, they obtained the seed of improved arabica cultivars from national coffee institutes or commercial breeders, who mass-produced the seed in seed gardens—plots of individual varieties whose crops were used exclusively for seed. But the F_1 coffees could not be propagated by seed; their seeds were *not* identical to the mother plant, so they would not have the same agronomic advantages as their hybrid parent. These F_1 coffees could only be propagated by some form of vegetative reproduction, which would ensure that the offspring were genetically identical to the parent.

The practical challenges of reproducing hybrid coffees had vexed coffee breeders since the early twentieth century. Breeders in the Dutch East Indies had tried to multiply hybrids by grafting, which was slow and ultimately unsatisfactory. But in the 1990s, new biotechnologies—especially somatic embryogenesis—made it possible to generate hundreds of

Figure 9.2. World Coffee Research field trial of F_1 coffees. (Photo by Leo Lombardini, © World Coffee Research)

thousands of genetically identical offspring (clones) in vitro from a single piece of plant tissue (see fig. 9.3). At its most simple, the process involved taking tissue (for example, leaf tissue) from a desirable parent and propagating it at the cellular level. The cells were then cultivated and propagated in a solid or liquid growth medium, producing thousands of genetically identical embryos. When these plantlets started to develop roots, they were transferred to a solid medium for further development until they were ready to be transferred to pots and raised in a nursery just like conventional coffee. While this technique is straightforward in theory, it is challenging (and expensive) in practice, which is why ECOM got involved in the project.[67]

While both the new generations of Catimors and F_1 coffees were promising in principle, in practice they faced a number of logistical and financial bottlenecks. The cost of renovation remained a significant obstacle. Few farmers had the resources to renovate their farms, as they were already reeling from cumulative economic and ecological crises. In Guatemala, for example, renovating a farm with conventional rust-resistant hybrids like ANACAFÉ 14 cost $8,000 per hectare, which was $3,000 per hectare more than it would cost to replant with traditional arabicas. Renovating with F_1 coffees would be even more expensive. "Although the investment can pay

Figure 9.3. Biotechnology laboratory for propagating F_1 coffees, La Cumplida, Nicaragua. (Photo by Bram deHoog, © World Coffee Research)

off after only a few years," wrote a USDA expert, "small coffee farmers are unable to take on this kind of economic burden."[68] By 2015, only about 10 percent of Guatemala's coffee area had been fully replanted. In some countries, governments offered farmers long-term loans to finance the renovation, although few offered the level or scope of support that Colombia offered its farmers.

Another challenge was expertise. Many countries, notably Mexico, Nicaragua, El Salvador, and Peru, did not have adequate agricultural research and extension infrastructures to confront the Big Rust. After several years—and vocal criticism from leading coffee organizations—the Mexican state launched programs to provide farmers with some measure of support. Two programs, first PROCAFÉ and later the Integrated Coffee Program (PIAC), developed a network of nurseries to propagate and distribute resistant seedlings. In 2016, the PIAC program had reportedly helped farmers in Mexico renovate 106,000 hectares of farmland—roughly 14 percent of the country's coffeelands.[69]

The private sector has also gotten involved in helping farmers renovate. In 2015, ECOM's nurseries began producing and distributing resistant varieties on a large scale for Starbucks. The coffee chain had launched a campaign to help its rust-afflicted suppliers in Mexico, Guatemala, and El Salvador renovate their farms. For every bag of coffee purchased by consumers in the United States, Starbucks would donate seventy cents—the price of a coffee seedling—to Conservation International, a large American NGO focused on environmental issues. Conservation International would purchase seedlings from one of ECOM's nurseries and distribute them to farmers. To be eligible for the program, the farms had to be certified by Starbucks's C.A.F.E. standards. In Chiapas, where the program was first rolled out, the main varieties distributed were Costa Rica 95, Guacamaya, and Marsellesa. By 2016, the program had distributed some thirty million seedlings to 6,200 affected families, contributing to the renovation of about 2,500 hectares of rust-infected farmland.[70]

In Nicaragua, ECOM provided loans and technical support to help 550 small farmers renovate their farms as part of the larger ECOM Coffee Renovation Facility. The program's goal, according to ECOM's CEO of coffee and cocoa, was to "provide farmers not only with financing to replace old, diseased plants with resistant varieties, but also technical assistance to help them make farming practices more sustainable." Funding for this project came from the private sector (ECOM and Starbucks), from international finance institutions (the International Finance Corporation and the Interamerican Development Bank), and the World Bank's Global Agriculture and Food Security Program.[71] In Peru, WCR and ECOM's Cafetalera Amazónica collaborated with Peru's Junta Nacional de Café in F_1 variety trials covering some 200 hectares in six regions.[72] These efforts are important, and they have considerable potential over the long term. But they still represent only a small percentage of the farmers afflicted by the rust.

The Big Rust has presented particularly serious challenges to organic coffee producers. Since the 1990s, organic coffee production had grown rapidly in parts of the Americas; Peru and Mexico were the world's two largest producers of certified organic coffee. But organic certification standards prevented farmers from using most fungicides, which were a key tool in disease management for conventional farmers. The standards did allow farmers to use copper fungicides, but unlike the systemics, copper sprays could not contain an epidemic that was already in progress. And in any case, even the copper fungicides were too expensive for many organic producers, who had been struggling even before the rust outbreak. In Mexico, the government distributed a fungicide called DR-43, which it claimed conformed to certified organic standards. But organic farmers balked at using it; because it had not been recognized by international certification organizations, farmers using it could lose their organic certification.[73]

In Peru, the agricultural attaché for the USDA feared that organic coffee farmers were facing "the total destruction of their fields."[74] Organic farmers throughout the Americas received far less economic or technical support than conventional producers. So out of necessity, many organic producers became "researchers on their own farms," sometimes with the support of international NGOs.[75] In Central America, CAFÉNICA (a federation of Nicaraguan smallholders), Biolatina (an organic certification agency), and Catholic Relief Services collaborated to publish a manual of best practices for organic coffee farmers, which listed a number of strategies for controlling the rust and strengthening coffee trees.[76]

Other farmers abandoned arabica and switched to robusta, as their counterparts in Africa and Asia had. Robusta had never been widely cultivated in the Americas because the arabicas have historically grown so well. But the ecological and economic niches for robusta in the Americas are expanding—slowly. As arabica has confronted a range of hazards— outbreaks of diseases and pests as well as changing temperatures and rainfall patterns—robusta has started to look more appealing, especially to lowland farmers. Demand for robusta coffee has also been growing. In 2013, Nestlé expanded the capacity of its soluble (instant) coffee plant in Toluca, Mexico, by a third. A new market segment for specialty robustas is also gaining traction. In 2012, the Coffee Quality Institute developed a quality-certification system for fine robusta coffees, similar to the system for evaluating arabica.[77] NGOs such as Catholic Relief Services see specialty robusta as a way of ensuring that farmers earn a sustainable living. [78] "There is a stubborn demand for Robusta in traditional European espresso blends," wrote Michael Sheridan of the CRS, "and the R[obusta] program opens new frontiers of possibility."[79]

The evolution of robusta production in the Americas has not yet been fully documented, but aggregate production statistics suggest some significant changes. Production in Mexico has remained steady at about two hundred thousand bags. Since the beginning of the Big Rust, robusta production in Guatemala has exploded. Before 2012, average production was about ten thousand bags. By 2017–18, it is expected to reach two hundred thousand bags. Production in Nicaragua expanded from zero (officially, at least) in 2013–14 to about twenty-five thousand bags in 2017–18.[80] The expansion of robusta has triggered some bitter debates, particularly in the specialty coffee community, which has historically focused on arabicas. Costa Rica had banned robusta cultivation in 1988 to preserve its reputation as a producer of high-quality coffee. But in 2016 Costa Rica's

National Coffee Congress, facing pressure from some growers and a favorable report on robusta cultivation from ICAFÉ, held a vote on overturning the rule. In the end, it remained in place: more than half of the congress's members had voted to allow robusta cultivation, but they were short of the two-thirds majority required to overturn the bill. Still, conversations about robusta persist because farmers, development agencies, and businesses see opportunities in the crop.[81] Barring further major catastrophes, it is unlikely that robusta cultivation in the Americas will ever surpass arabica, as it has elsewhere. But it will likely continue to expand in the lowlands.

Some farmers have abandoned coffee altogether and switched to other crops. Nowhere, however, have coffee farmers switched en masse to another crop like tea or rubber, as their counterparts in Asia and Africa had. Rather, these adaptations seem to have been mostly ad hoc, based on whatever crop worked best locally. Some cleared their farms of coffee plants and the shade trees associated with them, leading some observers to raise concerns that the rust could ultimately help contribute to deforestation.[82] In Peru, coffee farmers in areas badly affected by rust started planting coca. Many of them had cultivated coca before but had switched to coffee as part of programs to reduce illicit production. Farmers in Peru's Sandia province switched back to coca after several years of largely ineffective attempts to control the rust. In the Tinquimayo district, fifty-four of the sixty organic coffee farmers abandoned coffee for coca after the rust reduced the district's coffee production by 96 percent. The problem, according to the newspaper *El comercio*, was not that coca was more lucrative than coffee, but that technical assistance from the state and NGOs had been inadequate.[83]

THE BIG Rust may be under control for the moment, but as I write this recovery is still not complete. The coffeelands of Central and South America have adapted to the rust more slowly than those of Colombia. The Colombian experience was an important model, but it could not be fully reproduced elsewhere. The patterns of recovery varied considerably from one country to the next. In each country, recovery was shaped by the agroecological conditions, by the degree of engagement by farmer groups and institutions, and by the strength of the local and global coffee economies. If we take national coffee production as a measure of recovery, then Honduras rebounded relatively quickly, and by 2015, production was back up to pre-rust levels. Recovery in the other afflicted countries has taken much longer, as replanted areas waited to reach maturity or farmers grappled with other environmental and economic problems. By 2016–17, production in Costa Rica, El Salvador, and Mexico was still 10–30 percent below pre-rust levels; production in Ecuador and Peru was still down by more than a quarter.[84]

International organizations, the private sector, and NGOs have joined national governments and coffee institutions to help provide relief, research, and recovery. More farmers than ever before have renovated with resistant varieties, although many still have not done so. Early warning systems help people through the coffeelands prepare for difficult years. But behind the production statistics lie the stories of countless people whose lives were disrupted, temporarily or permanently, by the rust: the people whose families went hungry, who sold their farms, or who left the coffeelands in pursuit of a better life. A generation after the first set of outbreaks, the coffee farmers of Latin America have once again found ways to coexist with the rust—for the time being.

CHAPTER 10

Coffee Is Not (Necessarily) Forever

IN 2013, some friends and I went on a hike near the town of Sasaima, nestled in an idyllic agricultural area on the slopes of Cordillera Oriental in the Colombian state of Cundinamarca. We walked through lush farmland, with spectacular views across the Magdalena River Valley to the highlands of the Cordillera Central. The farmland was punctuated by what appeared to be scrub brush. These random patches of scrub proved to be abandoned plots of coffee, modern-day arabica graveyards. The neglected, skeletal trees grew tall and spindly. They had been badly defoliated, and small clumps of malformed fruit clung to their branches (see fig. 10.1). The rust, in tandem with other pressures, had done its work. Just a few hundred meters along the same path, we passed several well-tended coffee farms where rows of healthy-looking coffee plants—likely the new Castillo cultivar—grew vigorously with no sign of the rust (see fig. 10.2). There is nothing particularly exceptional about Sasaima, which is exactly the point. Since 1870, similar scenarios have played out around the world. Each of

Figure 10.1. Abandoned coffee farm, Sasaima, Colombia. (Photo by author)

Figure 10.2. Healthy coffee farm, Sasaima, Colombia. (Photo by author)

these farms—the failed farms and the successful ones—is an outcome of the interplay between local, regional, and global forces. In many places the rust has played, and will continue to play, a decisive role in determining whether coffee farming will succeed or fail.

The history of the coffee rust is a history of the coffee ecosystem as a whole. As coffee cultivation expanded and intensified, natural and human forces accidentally combined to produce landscapes that are particularly vulnerable to disease. The very forces that make coffee farms productive also make them vulnerable. The global coffee trade was built around arabica coffee, a species that was particularly susceptible to the rust. As the global coffee economy expanded, it often pushed arabica cultivation into hotter and more humid environments in which the rust could flourish. The logic of the global economy, where farmer income was tied to productivity, encouraged them to structure their farms in ways that accidentally encouraged the development of the rust. They increased production by simplifying the coffee agroecosystem: planting more densely, eliminating other plants, and reducing or limiting shade. This pursuit of productivity reduced or eliminated the forces that had previously kept the rust in check. These coffee farms were the ecological equivalent of a vast pile of kindling. All it needed was a spark—the rust fungus—to ignite the inferno. And in the mid-nineteenth century, the spark triggered the first epidemic in Ceylon and, from there, through the rest of the world.

The rust caused significantly more damage in some places than in others as it spread across the global coffeelands. Its impacts reverberated through the commodity chain, from the farmers and laborers to the mills, trading companies, roasters, and the end consumers, although these impacts were attenuated farther along the commodity chain. Its impacts have always been borne disproportionately by the farmers and laborers whose livelihoods depend on coffee. They could weather the rust if they had support, especially from public institutions. But if the outbreak was particularly severe, or sustained, they could face ruin. Some accounts of the rust have stressed its impact on *consumers*, but in fact the global rust epidemics caused barely a ripple in global coffee consumption. The explanation for this lies in the global structure of the coffee trade. While producers are typically rooted in particular places, traders and consumers are not. As the global coffee markets became fully integrated over the nineteenth century—at the same time the rust was spreading through Africa and Asia—production shortfalls in a particular area (other than Brazil, perhaps) could be offset with production from elsewhere.[1] This global dispersal of risk (at least for traders and consumers) is also found in other tropical commodities. For the past century, banana producers have also been grappling with severe epidemics—Panama and sigatoka disease, among others—that have scarcely affected consumers at all.

The coffee rust has triggered broader changes in coffee production and reshaped the global coffee economy. It set in motion a series of varietal revolutions that brought new varieties and species into production. The most important of these is robusta coffee, which now regularly accounts for 30–40 percent of global production. The rust epidemic explains how robusta coffee, with its famously indifferent cupping quality, first became a global commodity. It was, first and foremost, a response to the challenges of the rust. Its rust resistance made it a botanical success with the coffee planters in the Dutch East Indies; colonial governments, in conjunction with coffee roasters, helped make it a commercial success. During the 1920s, the Dutch government lobbied to create a space for it in the vast US market; in the 1930s, the French government used preferential tariffs to encourage French consumers to drink coffee from their colonies in Africa and Asia, most of which had adopted robusta after the rust decimated their arabica farms. Over the twentieth century, the coffee trade created spaces for robusta coffee in cheap coffee blends and instant coffee. The Timor hybrids, with resistance genes from robusta, have in turn triggered several generations of varietal revolutions, from the early Catimors and

Sarchimors released in the 1990s to the more recent F_1 coffees released after 2010, which farmers hope will find a place in the markets for mild coffees.

The rust is just one of a number of diseases and pests that threaten global coffee production. The same forces of globalization that moved the coffee rust around the globe have also moved other diseases and pests. The same commodity landscapes that favor the rust often are also suitable to other diseases and pests. Each of these has its own characteristics and history, but they are all shaped by similar forces. Farmers in Africa have to contend with the coffee berry disease (CBD), which is particularly harmful at higher altitudes, where the rust is rarely found. Just as the rust is an obstacle to cultivation at low altitudes, the CBD is an obstacle at higher altitudes. The coffee wilt, a viral disease, has recently been spreading through coffee farms in central and eastern Africa. For a long time, the wilt was contained to a small corner of Africa, but war and migration have started to move it across larger areas.[2] The coffee berry borer (known as *broca* in Spanish) originated in Africa; it reached Brazil in the 1920s, Central America in the 1970s, and Hawaii in 2010. Unlike the rust, the broca is not highly mobile, and it is usually spread anthropogenically. The borer has reached Hawaii— one of the most isolated coffee zones in the world—even before the more mobile rust. Farmers are often more concerned about the borer than the rust, since the borer attacks the coffee bean itself, producing defects that make it difficult or impossible to sell.[3] Changing weather patterns have also triggered outbreaks of previously minor diseases, such as the phoma (known in Colombia as the *muerte descendente del cafeto*).[4] Beyond these, the coffee plant can be afflicted by dozens of other diseases and pests that are continually expanding through the world's coffee farms and that each present a distinct challenge and a potential new cost to farmers.

The rust, along with these other diseases and pests, has made global coffee production more dependent on science and continued scientific innovation. Global coffee production depends on a transnational network of national coffee institutes, colonial and national botanical gardens, international development agencies, NGOs, agricultural colleges, research stations, and extension services. When the rust first broke out, scientists did important work in diagnosing and tracking the disease, but they could offer farmers little in the way of practical solutions. The first major scientific achievement was the development and dissemination of commercially viable strains of robusta after 1900. Plant breeding has remained essential in sustaining coffee production where levels of rust would otherwise make it impossible. Agricultural chemists have developed fertilizers and fungicides that have, likewise, made it possible for farmers to continue producing arabica coffee in zones with high levels of endemic rust. The science has evolved in tandem with the changing economic and environmental problems that the coffee industry has faced.

To consider the impact of these and other innovations, consider the counterfactual: what would the coffee industry look like today without the science? Without robusta, global coffee production today would be 30–40 percent smaller. The agricultural landscapes of Vietnam, Indonesia, and parts of Africa and Asia would look quite different from how they do now. Without chemical controls for rust, global arabica production would be considerably lower, although exact numbers are difficult to know. The data from the Big Rust suggest that yield losses of 15–20 percent are plausible. Chemical control has helped sustain arabica production in large parts of Brazil. In the absence of these controls and others, the volume and geographical distribution of global coffee production would look substantially different. Far fewer people across the global tropics would earn all or part of their livelihoods from coffee.

While these innovations have offered many benefits, they have also left a complicated legacy. Critics often associate coffee science with the particular model of technification promoted in the 1970s and 1980s. They rightly express concern about the impacts of agricultural chemicals on the health of farmers and laborers, of consumers, and of the coffee ecosystems as a whole. They worry about the destruction of Latin America's tropical forests and the rich biological diversity that they contain. But science is not a monolithic, unchanging enterprise. Scientists from different disciplinary backgrounds—plant breeders, agricultural chemists, and agroecologists, among others—have continually debated the best strategies for dealing with the rust. And the scientific conversations are themselves embedded in larger conversations with farmers, government agencies, and the coffee industry.

Until recently, therapeutic approaches (such as chemical control and resistant varieties) have dominated rust-control strategies. These approaches focus on one part of the disease system—historically, the pathogen or the host plant. These measures, alone or in tandem, have allowed farmers to continue producing coffee in places where the rust is otherwise a threat. But as this history has shown, therapeutic approaches can hasten the development of new rust strains that can overcome chemical-control schemes or the resistance genes in the coffee plant. These control strategies also require significant investments from farmers (and other stakeholders); in times of crisis, they have been severely weakened, leaving coffee farms newly vulnerable to the rust. Effective breeding programs require long-term institutional support, which has not always been forthcoming. Still, therapeutic approaches such as this will remain an important part of strategies to control the rust.

Since the 1990s, some scientists have explored more holistic strategies to managing the rust, strategies that focus on building resistance into the ecosystem as a whole. As early as the 1880s, Harry Marshall Ward's elegant field experiments demonstrated the correlations between cropping patterns and the rust. But until recently, therapeutic approaches prevailed. More holistic approaches to rust control have gained force since the 1990s, in part because of growing interest in economic, ecological, and social sustainability. Scientists working in the emergent disciplines of agroecology, agroforestry, and integrated pest management are developing more nuanced understandings of how the coffee ecosystem functions and of the role of the rust within that ecosystem. Their work is providing the foundations for new rust-control strategies. The goal, put simply, is to "structure and manage coffee ecosystems to maximize their preventive strengths, by enhancing multiple ecological control mechanisms."[5] John Vandermeer and Ivette Perfecto, at the University of Michigan, have done pioneering work on coffee agroecology, including studies on the complex web of forces that keep the coffee rust in check on farms with high levels of biodiversity. In Central America, Jacques Avelino and his collaborators have studied how the rust develops in different kinds of coffee farms. They have studied the relationship between shade and intensity of outbreaks, a relationship that turns out to be more complicated than had been previously imagined.

Reflecting the growing importance of such approaches, in 2015 the FAO organized an international conference on agroecological management of the coffee rust. Much of this work is still preliminary; as the conference organizer Alan Hruska concluded, "there is still much to learn about the interactions between key factors" in the coffee agroecosystem, such as "the local climate on farms, the density and composition of shade, patterns of rainfall and dew, and the role of other microorganisms as agents of biological control and other functions of the microbiome."[6] This inattention to ecological mechanisms was not accidental; previously, rust research had focused principally on therapeutic controls. But perhaps, as the coffee ecologists Vandermeer and Perfecto wrote, "when as many resources are devoted the more ecological aspects of agriculture as have been provided to chemistry-oriented productionist goals since World War II, recommendations for ecological management will be forthcoming."[7] The solutions to the coffee rust are not, in any case, solely technical.

Any effective rust-control program must begin with a central question: "Can this program help provide farmers with an economically and ecologically stable livelihood?" A technical solution that farmers cannot afford is not, in the end, a solution. Rust-control initiatives must be part of broader programs to manage the social and economic uncertainty that most coffee farmers face. Volatile coffee markets are a chronic problem. Now, as before, constant economic uncertainty makes it difficult for farmers to adapt their farms to the rust and to the many other challenges they face. The history of the coffee rust suggests that farmers can adapt to economic and ecological uncertainty when they have strong and sustained institutional support and access to credit. In places where the rust proves to be insurmountable, this support could help farmers can make a smooth transition from coffee to other crops. For much of the twentieth century, Colombia has been a model of how to build a strong and resilient coffee industry. But even Colombian farmers have struggled with adapting to ecological and economic challenges. Adaptation will be even more difficult in places where the economic and political weight of the coffee industry is much smaller than it was fifty—or even thirty—years ago. The recent partnerships between public institutions, NGOs, and the industry to support farmers have offered some relief, particularly for farmers who produce specialty coffees. If the coffee trade wants to ensure that coffee has a viable future as global demand increases and climate change threatens, then it must do more to ensure that coffee farmers, large and small, can earn a sustainable living from the coffee they produce.

The coffee rust has, like every other facet of the coffee ecosystem, been transformed by climate change. The Big Rust is a compelling example of how comparatively small changes in temperature, sunshine, and rainfall can have significant impact on the distribution and intensity of rust epidemics. Climate change has repercussions for every facet of the coffee ecosystem—the pathogen, the plant, the environment, and cropping practices. Scientists have recently developed models that predict how climate change will shape coffee production around the world.[8] But these models focus almost exclusively on abiotic factors, failing to take into account how those changes will affect biotic factors such as diseases and pests.[9] Entomologists have developed some predictions about how climate change will shape outbreaks of the coffee berry borer in East Africa, yet there has been no comparable regional or global study of the rust. Agroforestry can help coffee ecosystems address the intertwined challenges of the rust and of climate change. Shade, in particular, "can help mitigate against both the rust and against climate change," write Jacques Avelino and Gonzalo Rivas Platero. But still, they warn that "when we have optimal climatic systems for the rust, we must recognize that no control system will naturally keep the disease at low levels."[10] In those scenarios, chemical control and resistant varieties would still be necessary. Plant breeders are adding climate change, alongside disease resistance and quality, into their research agendas.

The title of this book is not a prediction, but a simple statement of fact. Coffee's future will be different from, and more fragile than, its past. If the book has a central message, it is that we cannot take coffee—or any of our crops—for granted. At the start of the nineteenth century the world's coffeelands were, for all practical purposes, free of major diseases and pests. Two centuries later, they are riddled with them. New diseases and pests, and new strains of established diseases and pests, are on the move. Once established, they are difficult to eradicate. And their impact is cumulative. Farmers now have to confront many problems at once—the rust *and* the borer in Central America, the rust *and* coffee berry disease in east Africa—with other diseases and pests on the way. These challenges have been aggravated by chronic economic uncertainty and, more recently, by climate change. In the face of such challenges many farmers have abandoned coffee, and as the challenges mount they will continue to do so. The tropics are littered with coffee graveyards, typically the product of environmental and economic problems operating in tandem. In Ceylon, tea now grows where coffee once flourished; once-vast coffeelands in frost-plagued southern Brazil have since been replanted in soy. Still, the history of the coffee rust also offers cause for hope: it is a story of constant and creative innovation, both by farmers and by scientists. It shows that farmers can, with the right kinds of support, adapt to these challenges. But if coffee *is* to be forever, then the central question—especially for poorer smallholders who produce most of the world's coffee—is whether they can get the support they need.

Notes

Chapter 1: The Devourer of Dreams

1. "Roya devora esperanzas."

2. Scholthof, "The Disease Triangle"; the question "Why is the disease a disease?" builds on ideas articulated in Lewis et al., "Sustainable Pest Management."

3. This account of coffee physiology draws upon Wrigley, *Coffee*, chap. 3; Cambrony and Coste, *Caféiers et cafés*, chap. 3. On biennial bearing, see Smith and Samach, "Constraints to Obtaining Consistent Annual Yields in Perennial Tree Crops. I."

4. Cerda et al., "Primary and Secondary Yield Losses Caused by Pests and Diseases."

5. George Marcus discusses the methodology of following as a way of studying globalization in "Ethnography in/of the World System"; other historians of tropical botany and agriculture have tracked similar transtropical connections. See Fernández Prieto, "Archipelago of Sugar"; Harwood, "The Green Revolution as a Process of Global Circulation."

6. Topik, "The Integration of the World Coffee Market."

7. Soluri, "Something Fishy"; Soluri, *Banana Cultures*; McCook, "Las epidemias liberales"; McCook, *States of Nature*, chap. 4. On diseases of tropical perennial crops generally, see Ploetz, "Diseases of Tropical Perennial Crops."

8. Olmstead and Rhode, "The Red Queen and the Hard Reds: Productivity Growth in American Wheat, 1800–1940."

9. Harwood, "The Green Revolution as a Process of Global Circulation." This network of relationships is similar to precompetitive research in the

pharmaceutical industry. See Tancredi, "Global Networks of Excellence"; Altshuler et al., "Opening Up to Precompetitive Collaboration."

10. As far as I can tell, this story was first told in Carefoot and Sprott, *Famine on the Wind*, 123. I explore this issue further in chapter 2.

11. McCook, "The Ecology of Taste."

12. Clarence-Smith, "Coffee Crisis."

Chapter 2: Coffee Rust Contained

1. Wintgens, "The Coffee Plant."

2. Sylvain, "Ethiopian Coffee," 117.

3. Berthaud, "L'origine et la distribution des caféiers dans le monde," 361–62.

4. Anthony et al., "Origin of Cultivated *Coffea arabica*"; Charrier and Eskes, "Botany and Genetics of Coffee"; Meyer, "Notes on Wild *Coffea arabica* from Southwestern Ethiopia, with Some Historical Considerations"; Sylvain, "Ethiopian Coffee"; Wrigley, *Coffee*; Wintgens, "The Coffee Plant."

5. Kushalappa, "Biology and Epidemiology," 16–76; Wellman, *Coffee*, 253–60.

6. Eskes, "Resistance," 223.

7. Eskes, 227.

8. Eskes, 227.

9. Eskes, 224–25; for a discussion of hyperparasites, see Waller, Bigger, and Hillocks, *Coffee Pests, Diseases and Their Management*, 174.

10. Koehler, *Where the Wild Coffee Grows*, 45–55.

11. Koehler, 56–67.

12. Sylvain, "Ethiopian Coffee," 124.

13. Schaefer, "Coffee Unobserved," 23–24; Wrigley, *Coffee*, 54–58.

14. Hattox, *Coffee and Coffeehouses*, 24–25.

15. Tuchscherer, "Commerce et production du café en mer Rouge."

16. Tuchscherer, "Coffee in the Red Sea Area," 54.

17. Um, *The Merchant Houses of Mocha*, 36.

18. Um, 36.

19. Varisco, "Agriculture in Al-Hamdānī's Yemen," 408–9.

20. Boivin, Fuller, and Crowther, "Old World Globalization and the Columbian Exchange"; Fuller and Boivin, "Crops, Cattle and Commensals across the Indian Ocean"; Watson, *Agricultural Innovation*.

21. Wrigley, *Coffee*, 13. To get a sense of the diversity of crops cultivated in Yemen, see Varisco, "Agriculture in Al-Hamdānī's Yemen."

22. Wrigley, *Coffee*, 13–15; Di Fulvio, *Le café dans le monde*, 85–86; Haarer, *Modern Coffee Production*, 349; Chevalier, *Les caféiers du globe*, 9.

23. La Roque [1726], cited in Wrigley, *Coffee*, 14.

24. Sylvain, "Le café du Yémen," 62.

25. Varisco, "Indigenous Plant Protection Methods in Yemen," 34.

26. Wrigley, *Coffee*, 40–50. See also Anthony et al., "Origin of Cultivated *Coffea arabica*."

27. Pendergrast, *Uncommon Grounds*, 10–12.

28. This argument is developed more fully in Cowan, *The Social Life of Coffee*.

29. Quoted in Pendergrast, *Uncommon Grounds*, 11.

30. François Valentijn [1726], quoted in McCants, "Poor Consumers as Global Consumers: The Diffusion of Tea and Coffee Drinking in the Eighteenth Century," 177.

31. Pendergrast, *Uncommon Grounds*, 45–62.

32. Clarence-Smith, "Spread of Coffee Cultivation in Asia."

33. Jussieu, "Histoire du café."

34. Auguste Chevalier's 1929 discussion of how coffee was introduced to the Americas remains one of the most complete and definitive accounts. See Chevalier, *Les caféiers du globe*.

35. Muthiah, *A Planting Century*, 109–12.

36. Topik, "Integration of the World Coffee Market"; Pendergrast, *Uncommon Grounds*; Jiménez, " 'From Plantation to Cup.' "

37. Clarence-Smith, "Coffee Crisis."

38. See, in particular Topik, "Integration of the World Coffee Market."

39. Clarence-Smith, "Coffee Crisis," 107.

40. The global spread of coffee is concisely and eloquently summarized in Jamieson, "Essence of Commodification," 281–83. William Clarence-Smith discusses how non-Europeans helped spread coffee in Asia in "Spread of Coffee Cultivation in Asia."

41. Chevalier, *Les caféiers du globe*, 54. Chevalier gives the 1775 figure as 45,933,941 "livres," French pounds. For the conversion to tons, I have assumed that Chevalier was referring to the livre de Paris, which is equivalent to 489.5 grams.

42. Hull, *Coffee Planting*, 108.

43. Hull, 152–53.

44. Hull, 39.

45. Dean, "Green Wave of Coffee."

46. Hull, *Coffee Planting*, 106.

47. These issues are characteristic of many monocultures, not just coffee. See Uekötter, "The Magic of One."

48. Chevalier, *Les caféiers du globe*, 60–61.

49. Laborie, *Coffee Planter of Saint Domingo*.

50. T. J. Barron describes coffee manuals and the system of "creeping" in "Science and the Ceylon Coffee Planters." On Laborie and other coffee manuals in the nineteenth century, see Samper K., "Modelos vs. prácticas."

51. Clarence-Smith and Topik, "Coffee and Global Development," 8–9.

52. Cramer, *Coffee Research in Indonesia*, 6. For a succinct overview of agricultural sciences in colonial Java, see Maat, *Science Cultivating Practice*; Maat, "Agricultural Sciences in Colonial Indonesia."

53. Hull, *Coffee Planting*, 239.

54. Chevalier, *Les caféiers du globe*, 61.

55. Rozier, *Cours complet d'agriculture*, 2:522, 526.

56. Hull, *Coffee Planting*, 267.

57. Waller, Bigger, and Hillocks, *Coffee Pests, Diseases and Their Management*, 47–50.

58. Hull, *Coffee Planting*, 268–69.

59. Hull, 275.

60. Gardner, *Extracts from a Report on the Coffee Blight of Ceylon*; Berkeley, "Notice of a Mould."

61. Nietner, *The Coffee Tree and Its Enemies*, 10.

62. Nietner, 10.

63. Goodwin, Cohen, and Fry, "Panglobal Distribution of a Single Clonal Lineage of the Irish Potato Famine Fungus"; Rosenberg, *The Cholera Years*; Arnold, "Indian Ocean as Disease Zone."

64. McCook, "Ephemeral Plantations"; Cramer, *Coffee Research in Indonesia*, 11.

65. Hull, *Coffee Planting*, 278.

66. Watt, *Economic Products of India*, 2:473.

67. Hefner, *Political Economy of Mountain Java*, 41.

68. Hull, *Coffee Planting*, 310.

69. Hull, 306.

Chapter 3: The Epicenter

1. Thwaites (1871) in Nietner, *The Coffee Tree and Its Enemies*, 23.

2. Webb, *Tropical Pioneers*, 16–17, 60; Thurber, *Coffee: From Plantation to Cup*, 90; Mills, *Ceylon under British Rule, 1795–1932*, 222. On initial tendencies for Europeans to capture existing coffee production from Sinhalese producers, see Jamieson, "The Essence of Commodification," 269–94.

3. Hull, *Coffee Planting*, 43.

4. Webb, *Tropical Pioneers*, 69–73.

5. Sabonadière, *The Coffee-Planter of Ceylon*, 22. Trollope quoted in Williams, *Deforesting the Earth*, 363. Production statistics from Webb, *Tropical Pioneers*, 113.

6. Webb, *Tropical Pioneers*, 5–10.

7. Thwaites (1871) in Nietner, *The Coffee Tree and Its Enemies*, 23.

8. Van der Plank, *Principles of Plant Infection*, 136–37; Zadoks and Schein, *Epidemiology and Plant Disease Management*, 151; Zadoks and van den Bosch, "On the Spread of Plant Disease."

9. Arnold, "Indian Ocean as a Disease Zone."

10. On the origins of the Wardian case, and global plant transfers, see McCook, "'Squares of Tropic Summer.'"

11. Wrigley, *Coffee*, 314.

12. Beachey, "The East African Ivory Trade in the Nineteenth Century."

13. For a succinct overview of these processes, see Kushalappa, "Biology and Epidmiology," 21–58.

14. Ferguson and Ferguson, *Planting Directory*, 13.

15. Ferguson and Ferguson, 13.

16. Russell (1871) in Nietner, *The Coffee Tree and Its Enemies*, 22.

17. Thwaites and Hooker, *Enumeratio Plantarum Zeylaniae*; Boulger and Grout, "Thwaites, George Henry Kendrick (1812–1882)."

18. Ainsworth, *History of Plant Pathology*, 7.

19. Price, "Berkeley, Miles Joseph (1803–1889)"; Massee, "Miles Joseph Berkeley, 1803–1889."

20. Berkeley, "*Hemileia vastatrix*," 1157.

21. On the origins of this circular, see "Correspondence respecting the Coffee-Leaf Disease in Ceylon."

22. "Coffee Leaf Disease in Ceylon, Answers to Circular of 12 February, 1875."

23. Hooker, "The Royal Gardens, Kew," 141.

24. Hooker, 142.

25. Data from Vanden Driesen, "Coffee Cultivation in Ceylon (2)." On the patterns of biennial bearing, see Wrigley, *Coffee*, 124, 230. Other tree crops follow similar bearing patterns: see Monselise and Goldschmidt, "Alternate Bearing in Fruit Trees."

26. Thurber, *Coffee: From Plantation to Cup*, 95.

27. Thwaites, "Ceylon Coffee Fungus," 726.

28. Hull, *Coffee Planting*, 112.

29. On the variety of fertilizers being used in Ceylon during the mid-1870s, see Hull, 238–62.

30. Thwaites, "Ceylon Coffee Fungus," 726.

31. Avelino, Willocquet, and Savary, "Effects of Crop Management Patterns on Coffee Rust Epidemics."

32. Berkeley, "*Hemileia vastatrix*," 1157. On the use of sulfur as a fungicide, see Ainsworth, *History of Plant Pathology*, 108–11.

33. Drayton, *Nature's Government*; Brockway, *Science and Colonial Expansion*.

34. Duncan, *Shadows of the Tropics*, 174.

35. Christy, *New Commercial Plants*, 1:5.

36. For a more detailed history of Liberian coffee, see McCook, "Ephemeral Plantations: The Rise and Fall of Liberian Coffee, 1870-1900"; Morris, *Notes on Liberian Coffee*.

37. Daniel Morris, in Crüwell, *Liberian Coffee in Ceylon*, xxvii.

38. Morris in Crüwell, xxxiii.

39. McCook, "Ephemeral Plantations: The Rise and Fall of Liberian Coffee, 1870-1900."

40. Ferguson and Ferguson, *Planting Directory*, 100.

41. Data from Vanden Driesen, "Coffee Cultivation in Ceylon (2)."

42. Ferguson, *Ceylon in 1893*, 68.

43. Quoted in Morris, "Coffee-Leaf Disease of Ceyon and Southern India."

44. Ferguson and Ferguson, *Planting Directory*, 13.

45. *Ceylon Observer* (Feb. 19, 1879). In "Misc. Rept. Ceylon Coffee Diseases."

46. For a concise overview of the changing place of the field sciences in the nineteenth and twentieth centuries, see Vetter, "Introduction."

47. On the new botany in England, see Drayton, *Nature's Government*, 244–45.

48. Ainsworth, *History of Mycology*, chap. 6; Ainsworth, *History of Plant Pathology*, 31–38; Egerton, "History of Ecological Sciences, Part 44," 314–16.

49. Thiselton-Dyer, "The Coffee-Leaf Disease of Ceylon," 122; Morris, *Campaign of 1879*, 117.

50. "Coffee Leaf-Disease," August 23, 1879.

51. Morris, "The Structure and Habit of *Hemileia vastatrix*," 516; Morris, *Campaign of 1879*, 123.

52. Quoted in Drayton, *Nature's Government*, 250.

53. Morris, *Campaign of 1879*, 172.

54. "Coffee Leaf-Disease," August 23, 1879.

55. Morris, *Campaign of 1879*, 153.

56. For a detailed overview of Ward's educational background, see Ayres, *Fungal Thread of Death*, chaps. 2, 3.

57. Ward, *Coffee Leaf Disease: Second Report*, 4.

58. Ward, *Coffee Leaf Disease: Third Report*, 5–6.

59. Ward, *Coffee Leaf Disease: Second Report.*, 10.

60. Ward, *Coffee Leaf Disease: Third Report*, 9.

61. Ward, 9.

62. Ward, 9.

63. Ward, 12.

64. Ward, 18–27.

65. Ward, 3.

66. Ward, 15.

67. Talbot, "Mr. Marshall Ward's Report on Leaf-Disease."

68. Nietner, *The Coffee Tree and Its Enemies*, 182–87.

69. "Coffee Leaf Disease and Mr. Schrottky's Remedy."

70. Thiselton-Dyer, "No Reward for a Remedy for Leaf-Disease."

71. Duncan, *Shadows of the Tropics*, 186.

72. Duncan, 172, 186; Ameer Ali, "Peasant Coffee in Ceylon," 55.

73. Duncan, *Shadows of the Tropics*, 186.

74. Quotations from "Government Gardens in Ceylon," 555.

75. Duncan, *Shadows of the Tropics*, 185.

76. Simmonds, *Tropical Agriculture*, 239. On coconut as the percentage of exports, see Wenzlhuemer, *From Coffee to Tea Cultivation in Ceylon*, 93.

77. Wenzlhuemer, *From Coffee to Tea Cultivation in Ceylon*, 92.

78. Vanden Driesen, "Coffee Cultivation in Ceylon (2)," 165–66.

79. Vanden Driesen, 169.

80. "Ceylon: General Planting Report," 90.

81. Herbert, "Peradeniya and the Plantation Raj," 138; Drayton, *Nature's Government*, 206–10.

82. Wenzlhuemer, *From Coffee to Tea Cultivation in Ceylon*, 72–23.

83. Webb, *Tropical Pioneers*, 133; Wenzlhuemer, *From Coffee to Tea Cultivation in Ceylon*, 76.

84. Wenzlhuemer, *From Coffee to Tea Cultivation in Ceylon*, 80.

85. Webb, *Tropical Pioneers*, 139.

86. Wenzlhuemer, *From Coffee to Tea Cultivation in Ceylon*, 81.

87. Figures from Webb, *Tropical Pioneers*, 137, table 5.5.

88. Vanden Driesen, "Coffee Cultivation in Ceylon (2)," 169.

89. Carefoot and Sprott, *Famine on the Wind*, 123.

90. Carefoot and Sprott, 123.

91. Ceylon export figures from Webb, *Tropical Pioneers*, 113; British consumption figures from Simmonds, *Tropical Agriculture*, 32, and Lock, *Coffee: Its Culture and Commerce*, 216.

92. Data on the origins of British coffee imports in 1884 from Lock, *Coffee: Its Culture and Commerce*, 167.

93. Willis, *Agriculture in the Tropics*, 65.

Chapter 4: Arabica Graveyards

1. Thurber, *Coffee: From Plantation to Cup*, 66.

2. Simmonds, *Tropical Agriculture*, 28.

3. Production figures calculated from Samper and Fernando, "Historical Statistics of Coffee," table A.15, 436–39.

4. Thurber, *Coffee: From Plantation to Cup*, 64.

5. On plant, animal, and human epidemics in the Indian Ocean basin, see Arnold, "Indian Ocean as Disease Zone"; Phoofolo, "Epidemics and Revolutions"; Storey, *Science and Power in Colonial Mauritius*.

6. Planter, "Indian Experiences," 199; "Planting Position and Prospects of Travancore," 526.

7. J. E. van der Plank draws a useful contrast between dispersal and migration (spread) in *Principles of Plant Infection*, 133.

8. This account is based on the models of dispersal described in Nagarajan and Singh, "Long-Distance Dispersion of Rust Pathogens."

9. Scheffer's observations reported in Abbay to Thiselton-Dyer, 21 May 1879.

10. Ferguson, *Ceylon in 1883*, 95.

11. The evolution of shipping in the Indian Ocean, including a concise overview of the Netherlands India Steam Navigation Company, is described in detail in Munro, *Maritime Enterprise and Empire*; J. N. F. M. à Campo describes the connection between shipping and empire in the Dutch East Indies in *Engines of Empire*.

12. Delacroix, *Maladies et ennemis des caféiers*, 43.

13. Hays, *Burdens of Disease*, 184, 187–90.

14. Most of this chronology is based upon Delacroix, *Maladies et ennemis des caféiers*. For Timor, see Lains e Silva, *Timor e a cultura do café*, 36–38; Leechman, "Story of *Hemileia vastatrix*."

15. For a discussion of the agricultural sciences in Puerto Rico under US domination, see McCook, *States of Nature*, chap. 3.

16. The outbreak was briefly mentioned in Orton, "Plant Diseases in 1903," 555. In the early 1950s, W. W. Diehl wrote a draft article on this event for the magazine *Chronica Botanica*, which was apparently circulated in typescript but never published. Fortunately, Frederick Wellman summarized Diehl's manuscript in *Hemileia vastatrix*, 9–12.

17. See, for example Zadoks, "On the Conceptual Basis of Crop Loss Assessment"; Nutter, Teng, and Royer, "Terms and Concepts for Yield, Crop Loss, and Disease Thresholds."

18. "Leaf Disease in Netherlands India," 198; Ukers, *All about Coffee* (1935), 188.

19. Samper and Fernando, "Historical Statistics of Coffee," 437, table A.15.

20. Campbell, "Coffee Production in Réunion and Madagascar," 70–71; Buis, *L'avenir du caféier*.

21. Ukers, *All about Coffee* (1935), 192, 210; Legarda, *After the Galleons*, 115, 117, 335; War Department, Office of the Secretary, "Coffee in the Philippines."

22. War Department, Office of the Secretary, "Coffee in the Philippines."

23. This idea of "belts" draws upon Cramer, *Coffee Research in Indonesia*, 79.

24. Elliot, *Gold, Sport, and Coffee Planting in Mysore*, 284, 399.

25. "Failure of Coffee Crops in Coorg."

26. Waller, Bigger, and Hillocks, *Coffee Pests, Diseases and Their Management*, 177.

27. Turing Mackenzie, "Leaf Disease and Coffee"; Wester, "Coffee in the Philippines," 40.

28. Mayne, "Control of Coffee Leaf Disease," 206.

29. Planter, "Indian Experiences."

30. Wester, "Coffee in the Philippines," 40.

31. Hefner, *Political Economy of Mountain Java*, 51; Clarence-Smith, "Coffee Crisis," 249, 256; Cramer, *"Hemileia vastatrix au Java,"* 348.

32. On diseases and the Brazilian rubber industry, see Dean, *Brazil and the Struggle for Rubber*.

33. Parr, "How a Planter Is Treated in Fiji," 140.

34. Busch, *Science and Agricultural Development*; Storey, *Science and Power in Colonial Mauritius*, 69–70.

35. Kumar, *Science and the Raj*, 1857–1905, 82–83.

36. "Coffee Leaf-Disease," April 1, 1892, 746.

37. Maat, *Science Cultivating Practice*, 54–59; Goss, *The Floracrats*, 46–47.

38. Cramer, *Coffee Research in Indonesia*, xvii.

39. Ainsworth, *History of Plant Pathology*, 108–11.

40. Ridley, "Dr. Burck's Method of Treatment of the Coffee-Leaf Disease in Java," 7–8.

41. Storck, "Cure for Leaf Disease in Fiji."

42. "Mr. Storck's Remedy for Coffee Leaf Disease," 911.

43. Grieq et al., "Coffee Leaf-Disease: Final Report of the Committee," 973.

44. Delacroix, *Maladies et ennemis des caféiers*, 49.

45. Ainsworth, *History of Plant Pathology*, 111–13; Ayres, "Alexis Millardet"; McCallan, "History of Fungicides."

46. Sadebeck, *Die wichtigeren Nutzpflanzen und deren Erzeugnisse aus den deutschen Colonien*; Mayne, "Control of Coffee Leaf Disease," 207.

47. Delacroix, *Maladies et ennemis des caféiers*, 49.

48. Raoul and Darolles, *Culture du caféier*, 25–29.

49. Buis, *L'avenir du caféier*, 13.

50. Elliot, *Gold, Sport, and Coffee Planting in Mysore*, 284; Ridley, "Dr. Burck's Method of Treatment of the Coffee-Leaf Disease in Java," 11.

51. Buis, *L'avenir du caféier*, 15.

52. Elliot, *Gold, Sport, and Coffee Planting in Mysore*, 284.

53. Delacroix, *Maladies et ennemis des caféiers*, 49.

54. Wrigley, *Coffee*, 324–26.

55. "Coffee Leaf-Disease," April 2, 1888.

56. Buis, *L'avenir du caféier*, 8.

57. Buis, 14.

58. Mayne, "Control of Coffee Leaf Disease," 207.

59. Elliot, *Gold, Sport, and Coffee Planting in Mysore*, 287.

60. Ridley, "Dr. Burck's Method of Treatment of the Coffee-Leaf Disease in Java," 6.

61. Bhattacharya, "Local History of a Global Commodity Production," 70–72; Clarence-Smith, "Spread of Coffee Cultivation in Asia."

62. "Leaf Disease in Netherlands India," 1069.

63. For a contemporary example of how germplasm moves through social networks, see Ellen and Platten, "Social Life of Seeds."

64. Windle, *Modern Coffee Planting*, 5.

65. "Coffee: 'Nalknaad.' To the Editor of the 'Asian'"; Richter, *Manual of Coorg*, 95; Anderson, *Jottings on Coffee and Its Culture in Mysore*, 50; "'Nakanaad Coffee'; and Crop Prospects," 329; "Hybrid Coffee in the Straits: Freedom of Coorg Coffee from Leaf Disease," 126.

66. Eskes, "Resistance," 210–11; Rodrigues and Eskes, "Resistance to Coffee Leaf Rust," 553–54; Elliot, *Gold, Sport, and Coffee Planting in Mysore*, 307, 311–13; Windle, *Modern Coffee Planting*, 5.

67. Hiern, "X. On the African Species of the Genus *Coffea*, Linn."

68. McCook, "Ephemeral Plantations," 88–92.

69. Chevalier, *Les caféiers du globe*, 177; Wellman, *Coffee*, 76–79; Hiern, "X. On the African Species of the Genus *Coffea*, Linn.," 171–72; Thurber, *Coffee: From Plantation to Cup*, 144.

70. Davis et al., "Taxonomic Conspectus of *Coffea*," 14.

71. Wellman, *Coffee*, 90, 78.

72. "Varieties of Liberian Coffee."

73. "Liberian Coffee and Tea in Java," 159.

74. McCook, "Ephemeral Plantations," 100–101.

75. Cramer, *Coffee Research in Indonesia*, 107. See also Cramer, "*Hemileia vastatrix* au Java," 389–93.

76. Cramer, *Coffee Research in Indonesia*, 43–45.

77. Cramer, 44.

78. Gomez et al., "Shift in Precipitation Regime Promotes Interspecific Hybridization of Introduced *Coffea* Species"; Gomez et al., "Favourable Habitats for *Coffea* Inter-Specific Hybridization."

79. "Hybrid Coffee in Mysore"; Windle, *Modern Coffee Planting*, 9, 138–39; Cameron, "Report on Coffee Leaf Disease in Coorg."

80. Cramer, *Coffee Research in Indonesia*, 46.

81. Cramer, 154.

82. Cramer, 44.

83. Cramer, 44–45.

84. Ainsworth, *History of Plant Pathology*, 48–51; Schafer, Roelfs, and Bushnell, "Contribution of Early Scientists to Knowledge of Cereal Rusts," 10–11.

85. These patterns are common to many plant pathogens. See Schumann and D'Arcy, *Hungry Planet*, 26–27, 31–32.

86. Clarence-Smith, "Coffee Crisis," 100–101, 118–19.

87. Eng, *Agricultural Growth in Indonesia*, 70–81; Cramer, *Coffee Research in Indonesia*, 9–10.

Chapter 5: Robusta to the Rescue

1. On commodities in the global economy, see Topik and Wells, "Commodity Chains in a Global Economy." On the integration of the global coffee market, see Topik, "The Integration of the World Coffee Market," especially pp. 32–35. On the coffee crisis in the Eastern Hemisphere, see Clarence-Smith, "Coffee Crisis."

2. Topik, *Political Economy of the Brazilian State*, chap. 3; Wickizer, *World Coffee Economy*, chap. 10.

3. Di Fulvio, *Le café dans le monde*, 30–31; Wickizer, *Coffee, Tea, and Cocoa*, 26–27. For statistics on average coffee prices, see Samper and Fernando, "Historical Statistics of Coffee," table A.22, 452; Topik, *Political Economy of the Brazilian State*, chap. 3.

4. The comments of India's trade commissioner are quoted in Sovani, *International Position of India's Raw Materials*, 108. On Indian coffee exports

and internal demand, see India, Office of the Agricultural Marketing Adviser, *Marketing of Coffee in India*, 46–47, 61. See also Ukers, *All about Coffee* (1935), 194; Di Fulvio, *Le café dans le monde*, 289–94.

5. Coleman, "Work on the Coffee Experiment Station, Balehonnur," 13.

6. Mayne, "Experiences of a Coffee Biologist in Mysore."

7. Windle, *Modern Coffee Planting*, 140.

8. Windle, 9, 139.

9. Windle, 8–9; Eskes, "Resistance," 179; Rodrigues, Bettencourt, and Rijo, "Races of the Pathogen and Resistance to Coffee Rust," 51.

10. Mayne, "Physiological Specialisation of *Hemileia vastatrix*," 510; Wellman, *Coffee*, 258–59; Wrigley, *Coffee*; Wellman, *Tropical American Plant Disease*, 494–95.

11. Mayne, "Physiological Specialisation of *Hemileia vastatrix*"; Coleman, "The Coffee-Planting Industry of South India," 308–9, 313.

12. Rodrigues, Bettencourt, and Rijo, "Races of the Pathogen and Resistance to Coffee Rust," 62; Avelino and Rivas Platero, "La roya anaranjada del cafeto," 8.

13. Mayne, "Control of Coffee Leaf Disease," 207.

14. Windle, *Modern Coffee Planting*, 135, 141–42.

15. Mayne, "Control of Coffee Leaf Disease," 207.

16. Mayne, 207.

17. Windle, *Modern Coffee Planting*, 150.

18. Mysore State, Department of Agriculture, *Coffee Experiment Station, Balehonnur*.

19. Windle, *Modern Coffee Planting*, 45.

20. Mayne, Narasimhan, and Sreenivasan, "Spraying of Coffee in South India"; Mayne, "Seasonal Periodicity of Coffee Leaf Disease"; Mayne, "Seasonal Periodicity of Coffee Leaf Disease Second Report."

21. Coleman, "The Coffee-Planting Industry of South India," 309.

22. Windle, *Modern Coffee Planting*, 157.

23. Mayne, Narasimhan, and Sreenivasan, "Spraying of Coffee in South India," i.

24. India, Office of the Agricultural Marketing Adviser, *Marketing of Coffee in India*, 40, 56–57.

25. Di Fulvio, *Le café dans le monde*, 119–26, 294–308 and the table "Répartition proportonelle de la production mondiale," 125. Five-year averages calculated from Samper and Fernando, "Historical Statistics of Coffee," 438.

26. Coleman, "Coffee in the Dutch East Indies"; Cramer, *Coffee Research in Indonesia*, 9–11; Maat, *Science Cultivating Practice*, 53–67; Goss, *The Floracrats*, chap. 4.

27. Davis et al., "Taxonomic Conspectus of *Coffea*," 474.

28. Cramer, *Coffee Research in Indonesia*, 13–14.

29. Cramer, 12.

30. Davis et al., "Taxonomic Conspectus of *Coffea*," 479.

31. Weiss, *Sacred Trees, Bitter Harvests*; Wrigley, *Coffee*, 54–58.

32. Wrigley, *Coffee*, 56–57.

33. Cramer, *Coffee Research in Indonesia*, 12, 114.

34. Cramer, 115; Wester, "Notes on Coffee in Java," 123; Coleman, "Coffee in the Dutch East Indies," 15.

35. Ferwerda, "Coffee Breeding in Java"; Coleman, "Coffee in the Dutch East Indies"; Cramer, *Coffee Research in Indonesia*, 128–34.

36. Ferwerda, "Coffee Breeding in Java," 263.

37. Cramer, *Coffee Research in Indonesia*, 114.

38. International Institute of Agriculture and Bally, *Coffee in 1931 and 1932*, 103; Coleman, "Coffee in the Dutch East Indies," 7, 13–15.

39. Ukers, *All about Coffee* (1935), 188; Wrigley, *Coffee*, 57; Pendergrast, *Uncommon Grounds*, 152–53.

40. Coleman, "Coffee in the Dutch East Indies," 6.

41. Cramer, *Coffee Research in Indonesia*, 38.

42. Quotation from Cramer, 38. See also Huitema, *De bevolkingskoffiecultuur op Sumatra*, 142–44; International Institute of Agriculture and Bally, *Coffee in 1931 and 1932*, 227.

43. International Institute of Agriculture and Bally, *Coffee in 1931 and 1932*, 103.

44. Viehover and Lepper, "Robusta Coffee," 286–87.

45. Ukers, *All about Coffee* (1922), 338.

46. Van Hall, "Robusta and Some Allied Coffee Species," 257.

47. Viehover and Lepper, "Robusta Coffee," 285. The calculation is based on data from Samper and Fernando, "Historical Statistics of Coffee," table A.15, 438, and table A.19, 444.

48. McCook, "The Ecology of Taste"; Coste, *Les caféiers*, 2:702.

49. Wickizer, *World Coffee Economy*, 55–57; Jiménez, "'From Plantation to Cup.'"

50. Ukers, *All about Coffee* (1935), 209, 250–51.

51. International Institute of Agriculture and Bally, *Coffee in 1931 and 1932*, 115.

52. Viehover and Lepper, "Robusta Coffee," 288.

53. Coste, "N.C.R.A. Circular Covers Four Important Subjects."

54. Wrigley, *Coffee*, 57; Di Fulvio, *Le café dans le monde*, 60.

55. Risbec, "Le café en Nouvelle-Calédonie (1)," 97–99.

56. Ukers, *All about Coffee* (1935), 183; Campbell, "Coffee Production in Réunion and Madagascar," 76–83; Buis, *L'avenir du caféier*.

57. Muthiah, *A Planting Century*, 108.

58. Muthiah, 118.

59. Coleman, "The Coffee-Planting Industry of South India," 304.

60. Cramer, *Coffee Research in Indonesia*, 178–79.

61. India, Office of the Agricultural Marketing Adviser, *Marketing of Coffee in India*, 49, 65; Coste, *Les caféiers*, 2:700.

62. Di Fulvio, *Le café dans le monde*, 279.

63. For data on global production between 1900 and 1940, see Di Fulvio, 119–21, 126.

Chapter 6: The "Malaria of Coffee"

1. Birmingham, "A Question of Coffee"; Birmingham, "The Coffee Barons of Cazengo"; McCook, "Ephemeral Plantations"; Henri Lecomte, *Le café*, 299–303; Silva, "Robusta Empire," chap. 2.

2. Di Fulvio, *Le café dans le monde*, 320–22; Bart, "Café des montagnes, café des plaines."

3. Eskes, "Resistance," 222–23.

4. This argument draws on some recent scholarship on host-pathogen coevolution in wild plants. See Burdon and Thrall, "Coevolution of Plants and Their Pathogens"; Carlsson-Granér and Thrall, "Host Resistance and Pathogen Infectivity"; Thrall and Burdon, "Evolution of Gene-for-Gene Systems in Metapopulations."

5. Grant, *A Walk across Africa*, 197.

6. Chevalier, *Les caféiers du globe*, 83, 88–89; Silva, "Robusta Empire," 83–86.

7. Chevalier, *Les caféiers du globe*, 86–87.

8. Sargos, "Une plantation dans le Kuilou (Congo Français)," 292.

9. Vergne, "Les plantations de café et de cacao de la maison Ancel-Seitz."

10. Sprott, *Coffee Planting in Kenya Colony*, 1; Tothill, *Agriculture in Uganda*, 314.

11. Kieran, "Arabica Production in East Africa"; Di Fulvio, *Le café dans le monde*, 344–45; Haarer, *Modern Coffee Production*, 353–55.

12. Haarer, *Modern Coffee Production*, 352.

13. "German Colonies in Tropical Africa," 412.

14. Kieran, "Arabica Production in East Africa," 59; McDonald, *Coffee Growing*, 17; "German Colonies in Tropical Africa and the Pacific," 179.

15. On the development of international plant regulations in this period, see Castonguay, "Creating an Agricultural World Order."

16. "Coffee-Leaf Disease in Central Africa," 363.

17. British Central Africa Chamber of Agriculture and Commerce to H. M. Acting Commissioner, undated (1900), p. 6, FO 2/672: "Coffee Seed for British Africa. Coffee Leaf Disease Regulations, B.C.A.," The National Archives, Kew, United Kingdom.

18. Pauly, "Beauty and Menace of the Japanese Cherry Trees."

19. "Coffee-Leaf Disease in Central Africa," 362.

20. Brode, *British and German East Africa*, 36–37.

21. Brode, 38.

22. Kieran, "Arabica Production in East Africa," 63; McDonald, *Coffee Growing*, 17–18.

23. McDonald, *Coffee Growing*, 17.

24. Hill, *Planters' Progress*, 32–33; McDonald, *Coffee Growing*, 18.

25. Tothill, *Agriculture in Uganda*, 316.

26. Gowdy to Prain, November 4, 1912.

27. Simpson, "Coffee Leaf Disease in Uganda."

28. Small, "Coffee Cultivation in Uganda," 53.

29. McDonald, *Coffee Growing*, 17.

30. Hodge, *Triumph of the Expert*, 54–57; Bonneuil, "Mettre en ordre et discipliner les tropiques."

31. "List of Staffs of the Royal Botanic Gardens, Kew"; Masefield, *Agriculture in the British Colonies*, 68.

32. McDonald, *Coffee Growing*, 18. Dowson was a high-achieving graduate of Cambridge University, on his first job. For an overview of his life, see Garrett, "Pioneer Leaders in Plant Pathology."

33. Small, "Coffee Cultivation in Uganda," 53. Like Dowson, Small had been nominated to his position by the Royal Botanic Gardens at Kew. See "Miscellaneous Notes," 90.

34. Brown and Hunter, *Planting in Uganda*, xv.

35. Hill, *Planters' Progress*, 33.

36. International Institute of Agriculture and Bally, *Coffee in 1931 and 1932*, 78.

37. Iliffe, *Modern History of Tanganyika*, 271–76, 281–84; Rowe, *The World's Coffee*, chaps. 5–7.

38. McDonald, *Coffee Growing*, 89.

39. Kenya, Department of Agriculture, *Coffee Conference*, 11.

40. Waller, Bigger, and Hillocks, *Coffee Pests, Diseases and Their Management*, 68–76 (borer); 79–84 (Antestia); 132–36 (thrips).

41. McDonald, *Coffee Growing*, 98.

42. For a current overview of coffee berry disease, see Waller, Bigger, and Hillocks, *Coffee Pests, Diseases and Their Management*, 211–30.

43. Haarer, *Modern Coffee Production*, 304–8.

44. Masefield, *Agriculture in the British Colonies*, 73; Hodge, *Triumph of the Expert*, 96, 109.

45. Tothill, *Agriculture in Uganda*, 316.

46. Leechman, "Story of *Hemileia vastatrix*," 19.

47. Mayne, "The Experiences of a Coffee Biologist in the Jungles of Mysore."

48. McDonald, *Coffee Growing*, 165.

49. Quoted in Hansford, "Diseases of Coffee," 382.

50. Leechman, "Story of *Hemileia vastatrix*," 22.

51. McDonald, *Coffee Growing*, 93.

52. Leechman, "Story of *Hemileia vastatrix*," 22.

53. Tothill, *Agriculture in Uganda*, 317–18.

54. Thomas, "Robusta Coffee," 293.

55. For a brief biographical sketch of Maitland, see Kew Guild, "Thomas Douglas Maitland."

56. Thomas, "Robusta Coffee," 305.

57. Wrigley, "Aspects of Economic History"; Daviron and Ponte, *The Coffee Paradox*, 85–86.

58. For a statistical overview of coffee production in Africa between 1910 and 1946, see Di Fulvio, *Le café dans le monde*, 326–27.

59. Leplae, *Les plantations de café au Congo belge*, 63–67; Coste, *Les caféiers*, 2:473.

60. Masefield, *Agriculture in the British Colonies*, 73; Haarer, *Modern Coffee Production*, 370.

61. Haarer, *Modern Coffee Production*, 365; Di Fulvio, *Le café dans le monde*, 340.

62. Di Fulvio, *Le café dans le monde*, 345–51.

63. Leechman, "Story of *Hemileia vastatrix*," 7.

Chapter 7: Coffee, Cold War, and Colonial Modernization

1. Wellman and Cowgill, "Coffee Rust Survey Mission" 16.

2. On coffee cultivation in Cameroon, see Coste, *Les caféiers*, 2:408–19.

3. Hodge, *Triumph of the Expert*, chap. 7.

4. For a concise overview of the Point IV program, see Rist, *The History of Development*, 69–79.

5. Wellman and Cowgill, "Coffee Rust Survey Mission," 29.

6. Quotation from Pendergrast, *Uncommon Grounds*, 259.

7. Data from Coste, *Les caféiers*, 2:385, table 59.

8. For brief overviews of coffee cultivation in the Ivory Coast, the Belgian Congo, Angola, and Uganda, see Krug and De Poerck, *World Coffee Survey*, 35–47, 85–104, 112–20, 120–30. Statistics on arabica and robusta production are taken from Euverte, "La culture du caféier en Afrique continentale," 17.

9. Wrigley, *Coffee*, 511–19; Pendergrast, *Uncommon Grounds*, 235–39.

10. Wellman and Cowgill, "Coffee Rust Survey Mission," 29.

11. The chronology for West Africa is documented in Razafindramamba, "Biologie de la rouille du caféier," 178.

12. Wellman, *Coffee*, 255.

13. Krug and De Poerck, *World Coffee Survey*, 39–41; Haarer, *Modern Coffee Production*, 315.

14. Haarer, *Modern Coffee Production*, 298.

15. Wellman and Cowgill, "Coffee Rust Survey Mission," 21.

16. There is an extensive literature on the Green Revolution and global agriculture. For a useful starting point, see Kumar et al., "Roundtable"; Harwood, "Has the Green Revolution Been a Cumulative Learning Process?"

17. Bonneuil, "Development as Experiment"; McCann, *Maize and Grace*, 120–39.

18. Coste, *Les caféiers*, 2:327–30; Jones, "Coffee."

19. M. Meiffren gives a good contemporary account of the wilt in *Les maladies du caféier*, 9–54. For a recent scientific review of the coffee wilt disease, see Waller, Bigger, and Hillocks, *Coffee Pests, Diseases and Their Management*, 231–39.

20. Waller, Bigger, and Hillocks, *Coffee Pests, Diseases and Their Management*, 231–32; Meiffren, *Les maladies du caféier*, 9–54.

21. Wellman and Cowgill, "Coffee Rust Survey Mission," 48.

22. Rayner, "Rust Disease of Coffee 4: Control by Fungicide," 310–11.

23. Saraiva, "Fascist Labscapes."

24. This account builds on Rodrigues, "Branquinho D'Oliveira: Esboço"; Rodrigues, "A Portuguese Leader in Plant Pathology." For a fuller account of the politics and economics of the CIFC, see Silva, "Robusta Empire," 230–39.

25. Castelo, "Scientific Research and Portuguese Colonial Policy"; Shepherd, *Development and Environmental Politics*, 85.

26. Rodrigues, "Branquinho D'Oliveira: Esboço"; Rodrigues, "A Portuguese Leader in Plant Pathology."

27. CIFC, *Progress Report, 1960–1965*, 4.

28. For a fuller discussion of resistance testing, see Eskes, "Resistance," 192–210.

29. CIFC, 5–7; Rayner, "Rust Disease of Coffee 3: Resistance," 262–63.

30. Wellman, *Coffee*, 140–44; Eskes and Leroy, "Coffee Selection and Breeding," 60–61.

31. Rodrigues et al., "Importância do Hibrido de Timor."

32. Bettencourt, *Considerações gerais sobre o híbrido de Timor*, 1–8; Rodrigues et al., "Importância do Hibrido de Timor." For an agronomist's view of coffee cultivation on Timor in the 1950, see Lains e Silva, *Timor e a cultura do café*, 44–48. On postwar development schemes in Timor, see Shepherd, *Development and Environmental Politics*, chap. 3.

33. Rodrigues et al., "Importância do Hibrido de Timor," 1–5; Bettencourt, *Considerações gerais sobre o híbrido de Timor*, 8–13.

34. For an overview of decolonization in Africa, see Birmingham, *Decolonization of Africa*.

35. Talbot, *Grounds for Agreement*, 51–60.

36. Tourte, *La recherche agricole en Afrique tropicale*, 6:128–30.

37. Drachoussof, "Historique des recherches en agronomie tropicale africaine."

38. Krug and De Poerck, *World Coffee Survey*, 179.

39. Castelo, "Scientific Research and Portuguese Colonial Policy."

40. Rodrigues, "A Portuguese Leader in Plant Pathology," 44.

41. Silva, "Robusta Empire," 237–38.

42. Capot, "Les hybrides 'Arabusta.'" On colchicine in plant breeding, see Murphy, *Plant Breeding and Biotechnology*, 39–40. On arabusta and rust resistance, see Eskes, "Resistance," 272.

43. Meyer et al., *FAO Coffee Mission to Ethiopia, 1964–1965*, vii–ix.

44. Eskes, "Resistance," 222–23.

45. Rayner, "Rust Disease of Coffee 2: Spread of the Disease," 222–24.

Chapter 8: A Plague Foretold

1. Wellman and Echandi, "Coffee Rust in 1980," 969.

2. Schieber, "Coffee Rust in Latin America," 492.

3. Krug and De Poerck, *World Coffee Survey*, 298–99.

4. For a broad overview of intensification in Central America after World War II, see Samper K., "Trayectoria y viabilidad," 30–41. For an overview of

research and extension programs in Brazil in the 1960s, see Krug and De Poerck, *World Coffee Survey*, 294–97.

5. Carvalho et al., "Breeding Programs."

6. Muller, "La rouille sur le continent américain," 24.

7. Wellman, "Rust of Coffee in Brazil," 540.

8. Schieber, "Coffee Rust in Latin America," 493.

9. Bowden, Gregory, and Johnson, "Wind Transport of Coffee Leaf Rust."

10. Botany Correspondent, "Brazil."

11. Menchú, "Algunos datos sobre la 'roya del café,'" 14.

12. Waller, "Coffee Rust," 388.

13. Wellman, "Rust of Coffee in Brazil," 540.

14. Muller, "La rouille sur le continent américain," 24.

15. Muller, 26.

16. The Brazilian programs are neatly summarized in Penagos Dardón, "La roya del cafeto en Guatemala," 38–53.

17. Schieber, "Coffee Rust in Latin America," 493; Schieber, "Present Status of Coffee Rust in South America," 377; Martinez et al., "Presença de esporos de *Hemileia vastatrix* Berk & Br."

18. On the term "agroecological imperative" see Rice, "Transforming Agriculture," xxxiii–xxxiv.

19. Penagos Dardón, "La roya del cafeto en Guatemala," 44.

20. Penagos Dardón, "La roya del cafeto en Guatemala."

21. Coordenadoria de Assistência Técnica Integral, *Ferrugem do cafeeiro*, 2.

22. Waller, "Coffee Rust," 396.

23. Monaco, "Coffee Rust in Brazil," 62.

24. IBC, *Cultura do café no Brasil*, 346.

25. Waller, "Coffee Rust," 397.

26. Wellman and Echandi, "Coffee Rust in 1980," 969.

27. Wellman and Echandi, 969.

28. Monaco, "Coffee Rust in Brazil," 69.

29. Schieber, "Coffee Rust in Latin America," 502; Wellman and Echandi, "Coffee Rust in 1980," 970.

30. Wellman and Echandi, "Coffee Rust in 1980," 970.

31. For an overview, see Ploetz, "Diseases of Tropical Perennial Crops."

32. Monaco, "Coffee Rust in Brazil," 66–67.

33. Schieber, "Coffee Rust in Latin America," 503.

34. Monaco, "Coffee Rust in Brazil," 65.

35. Wellman and Echandi, "Coffee Rust in 1980," 970.

36. Kushalappa and Eskes, "Advances in Coffee Rust Research."

37. Carvalho, "Pesquisas sobre a resistência," 134–35; Eskes, "Qualitative and Quantitative Variation in Coffee Leaf Rust," 31–32; Monaco, "Coffee Rust in Brazil," 67.

38. Monaco, "Coffee Rust in Brazil."

39. Monaco, 70.

40. Muller, "La rouille sur le continent américain," 25–27; Instituo Interamericano de Ciencias Agrícolas, *Reunión técnica sobre las royas del cafeto*.

41. M. Muyshondt cited in Schieber, "Coffee Rust in Latin America," 505.

42. Schieber, "Observaciones comparativas sobre la roya del cafeto," 19.

43. Organismo Internacional Regional De Sanidad Agropecuaria, "Informe de la misión OIRSA en Brasil."

44. "Roya del café no será una calamidad nacional"; Asociación Nacional del Café [ANACAFÉ], "Reunión internacional."

45. Valenzuela Samper, "La temible roya," 6.

46. Sarria, "Campaña de prevención contra la roya," 13–14.

47. "La 'roya' llegó a Nicaragua por correo"; Vega M., "La vulnerable zona norte abrió su paso a la roya"; "Nicaragua no puede todavía con la roya."

48. Samper K., "Trayectoria y viabilidad," 30–32.

49. Penagos Dardón, "La roya del cafeto en Guatemala."

50. "Imposible erradicar totalmente la roya"; Otero, "Coffee Rust in the Americas," 94.

51. ANACAFÉ, "La roya del cafeto *Hemileia vastatrix*"; Otero, "Coffee Rust in the Americas"; Llano, "Orange Coffee Rust in Nicaragua."

52. "Esperanza de erradicar la roya del cafeto en Nicaragua," 7; "Alentadora campaña contra 'la roya.'"

53. Waller, "Coffee Rust"; Rice, "Transforming Agriculture"; Schuppener, Harr, and Sequeira, "First Occurrence of the Coffee Leaf Rust *Hemileia vastatrix* in Nicaragua"; Deutsche Gesellschaft für Technische Zusammenarbeit, *Lucha contra la roya del café*.

54. Otero, "Coffee Rust in the Americas."

55. Vega, "Países centroamericanos forman bloque para control de la roya"; Schieber and Zentmyer, "Spread of Coffee Rust," 7.

56. Rice, "Transforming Agriculture," 60–70; "Roya del café no se desplaza hacia C.R."

57. Schieber and Zentmyer, "Spread of Coffee Rust," 9.

58. "Peligro de que llegue la roya es iminente"; Vega, "Temen que roya puede estar en Valle Central."

59. Dao Dao, *La sanidad agropecuaria en Latinoamérica y en el Caribe*, 12.

60. Schieber and Zentmyer, "Coffee Rust in the Western Hemisphere," 89–90; Schieber and Zentmyer, "Spread of Coffee Rust," 1–14; Waller, "Coffee Rust," 388–89.

61. "Colombia declara cuarentena por brote de roya del café."

62. Asociación de Academias de la Lengua Española, "Caer la roya."

63. Velasquez, "A Berlusconi le cayó la roya."

64. Cartagena Ortega, "¿A los cafeteros les cayó la roya?"

65. Aterciopelados, "Luz azul."

66. "Le cayó la roya a Colombia afirma *Wall Street Journal*"; "A Don José Gómez le cayó la roya."

67. Bulmer-Thomas, *Economic History of Latin America*, chaps. 10–11.

68. Margolis, "Natural Disaster and Socioeconomic Change"; Wrigley, *Coffee*, 539–40.

69. "No hemos tirado la toalla contra la roya," 2.

70. PROMECAFÉ, *Sétima reunión del Consejo Asesor*; Fernández, "Central American Coffee Rust Project," 84–92; "Protección al cultivo del café"; Carvalho et al., "Breeding Programs," 323–25.

71. From a 1981 USAID/ROCAP report, cited in Rice, "A Place Unbecoming," 569.

72. Samper K., "Trayectoria y viabilidad," 27, 37, 39–41; Wintgens, *Coffee*, 42–43; Wrigley, *Coffee*, 390–91; Naranjo, Samper K., and Sfez, *Entre la tradición y el cambio*.

73. Waller, Bigger, and Hillocks, *Coffee Pests, Diseases and Their Management*, 192–94; Wellman, *Coffee*, 260–62.

74. Waller, "Coffee Rust," 399.

75. Muller, "La rouille sur le continent américain," 226–27.

76. Waller, "Coffee Rust," 400–401.

77. Waller, 401.

78. Vega M., "Roya no ha detenido auge en la producción de café"; "Intensifican control sobre roya del café y el moho azul."

79. Schieber, "Present Status of Coffee Rust in South America," 380.

80. Echeverri R., "Variedades resistentes a la roya del cafeto," 9.

81. "La roya en México."

82. Carvalho, "Pesquisas sobre a resistência," 134.

83. Echeverri R., "Variedades resistentes a la roya del cafeto," 9.

84. Carvalho et al., "Breeding Programs," 326–29.

85. Kushalappa and Eskes, "Advances in Coffee Rust Research," 525.

86. Marshall and Pryor, "Multiline Varieties and Disease Control."

87. Browning and Frey, "Multiline Cultivars as a Means of Disease Control," 355; Mundt, "Multiline Cultivars and Cultivar Mixtures."

88. Moreno Ruiz, "Obtención de variedades de café."

89. Buriticá Céspedes, "La roya del cafeto en Colombia"; Gómez and Bustamante, "Las enfermedades del café."

90. Samper K., "Trayectoria y viabilidad," 32.

91. Estimates from Rice, "A Place Unbecoming," 564.

92. Fernández and Muschler, "Sostentibilidad de los sistemas de cultivo de café," 74.

93. "El Viejo Caldas."

94. Data from Rice, "A Place Unbecoming," 564.

95. Hernández Paz and ANACAFÉ, Manual de caficultura Guatemala, 33; Samper K., "Trayectoria y viabilidad."

96. Avelino, Muller, et al., "La roya anaranjada," 216–18; Rivillas Osorio et al., La roya del cafeto en Colombia, 15–16; IBC, Cultura do café no Brasil, 343; Zambolim, "Coffee Leaf Rust in Brazil"; Deutsche Gesellschaft für Technische Zusammenarbeit, Lucha contra la roya del café, 13.

97. Avelino, Cristancho, et al., "Coffee Rust Crises," 310; Zambolim, "Coffee Leaf Rust in Brazil," 4.

98. Data from Rice, "A Place Unbecoming," 564.

99. Vandermeer, Jackson, and Perfecto, "Qualitative Dynamics of the Coffee Rust Epidemic," 210.

100. Avelino, Willocquet, and Savary, "Effects of Crop Management Patterns on Coffee Rust Epidemics"; Avelino, Romero-Gurdián, et al., "Landscape Context and Scale."

101. For discussions of technification, see Samper K., "Trayectoria y viabilidad," 53–55; Guadarrama-Zugasti, "Coffee Farming in Veracruz"; Rice, "A Place Unbecoming."

102. ICAFÉ, Manual de recomendaciones, 108.

103. Moraes, A ferrugem do cafeeiro, 33.

104. Nares, "Colombia: Exporters Content, Growers Unhappy," 61.

105. Nares, "Will Colombia Be Able to Produce High Quality Milds 10 Years from Now?," 16.

106. Fridell, Coffee, 299–300; Waller, "Coffee Rust," 400–401.

107. IBC, Cultura do café no Brasil, 344.

108. Nares, "Will Colombia Be Able to Produce High Quality Milds 10 Years from Now?," 16.

109. Avelino, Muller, et al., "La roya anaranjada."

Chapter 9: The Big Rust

1. The term "Big Rust" was coined by Peter Baker to refer to the outbreaks in Central America. I expand the term to include all of the outbreaks in the Americas from 2007 to 2017. See Baker, "The 'Big Rust.'"

2. Avelino, Cristancho, et al., "Coffee Rust Crises."

3. Sources do not always agree about the size of losses due to the rust. The figures here are derived from International Coffee Organization, "Total Production by All Exporting Countries." For other estimates, see also Baker, "The 'Big Rust,'" 37–38; Avelino, Cristancho, et al., "Coffee Rust Crises," 306–7; Virginio Filho and Astorga Domian, *Control de la roya del café*, 15. On aggregate losses in Central America, see International Coffee Organization, *ICO Annual Review, 2013–14*.

4. See, for example, Bacon et al., "Vulnerability to Cumulative Hazards."

5. PROMECAFÉ, *Plan de acción* 2013.

6. Topik, Talbot, and Samper, "Globalization and the Latin American Coffee Societies"; Samper K. and Topik, *Crisis y transformaciones del mundo del café*; Daviron and Ponte, *The Coffee Paradox*.

7. Fridell, *Coffee*, 63.

8. Goodman, "International Coffee Crisis," 3.

9. This overview builds on Avelino, Cristancho, et al., "Coffee Rust Crises"; Topik, Talbot, and Samper, "Globalization and the Latin American Coffee Societies."

10. Topik, Talbot, and Samper, "Globalization and the Latin American Coffee Societies," 7–8; Goodman, "International Coffee Crisis," 8–17; Morris, *Coffee: A Global History,* chap. 6.

11. World Coffee Research, "Caturra"; World Coffee Research, "Bourbon."

12. Rivillas Osorio et al., *La roya del cafeto en Colombia*, 11.

13. Quoted in Vossen, "Cup Quality of Disease-Resistant Cultivars," 324.

14. Sweet Maria's, "Costa Rica: Can a Coffee Be Too Perfect?"

15. Vossen, "Cup Quality of Disease-Resistant Cultivars." World Coffee Research's variety catalog describes most of these hybrids as having "low" or "very low" cupping potential. See World Coffee Research, "Coffee Varieties of Mesoamerica and the Caribbean."

16. Orozco Miranda, "Roya del cafeto en Guatemala," 29.

17. Sánchez Víquez, "Cafetaleros temen," 2A.

18. Picado Umaña, Ledezma Díaz, and Granados Porras, "Territorio de coyotes, agroecosistemas y cambio tecnológico en una región cafetalera de Costa Rica"; Guadarrama-Zugasti, "Coffee Farming in Veracruz"; Guhl, "Coffee Production in Colombia"; Sick, "Coping with Crisis."

19. Hausermann and Hernández, "Los sustentos del café."

20. Quoted in Sick, "Coping with Crisis," 260.

21. Avelino and Rivas Platero, "La roya anaranjada del cafeto," 3–4.

22. Baker, "The 'Big Rust.'"

23. Avelino, Cristancho, et al., "Coffee Rust Crises."

24. Vandermeer, Perfecto, and Liere, "Evidence for Hyperparasitism of Coffee Rust"; Vandermeer, Jackson, and Perfecto, "Qualitative Dynamics of the Coffee Rust Epidemic"; Vandermeer and Rohani, "Interaction of Regional and Local"; Avelino, Romero-Gurdián, et al., "Landscape Context and Scale."

25. International Coffee Organization, "ICO Indicator Prices."

26. International Coffee Organization, *World Coffee Trade (1963–2013)*, 18; Avelino, Cristancho, et al., "Coffee Rust Crises," 307.

27. "391. Coffee Leaf Rust Update: Nicaragua."

28. "388. Coffee Leaf Rust Update: Guatemala."

29. "390. Coffee Leaf Rust Update: El Salvador."

30. PROMECAFÉ, *Coffee Crisis in Mesoamerica*, 2.

31. Sheridan, "Leaf Rust Fallout."

32. Kumari Drapkin, "Coffee Plague behind Recent Wave of Immigrants."

33. Moreno R. and Alvarado A., *La variedad Colombia*, 7. For an overview of how Colombian coffee farmers adapted to changing market conditions, see Forero Álvarez, "Colombian Family Farmers' Adaptations."

34. Cristancho et al., "Outbreak of Coffee Leaf Rust"; Rivillas Osorio et al., *La roya del cafeto en Colombia*.

35. Vossen, Bertrand, and Charrier, "Next Generation Variety Development"; Alvarado A., Posada S., and Cortina G., "Castillo."

36. "¿Por qué el programa PSF es clave para recuperar la producción cafetera?"; "331. Farmer Perspectives on Castillo"; USDA, Foreign Agricultural Service, "2017 Coffee Annual: Colombia," 3. Data on the distribution of farm sizes in Colombia from Forero Álvarez, "Estrategias adaptivas," 47.

37. Sheridan, "A Simple Question."

38. "437. Our Castillo Samples Surprised George Howell."

39. Rivillas Osorio, "El manejo de la roya del cafeto," 12; Moreno Ruiz, "TABI."

40. USDA, Foreign Agricultural Service, "2011 Coffee Annual: Colombia," 3; USDA, Foreign Agricultural Service, "2013 Coffee Semi-Annual: Colombia," 2–4.

41. "331. Farmer Perspectives on Castillo."

42. USDA, Foreign Agricultural Service, "2012 Coffee Semi-Annual: Colombia," 3.

43. Charrier and Eskes, "Botany and Genetics of Coffee," 514; Waller, Bigger, and Hillocks, *Coffee Pests, Diseases and Their Management*, 184–85. For an overview of the total costs for applying a traditional copper fungicide and a systemic fungicide, see Rivillas Osorio et al., *La roya del cafeto en Colombia*, 37–38, tables 6 and 7.

44. Rivillas Osorio et al., *La roya del cafeto en Colombia*, 15.

45. "Los cafeteros continúan trabajando por una 'Colombia sin Roya,'" 21.

46. USDA, Foreign Agricultural Service, "2013 Coffee Annual: Colombia," 3.

47. "Paro cafetero"; "341. A Closer Look at Colombia's Coffee Strike."

48. Rivillas Osorio, "El manejo de la roya del cafeto," 12.

49. Hoffmann, *The World Atlas of Coffee*, 189.

50. "345. Coffee Rust."

51. PROMECAFÉ, "Coffee Crisis in Mesoamerica," 4.

52. World Coffee Research and PROMECAFÉ, *First International Coffee Rust Summit*. On the importance of transnational networks and knowledge exchange, see Neill, *Networks in Tropical Medicine*.

53. USDA, Foreign Agricultural Service, "2015 Coffee Annual: El Salvador."

54. Baker, "The 'Big Rust,'" 41.

55. Alonzo, "Cafetaleros adquieren fungicidas contra roya."

56. USDA, Foreign Agricultural Service, "Situation Update: Coffee Rust in Mexico," 3.

57. Baca Castellón, " 'Queda mucho por aprender.' "

58. See, for example Thrupp, "Pesticides and Policies"; Soluri, "Accounting for Taste."

59. "Contra roya, reparte Sagarpa químicos tóxicos para la planta y los productores."

60. Avelino and Rivas Platero, "La roya anaranjada del cafeto," 5.

61. Virginio Filho and Astorga Domian, *Control de la roya del café*, 131:77–79.

62. Avelino, Cristancho, et al., "Coffee Rust Crises," 315; Vossen, Bertrand, and Charrier, "Next Generation Variety Development," 245–46.

63. Reuters, "Starbucks Buys First Coffee Farm, Will Research Devastating Leaf Rust"; Starbucks Coffee Company, "Growing the Future of Coffee One Tree at a Time."

64. World Coffee Research, "About."

65. Vossen, Bertrand, and Charrier, "Next Generation Variety Development." On ecologically intensive production, see Ahmadi, Bertrand, and Glaszmann, "Rethinking Plant Breeding."

66. "New Rust-Resistant Hybrid Centroamericano Scores 90+ at Nicaragua CoE"; World Coffee Research, "Centroamericano."

67. Vossen, Bertrand, and Charrier, "Next Generation Variety Development," 250; Etienne, Anthony, et al., "Biotechnological Applications for the Improvement of Coffee"; Etienne, Bertrand, et al., "Un exemple de transfert de tecnologie réussi."

68. USDA, Foreign Agricultural Service, "2017 Coffee Annual: Guatemala," 3.

69. USDA, Foreign Agricultural Service, "2017 Coffee Annual: Mexico," 5.

70. "Along with Coffee Trees, New Jobs Grow"; "Starbucks donará"; "Starbucks' 'One Tree for Every Bag' Sustainable Coffee Partnership."

71. Inter-American Development Bank, "IDB Helps Nicaraguan Farmers."

72. "Instalan cerca de 200 hectáreas con café de alta calidad y resistente a la roya."

73. Henríquez, "Se aplicará producto biológico."

74. USDA, Foreign Agricultural Service, "2016 Coffee Annual: Peru."

75. Soto, "Manejo de la roya," 65.

76. Shriver, Largaespada, and Gutiérrez, *Sustainable Good Agriculture Practices Manual.*

77. Uganda Coffee Development Authority and Coffee Quality Institute, "Fine Robusta Coffee Standards and Protocols."

78. "317. Questions on the Great Robusta Debate."

79. "316. CRS and the Great Debate."

80. USDA, Foreign Agricultural Service, "PS&D (Production, Supply, and Distribution)."

81. Granados, "Costa Rica no producirá café robusta"; ICAFÉ, *Informe de Comisión de Café Robusta.*

82. "Fighting Coffee Rust in Latin America and the Caribbean."

83. Fernández, "La coca le sigue ganando al café."

84. International Coffee Organization, "Total Production by All Exporting Countries"; United States, Foreign Agricultural Service, "Coffee: World Markets and Trade."

Chapter 10: Coffee Is Not (Necessarily) Forever

1. Topik, "Integration of the World Coffee Market."

2. Rutherford, "Current Knowledge of Coffee Wilt Disease, a Major Constraint to Coffee Production in Africa."

3. Messing, "The Coffee Berry Borer (*Hypothenemus hampei*) Invades Hawaii"; Steiman, "Coffee Berry Borer in Hawai'i."

4. Gil-Vallejo and Leguizamón-Caycedo, *La muerte descendente del cafeto* (Phoma *spp.*).

5. Avelino, Cristancho, et al., "Coffee Rust Crises," 316.

6. Hruska, "El manejo de enfermedades en Centroamérica."

7. Vandermeer, Jackson, and Perfecto, "Qualitative Dynamics of the Coffee Rust Epidemic," 217.

8. Ovalle-Rivera et al., "Projected Shifts in *Coffea arabica* Suitability"; Bunn et al., "A Bitter Cup."

9. This problem is not unique to studies of coffee: see Newton, Johnson, and Gregory, "Implications of Climate Change"; Gregory et al., "Integrating Pests and Pathogens."

10. Avelino and Rivas Platero, "La roya anaranjada del cafeto," 11.

Bibliography

"316. CRS and the Great Debate." *CRS Coffeelands* (blog), November 7, 2012. http://coffeelands.crs.org/2012/11/316-crs-and-the-great-debate/.

"317. Questions on the Great Robusta Debate." *CRS Coffeelands* (blog), November 8, 2012. http://coffeelands.crs.org/2012/11/317-questions-on-the-great-robusta-debate/.

"331. Farmer Perspectives on Castillo." *CRS Coffeelands* (blog), January 28, 2013. http://coffeelands.crs.org/2013/01/farmer-perspectives-on-castillo/.

"341. A Closer Look at Colombia's Coffee Strike." *CRS Coffeelands* (blog), March 14, 2013. http://coffeelands.crs.org/2013/03/the-colombian-coffee-strike-what-does-it-mean/.

"345. Coffee Rust: The Long Haul." *CRS Coffeelands* (blog), April 8, 2013. http://coffeelands.crs.org/2013/04/345-coffee-rust-the-long-haul/.

"388. Coffee Leaf Rust Update: Guatemala." *CRS Coffeelands* (blog), February 18, 2014. http://coffeelands.crs.org/2014/02/388-coffee-leaf-rust-update-guatemala/.

"390. Coffee Leaf Rust Update: El Salvador." *CRS Coffeelands* (blog), February 20, 2014. http://coffeelands.crs.org/2014/02/390-coffee-leaf-rust-update-el-salvador/.

"391. Coffee Leaf Rust Update: Nicaragua." *CRS Coffeelands* (blog), February 21, 2014. http://coffeelands.crs.org/2014/02/391-coffee-leaf-rust-update-nicaragua/.

"437. Our Castillo Samples Surprised George Howell." *CRS Coffeelands* (blog), December 9, 2014. http://coffeelands.crs.org/2014/12/437-the-crs-colombian-varietal-cuppings-george-howell/.

"A Don José Gómez le cayó la roya." *El tiempo*. February 17, 2002. https://www.eltiempo.com/archivo/documento/MAM-1314671.

Abbay, Richard. Letter to William Thiselton-Dyer, May 21, 1879. Miscellaneous Report: Ceylon Coffee Diseases, 1871–1887. Library and Archives, Royal Botanic Gardens, Kew, folio 68.

Ahmadi, Nourollah, Benoît Bertrand, and Jean-Christophe Glaszmann. "Rethinking Plant Breeding." In *Cultivating Biodiversity to Transform Agriculture*, edited by Étienne Hainzelin, 91–140. Dordrecht: Springer Netherlands, 2013. https://doi.org/10.1007/978-94-007-7984-6_4.

Ainsworth, G. C. *Introduction to the History of Mycology*. Cambridge: Cambridge University Press, 1976.

———. *Introduction to the History of Plant Pathology*. Cambridge: Cambridge University Press, 1981.

"Alentadora campaña contra 'la roya.'" *La prensa libre*, September 20, 1977.

"Along with Coffee Trees, New Jobs Grow from Starbucks One Tree for Every Bag Commitment." 1912 Pike, March 10, 2016. https://1912pike.com/along-with-coffee-trees-new-jobs-grow-from-starbucks-one-tree-for-every-bag-commitment/.

Alonzo, Areli. "Cafetaleros adquieren fungicidas contra roya." DEGUATE.com, July 1, 2014. http://www.deguate.com/artman/publish/ecofin_noticias/cafetaleros-adquieren-fungicidas-contra-roya.shtml.

Altshuler, Jill S., Erin Balogh, Anna D. Barker, Stephen L. Eck, Stephen H. Friend, Geoffrey S. Ginsburg, Roy S. Herbst, Sharyl J. Nass, Christopher M. Streeter, and John A. Wagner. "Opening Up to Precompetitive Collaboration." *Science Translational Medicine* 2, no. 52 (October 2010): 52cm26. https://doi.org/10.1126/scitranslmed.3001515.

Alvarado A., G., H. E. Posada S., and H. A. Cortina G. "Castillo: Nueva variedad de café con resistencia a la roya." *Avances técnicos CENICAFÉ*, no. 337 (July 2005). http://biblioteca.cenicafe.org/handle/10778/401.

Ameer Ali, A. C. L. "Peasant Coffee in Ceylon during the 19th Century." *Ceylon Journal of Historical and Social Studies* 2, no. 1 (1972): 50–59.

ANACAFÉ. "La roya del cafeto *Hemileia vastatrix* Berk y Br. y la situación actual en la Republica de Nicaragua a Octubre 1978." *Revista cafetalera*, no. 181 (1979): 18–19.

———. "Reunión internacional sobre prevención contra la roya del cafeto, Costa Rica." *Revista cafetalera*, no. 108 (November 1971): 30–41.

Anderson, Graham. *Jottings on Coffee and Its Culture in Mysore*. Bangalore: Caxton Press, 1879.

Anthony, F., M. C. Combes, C. Astorga, B. Bertrand, G. Graziosi, and P. Lashermes. "The Origin of Cultivated *Coffea arabica* L. Varieties Revealed by AFLP and SSR Markers." *Theoretical and Applied Genetics* 104, no. 5 (2002): 894–900. https://doi.org/10.1007/s00122-001-0798-8.

Arnold, David. "The Indian Ocean as a Disease Zone, 1500–1950." *South Asia: Journal of South Asian Studies* 14, no. 2 (1991): 1–21.

Asociación de Academias de la Lengua Española. "Caer la roya." In *Diccionario de americanismos*, 344. Madrid: Santillana, 2010.

Aterciopelados. "Luz Azul." Track 1 on *Gozo poderoso*. BMG, 2000, compact disc.

Avelino, J., L. Willocquet, and S. Savary. "Effects of Crop Management Patterns on Coffee Rust Epidemics." *Plant Pathology* 53, no. 5 (October 2004): 541–47. https://doi.org/10.1111/j.1365-3059.2004.01067.x.

Avelino, Jacques, Marco Cristancho, Selena Georgiou, Pablo Imbach, Lorena Aguilar, Gustavo Bornemann, Peter Läderach, Francisco Anzueto, Allan J. Hruska, and Carmen Morales. "The Coffee Rust Crises in Colombia and Central America (2008–2013): Impacts, Plausible Causes and Proposed Solutions." *Food Security* 7, no. 2 (March 2015): 303–21. https://doi.org/10.1007/s12571-015-0446-9.

Avelino, Jacques, Raoul Muller, Albertus Eskes, Rodney Santacreo, and Francisco Holguín. "La roya anaranjada del cafeto: Mito y realidad." In *Desafíos de la caficultura en Centroamérica*, edited by Benoît Bertrand and Bruno Rapidel, 193–241. San José, Costa Rica: Agroamerica, 1999.

Avelino, Jacques, and Gonzalo Galileo Rivas Platero. "La roya anaranjada del cafeto," March 12, 2013. http://hal.archives-ouvertes.fr/hal-01071036.

Avelino, Jacques, Alí Romero-Gurdián, Héctor F. Cruz-Cuellar, and Fabrice A. J. Declerck. "Landscape Context and Scale Differentially Impact Coffee Leaf Rust, Coffee Berry Borer, and Coffee Root-Knot Nematodes." *Ecological Applications* 22, no. 2 (March 2012): 584–96. https://doi.org/10.1890/11-0869.1.

Ayres, Peter G. "Alexis Millardet: France's Forgotten Mycologist." *Mycologist* 18, no. 1 (February 2004): 23–26.

———. *Harry Marshall Ward and the Fungal Thread of Death*. St. Paul: APS Press, 2005.

Baca Castellón, Lucydalia. "'Queda mucho por aprender.'" *La prensa*. September 13, 2013. http://www.laprensa.com.ni/2013/09/13/economia/162280-queda-mucho-por-aprender.

Bacon, Christopher M., William A. Sundstrom, Iris T. Stewart, and David Beezer. "Vulnerability to Cumulative Hazards: Coping with the Coffee Leaf Rust Outbreak, Drought, and Food Insecurity in Nicaragua." *World Development*, no. 93 (May 2017): 136–52. https://doi.org/10.1016/j.worlddev.2016.12.025.

Baggaley, Kate. "The World's Bananas Are Under Attack." *Popular Science*, September 13, 2017. https://www.popsci.com/worlds-bananas-under-attack-disease.

Baker, Peter. "The 'Big Rust': An Update on the Coffee Leaf Rust Situation." *Coffee and Cocoa International* 40, no. 6 (January 2014): 37–39.

Barron, T. J. "Science and the Nineteenth-Century Ceylon Coffee Planters." *Journal of Imperial and Commonwealth History* 16, no. 1 (1987): 5–23.

Bart, F. "Café des montagnes, café des plaines." *Etudes rurales* 180, no. 2 (2007): 35–48.

Beachey, R. W. "The East African Ivory Trade in the Nineteenth Century." *Journal of African History* 8, no. 2 (1967): 269–90.

Berkeley, Miles J. "*Hemileia vastatrix.*" *Gardeners' Chronicle* (November 6, 1869), 1157.

———. "Notice of a Mould Attacking the Coffee Plantations in Ceylon." *Journal of the Horticultural Society of London*, no. 4 (1849): 7–9.

Berthaud, J. "L'origine et la distribution des caféiers dans le monde." In *Le commerce du café avant l'ère des plantations coloniales: Espaces, réseaux, sociétés (XV*ᵉ*-XIX*ᵉ*siècle)*, edited by Michel Tuchscherer, 361–70. Cairo: Institut Français d'Archéologie Orientale, 2001.

Bettencourt, A. J. *Considerações gerais sobre o híbrido de Timor: Origem e possibilidades de cultivo.* Instituto Agronômico de Campinas, Circular 23. Campinas: Instituto Agronômico de Campinas, 1973.

Bhattacharya, Bhaswati. "Local History of a Global Commodity Production of Coffee in Mysore and Coorg in the Nineteenth Century." *Indian Historical Review* 41, no. 1 (June 2014): 67–86. https://doi.org/10.1177/0376983614521734.

Birmingham, David. "The Coffee Barons of Cazengo." *Journal of African History* 19, no. 4 (1978): 523–38.

———. *The Decolonization of Africa.* Athens: Ohio University Press, 1995.

———. "A Question of Coffee: Black Enterprise in Angola." *Canadian Journal of African Studies* 16, no. 2 (1982): 343–46.

Boivin, Nicole, Dorian Q. Fuller, and Alison Crowther. "Old World Globalization and the Columbian Exchange: Comparison and Contrast." *World Archaeology* 44, no. 3 (2012): 452–69. https://doi.org/10.1080/00438243.2012.729404.

Bonneuil, C. "Development as Experiment: Science and State Building in Late Colonial and Postcolonial Africa, 1930–1970." *Osiris*, no. 15 (2000): 258–81.

———. "Mettre en ordre et discipliner les tropiques: Les sciences du végétal dans l'empire français, 1870–1940." PhD thesis, Université de Paris 7, 1997.

Botany Correspondent. "Brazil: Death in the Pot." *Nature* 226, no. 5250 (June 1970): 997–98. https://doi.org/10.1038/226997a0.

Boulger, G. S., and Andrew Grout. "Thwaites, George Henry Kendrick (1812–1882)." In *Oxford Dictionary of National Biography*. Oxford: Oxford University Press, 2004. http://www.oxforddnb.com/view/article/27416.

Bowden, J., P. H. Gregory, and C. G. Johnson. "Possible Wind Transport of Coffee Leaf Rust across the Atlantic Ocean." *Nature* 229, no. 5285 (February 1971): 500–501. https://doi.org/10.1038/229500b0.

British Central Africa Chamber of Agriculture and Commerce to H. M. Acting Commissioner, undated (1900), p. 6, FO 2/672: "Coffee Seed for British Africa. Coffee Leaf Disease Regulations, B.C.A.," The National Archives, Kew, United Kingdom.

Brockway, Lucile. *Science and Colonial Expansion: The Role of the British Royal Botanic Gardens*. New Haven: Yale University Press, 2002.

Brode, Heinrich. *British and German East Africa: Their Economic and Commercial Relations*. London: E. Arnold, 1911.

Brown, Ernest, and H. H. Hunter. *Planting in Uganda: Coffee, Para Rubber, Cocoa*. London: Longmans, 1913.

Browning, J. A., and K. J. Frey. "Multiline Cultivars as a Means of Disease Control." *Annual Review of Phytopathology* 7, no. 1 (1969): 355–82. https://doi.org/10.1146/annurev.py.07.090169.002035.

Buis, J. *L'Hemileia et l'avenir du caféier à Madagascar et à la Réunion*. Paris: A. Challamel, 1907.

Bulmer-Thomas, Victor. *The Economic History of Latin America since Independence*. 3rd ed. New York: Cambridge University Press, 2014.

Bunn, Christian, Peter Läderach, Oriana Ovalle-Rivera, and Dieter Kirschke. "A Bitter Cup: Climate Change Profile of Global Production of Arabica and Robusta Coffee." *Climatic Change* 129, no. 1–2 (December 2014): 89–101. https://doi.org/10.1007/s10584-014-1306-x.

Burdon, Jeremy J., and Peter H. Thrall. "Coevolution of Plants and Their Pathogens in Natural Habitats." *Science* 324, no. 5928 (May 2009): 755–56. https://doi.org/10.1126/science.1171663.

Buriticá Céspedes, Pablo. "La roya del cafeto en Colombia: Realizaciones de impacto nacional e internacional en el siglo XX." *Revista Facultad Nacional de Agronomía, Medellín* 63, no. 1 (2010): 5285–92.

Busch, Lawrence. *Science and Agricultural Development*. Totowa, NJ: Allanheld, Osmun, 1981.

Cambrony, H., and René Coste. *Caféiers et cafés*. Paris: Maisonneuve, 1989.

Cameron, John. "Report on Coffee Leaf Disease in Coorg." *Tropical Agriculturist*, no. 18 (1899): 745–52, 823–26b.

Campbell, Gwyn. "The Origins and Development of Coffee Production in Réunion and Madagascar, 1711–1972." In *The Global Coffee Economy in Africa, Asia and Latin America, 1500–1989*, edited by W. G. Clarence-Smith and Steven Topik, 67–99. Cambridge: Cambridge University Press, 2003.

Campo, Joseph Norbert Frans Marie à. *Engines of Empire: Steamshipping and State Formation in Colonial Indonesia*. Hilversum, Neth.: Verloren, 2002.

Capot, J. "L'amélioration du caféier en Côte d'Ivoire: Les hybrides 'Arabusta.'" *Café, cacao, thé* 16, no. 1 (March 1972): 3–18.

Carefoot, G. L., and E. R. Sprott. *Famine on the Wind: Man's Battle against Plant Disease*. Don Mills: Longmans, 1967.

Carlsson-Granér, Ulla, and Peter H. Thrall. "Host Resistance and Pathogen Infectivity in Host Populations with Varying Connectivity." *Evolution* 69, no. 4 (April 2015): 926–38. https://doi.org/10.1111/evo.12631.

Cartagena Ortega, Juan Diego. "¿A los cafeteros les cayó la roya?" *El Colombiano*, February 3, 2014. https://www.elcolombiano.com/historico /jugadores_de_la_seleccion_colombia_no_tienen_buen_presente -AWEC_280451.

Carvalho, A. "Pesquisas sobre a resistência do cafeeiro à *Hemileia vastatrix* em São Paulo." *Garcia de orta: Serie de estudos agronomicos* 9, no. 1–2 (1982): 129–36.

Carvalho, A., A. B. Eskes, Jaime Castillo Zapata, M. S. Sreenivasan, Jorge Hernán Echeverri R., C. E. Fernandez, and L. C. Fazuoli. "Breeding Programs." In *Coffee Rust: Epidemiology, Resistance, and Management*, edited by Ajjamada C. Kushalappa and Albertus B. Eskes, 295–335. Boca Raton: CRC, 1989.

Castelo, Cláudia. "Scientific Research and Portuguese Colonial Policy: Developments and Articulations, 1936–1974." *História, ciências, saúde* (Manguinhos) 19, no. 2 (June 2012): 391–408. https://doi.org/10.1590 /S0104-59702012000200003.

Castonguay, Stéphane. "Creating an Agricultural World Order: Regional Plant Protection Problems and International Phytopathology, 1878–1939." *Agricultural History* 84, no. 1 (January 2010): 46–73. https://doi.org/10.3098 /ah.2010.84.1.46.

Cerda, Rolando, Jacques Avelino, Christian Gary, Philippe Tixier, Esther Lechevallier, and Clémentine Allinne. "Primary and Secondary Yield Losses Caused by Pests and Diseases: Assessment and Modeling in Coffee." *PLOS ONE* 12, no. 1 (January 2017): e0169133. https://doi.org/10.1371/journal .pone.0169133.

"Ceylon: General Planting Report." *Tropical Agriculturist*, no. 2 (August 1882): 90–92.

Charrier, A., and A. B. Eskes. "Botany and Genetics of Coffee." In *Coffee: Growing, Processing, Sustainable Production: A Guidebook for Growers, Processors, Traders and Researchers*, edited by Jean Nicolas Wintgens, 25–56. Weinheim, Germany: Wiley-VCH, 2004.

Chevalier, Auguste. *Les caféiers du globe*. Paris: Paul Lechevalier, 1929.

Christy, Thomas. *New Commercial Plants: With Directions How to Grow Them to the Best Advantage*. 11 vols. London: Christy, 1878–89.

CIFC. *Progress Report, 1960–1965*. Oeiras, Portugal: Estação Agronómica Nacional, 1965.

Clarence-Smith, W. G. "The Coffee Crisis in Asia, Africa, and the Pacific, 1870–1914." In *The Global Coffee Economy in Africa, Asia and Latin America, 1500–1989*, edited by W. G. Clarence-Smith and Steven Topik, 100–119. Cambridge: Cambridge University Press, 2003.

———. "The Spread of Coffee Cultivation in Asia, from the Seventeenth to the Early Nineteenth Century." In *Le commerce du café avant l'ère des plantations coloniales: Espaces, réseaux, sociétés (XV'-XIX'siècle)*, edited by Michel Tuchscherer, 371–84. Cairo: Institut Français d'Archéologie Orientale, 2001.

Clarence-Smith, W. G., and Steven Topik. "Introduction: Coffee and Global Development." In *The Global Coffee Economy in Africa, Asia and Latin America, 1500–1989*, edited by W. G. Clarence-Smith and Steven Topik, 1–17. Cambridge: Cambridge University Press, 2003.

"Coffee Leaf Disease and Mr. Schrottky's Remedy." *Tropical Agriculturist*, no. 1 (July 1, 1881): 91.

"Coffee-Leaf Disease in Central Africa (Preventive Measures)." *Bulletin of Miscellaneous Information* (Royal Gardens, Kew) 1893, no. 84 (1893): 361–63.

"Coffee Leaf Disease in Ceylon, Answers to Circular of 12 February, 1875," 1875. FO 83/486. The National Archives of the United Kingdom, Kew.

"Coffee Leaf-Disease." *Gardeners' Chronicle*, no. 12 (August 23, 1879): 240.

"Coffee Leaf-Disease." *Tropical Agriculturist*, no. 7 (April 2, 1888): 712.

"Coffee Leaf-Disease." *Tropical Agriculturist*, no. 11 (April 1, 1892): 746.

"Coffee: 'Nalknaad.' To the Editor of the 'Asian.'" *Tropical Agriculturist*, no. 1 (1882): 966.

Coleman, Leslie C. "The Coffee-Planting Industry of South India." *Empire Journal of Experimental Agriculture* 1, no. 2 (1933): 303–14.

———. "The Improvement of Coffee in the Dutch East Indies." *Bulletin of the Mysore Department of Agriculture*, no. 15 (1931): 3–19.

———. "Report of Work on the Coffee Experiment Station, Balehonnur for the Years 1925–1930." *Bulletin of the Mysore Coffee Experiment Station*, no. 3 (1930): 1–23.

"Colombia declara cuarentena por brote de roya del café." *La nación*, September 30, 1983.

"Contra roya, reparte Sagarpa químicos tóxicos para la planta y los productores." *La jornada Veracruz*, October 27, 2014. http://www.jornadaveracruz .com.mx/Post.aspx?id=141026_234640_539.

Coordenadoria de Assistência Técnica Integral. *Ferrugem do cafeeiro: Instrucões sobre pulverizadores*. Instruções práticas 111. São Paulo: CATI, 1972.

"Correspondence respecting the Coffee-Leaf Disease in Ceylon," 1874. CO 882/2/14. The National Archives, Kew, United Kingdom.

Coste, Felix. "N.C.R.A. Circular Covers Four Important Subjects." *Spice Mill*, March 1921, 402.

Coste, René. *Les caféiers et les cafés dans le monde*. Vol. 2, *Les cafés*. Paris: Larose, 1961.

Cowan, Brian William. *The Social Life of Coffee: The Emergence of the British Coffeehouse*. New Haven: Yale University Press, 2005.

Cramer, P. J. S. *A Review of Literature of Coffee Research in Indonesia*. Miscellaneous Publications Series, no. 15. Turrialba: SIC Editorial, Inter-American Institute of Agricultural Sciences, 1957.

———. "L'influence de l'*Hemileia vastatrix* sur la culture du café au Java." *L'agronomie tropicale* (Brussels), no. 2 (1910): 341–49, 391–94.

Cristancho, M. A., Y. Rozo, C. Escobar, C. A. Rivillas, and A. L. Gaitán. "Outbreak of Coffee Leaf Rust (*Hemileia vastatrix*) in Colombia." *New Disease Reports* 25, no. 19 (2012). https://doi.org/doi:10.5197/j.2044-0588.2012.025.019.

Crüwell, G. A. *Liberian Coffee in Ceylon: The History of the Introduction and Progress of the Cultivation up to April, 1878*. Colombo: A.M. and J. Ferguson, 1878.

Dao Dao, Federico. *La sanidad agropecuaria en Latinoamérica y en el Caribe*. San José, Costa Rica: Instituto Interamericano de Cooperación para la Agricultura, 1979.

Daviron, Benoît, and Stefano Ponte. *The Coffee Paradox: Global Markets, Commodity Trade, and the Elusive Promise of Development*. London: Zed Books, 2005.

Davis, Aaron P., Rafael Govaerts, Diane M. Bridson, and Piet Stoffelen. "An Annotated Taxonomic Conspectus of the Genus *Coffea* (Rubiaceae)." *Botanical Journal of the Linnean Society* 152, no. 4 (2006): 465–512. https:// doi.org/10.1111/j.1095-8339.2006.00584.x.

Dean, Warren. *Brazil and the Struggle for Rubber: A Study in Environmental History*. Cambridge: Cambridge University Press, 1987.

———. "The Green Wave of Coffee: Beginnings of Tropical Agricultural Research in Brazil (1885–1900)." *Hispanic American Historical Review* 69, no. 1 (February 1989): 91–115.

Delacroix, Georges. *Les maladies et les ennemis des caféiers*. 2nd ed. Paris: A. Challamel, 1900.

Deutsche Gesellschaft für Technische Zusammenarbeit. *Lucha contra la roya del café*. Eschborn: Deutsche Gesellschaft für Technische Zusammenarbeit, 1979.

Di Fulvio, Antonio. *Le café dans le monde*. Rome: Institut International D'agriculture, 1947.

Drachoussof, M. V. "Historique des recherches en agronomie tropicale africaine." In *Amélioration et protection des plantes vivrières tropicales*, edited by Claude-André Saint-Pierre and Yves Demarly, 5–12. Brussels: Libbey Eurotext, 1989.

Drayton, Richard. *Nature's Government: Science, Imperial Britain, and the "Improvement" of the World*. New Haven: Yale University Press, 2000.

Duncan, J. S. *In the Shadows of the Tropics: Climate, Race and Biopower in Nineteenth Century Ceylon*. Aldershot, UK: Ashgate, 2007.

Echeverri R., Jorge Hernán. "Variedades resistentes a la roya del cafeto." *Revista cafetalera*, no. 227 (February 1983): 5–9.

Egerton, Frank N. "History of Ecological Sciences, Part 44: Phytopathology during the 1800s." *Bulletin of the Ecological Society of America* 93, no. 4 (October 2012): 303–39. https://doi.org/10.1890/0012-9623-93.4.303.

"El Viejo Caldas." *Semana*. July 30, 1990.

Ellen, Roy, and Simon Platten. "The Social Life of Seeds: The Role of Networks of Relationships in the Dispersal and Cultural Selection of Plant Germplasm." *Journal of the Royal Anthropological Institute* 17, no. 3 (2011): 563–84.

Elliot, Robert Henry. *Gold, Sport, and Coffee Planting in Mysore*. Westminster: Archibald, Constable, 1894.

Eng, Pierre van der. *Agricultural Growth in Indonesia: Productivity Change and Policy Impact since 1880*. New York: St. Martin's Press, 1996.

Eskes, Albertus B. "Qualitative and Quantitative Variation in Pathogenicity of Races of Coffee Leaf Rust (*Hemileia vastatrix*) Detected in the State of São Paulo, Brazil." *Netherlands Journal of Plant Pathology* 89, no. 1–2 (1983): 31–45.

————. "Resistance." In *Coffee Rust: Epidemiology, Resistance, and Management*, edited by Albertus B. Eskes and Ajjamada C. Kushalappa, 175–291. Boca Raton: CRC, 1989.

Eskes, Albertus B., and Thierry Leroy. "Coffee Selection and Breeding." In *Coffee: Growing, Processing, Sustainable Production; A Guidebook for Growers, Processors, Traders and Researchers*, edited by Jean Nicolas Wintgens, 57–86. Weinheim, Germany: Wiley-VCH, 2004.

"Esperanza de erradicar la roya del cafeto en Nicaragua." *La prensa libre*, August 31, 1977.

Etienne, Hervé, F. Anthony, S. Dussert, D. Fernandez, P. Lashermes, and B. Bertrand. "Biotechnological Applications for the Improvement of Coffee (*Coffea arabica* L.)." *In Vitro Cellular and Developmental Biology: Plant* 38, no. 2 (March 2002): 129–38.

Etienne, Hervé, Benoît Bertrand, Christophe Montagnon, Roberto Bodadilla Landey, Eveline Dechamp, Isabelle Jourdan, Edgardo Alpizar, Eduardo Malo, and Frédéric Georget. "Un exemple de transfert de technologie réussi dans le domaine de la micropropagation: La multiplication *Coffea arabica* par embryogenèse somatique." *Cahiers Agricultures* 21, no. 2–3 (2012): 115–24.

Euverte, G. "La culture du caféier en Afrique continentale: Afrique occidentale française, Congo Belge, Afrique orientale Anglaise." *Agronomie tropicale* 10, no. 2 (1955): 241–57.

"Failure of Coffee Crops in Coorg." *Tropical Agriculturist*, no. 2 (February 1883): 636.

Ferguson, Alastair, and J. M. Ferguson. *The Planting Directory for India and Ceylon*. Colombo, 1878.

Ferguson, John. *Ceylon in 1883: The Leading Crown Colony of the British Empire*. London: S. Low, Marston, Searle, and Rivington, 1883. http://archive.org/details/ceyloninleading01ferggoog.

————. *Ceylon in 1893*. London: J. Haddon, 1893.

Fernández, Carlos Enrique. "Central American Coffee Rust Project." In *Coffee Rust in the Americas*, edited by Robert H. Fulton, 84–92. St. Paul: American Phytopathological Society, 1984.

————. "La coca ilegal le sigue ganando al café orgánico de Sandia." *El Comercio*, July 21, 2016. http://elcomercio.pe/peru/puno/coca-ilegal-le-sigue-ganando-cafe-organico-sandia-238857.

Fernández, Carlos E., and R. G. Muschler. "Aspectos de la sostenibilidad de los sistemas de cultivo de café en América Central." In *Desafíos de la caficultura en Centroamérica*, edited by Benoît Bertrand and Bruno Rapidel, 69–96. San José, Costa Rica: Agroamerica,1999.

Fernández Prieto, Leida. "Mapping the Global and Local Archipelago of Scientific Tropical Sugar: Agriculture, Knowledge, and Practice, 1790–1880." In *Global Scientific Practice in an Age of Revolutions, 1750–1850*, edited by Patrick Manning and Daniel Rood, 181–98. Pittsburgh: University of Pittsburgh Press, 2016.

Ferwerda, F. P. "Coffee Breeding in Java." *Economic Botany* 2, no. 3 (1948): 258–72.

"Fighting Coffee Rust in Latin America and the Caribbean." Feed the Future. Accessed August 4, 2017. https://www.feedthefuture.gov/article /fighting-coffee-rust-latin-america-and-caribbean.

Forero Álvarez, Jaime. "Colombian Family Farmers' Adaptations to New Conditions in the World Coffee Market." *Latin American Perspectives* 37, no. 2 (2010): 93–110.

——. "Estrategias adaptivas de la caficultura colombiana." In *Crisis y transformaciones del mundo del café: Dinámicas locales y estrategias nacionales en un periodo de adversidad e incertidumbre*, edited by Mario Samper K. and Steven Topik, 37–83. Bogota: Pontificia Universidad Javeriana, 2012.

Fridell, Gavin. *Coffee.* Cambridge: Polity Press, 2014.

Fuller, Dorian Q., and Nicole Boivin. "Crops, Cattle and Commensals across the Indian Ocean." *Études Océan Indien*, no. 42–43 (January 2009): 13–46. https://doi.org/10.4000/oceanindien.698.

Gardner, George. *Extracts from a Report by George Gardner, Esq. on the Coffee Blight of Ceylon, Addressed to the Secretary of the Government.* Peradeniya: Royal Botanic Gardens, 1848.

Garrett, S. D. "Pioneer Leaders in Plant Pathology: W. J. Dowson." *Annual Review of Phytopathology* 19, no. 1 (1981): 29–34. https://doi.org/10.1146 /annurev.py.19.090181.000333.

"German Colonies in Tropical Africa." *Bulletin of Miscellaneous Information* (Royal Gardens, Kew) 1894, no. 96 (December 1894): 410–12. https://doi.org /10.2307/4115497.

"German Colonies in Tropical Africa and the Pacific." *Bulletin of Miscellaneous Information* (Royal Gardens, Kew) 1896, no. 117/118 (January 1896): 174–85. https://doi.org/10.2307/4118338.

Gil-Vallejo, Luis Fernando, and Jairo Eduardo Leguizamón-Caycedo. *La muerte descendente del cafeto (Phoma spp.).* Avances Técnicos Cenicafé 278. Chinchina, Colombia: CENICAFÉ, August 2010. http://www.cenicafe.org /es/publications/avt0278.pdf.

Gomez, C., A. Batti, D. Le Pierrès, C. Campa, S. Hamon, A. De Kochko, P. Hamon, F. Huynh, M. Despinoy, and V. Poncet. "Favourable Habitats for

Coffea Inter-Specific Hybridization in Central New Caledonia: Combined Genetic and Spatial Analyses." *Journal of Applied Ecology* 47, no. 1 (2010): 85–95.

Gomez, Céline, Marc Despinoy, Serge Hamon, Perla Hamon, Danyela Salmon, Doffou Sélastique Akaffou, Hyacinthe Legnate, Alexandre de Kochko, Morgan Mangeas, and Valérie Poncet. "Shift in Precipitation Regime Promotes Interspecific Hybridization of Introduced *Coffea* Species." *Ecology and Evolution* 6, no. 10 (May 2016): 3240–553 https://doi.org/10.1002/ece3.2055.

Gómez, Gabriel Cadena, and A. B. Bustamante. "Las enfermedades del café: Logros y desafíos para la caficultura colombiana del siglo XXI." *Manejo Integrado de Plagas y Agroecología*, no. 77 (2006): 89–93.

Goodman, David. "The International Coffee Crisis: A Review of the Issues." In *Confronting the Coffee Crisis: Fair Trade, Sustainable Livelihoods and Ecosystems in Mexico and Central America*, edited by Christopher M Bacon, V. Ernesto Méndez, Stephen R. Gleissman, David Goodman, and Jonathan A. Fox, 3–25. Cambridge: Massachusetts Institute of Technology Press, 2008.

Goodwin, S. B., B. A. Cohen, and W. E. Fry. "Panglobal Distribution of a Single Clonal Lineage of the Irish Potato Famine Fungus." *Proceedings of the National Academy of Sciences* 91, no. 24 (November 1994): 11591–95.

Goss, Andrew. *The Floracrats: State-Sponsored Science and the Failure of the Enlightenment in Indonesia*. Madison: University of Wisconsin Press, 2011.

"Government Gardens in Ceylon." *Tropical Agriculturist*, no. 1 (December 1881): 555–56.

Gowdy, W. Letter to David Prain, November 4, 1912. Miscellaneous Report: Uganda—Coffee Diseases and Brown Blast, 1912–1928. Library and Archives, Royal Botanic Gardens, Kew.

Granados, Greivin. "Costa Rica no producirá café robusta." *La prensa libre*, October 11, 2016. http://www.laprensalibre.cr/Noticias/detalle/88103/costa-rica -no-producira-cafe-robusta-.

Grant, James Augustus. *A Walk across Africa; or, Domestic Scenes from My Nile Journal*. Edinburgh, London: W. Blackwood and Sons, 1864.

Gregory, Peter J., Scott N. Johnson, Adrian C. Newton, and John S. I. Ingram. "Integrating Pests and Pathogens into the Climate Change/Food Security Debate." *Journal of Experimental Botany* 60, no. 10 (July 2009): 2827–38. https://doi.org/10.1093/jxb/erp080.

Grieq, George, W. Taylor, Giles F. Walker, F. G. A. Lane, and E. H. Skrine. "Coffee Leaf-Disease: Final Report of the Committee Appointed to Inspect Mr. Schrottky's Carbolic Treatment for Leaf-Disease on Claverton, Dikoya, Ceylon." *Tropical Agriculturist*, no. 2 (June 1883): 972–73.

Guadarrama-Zugasti, Carlos. "A Grower Typology Approach to Assessing the Environmental Impact of Coffee Farming in Veracruz, Mexico." In *Confronting the Coffee Crisis: Fair Trade, Sustainable Livelihoods and Ecosystems in Mexico and Central America*, edited by Christopher M Bacon, V. Ernesto Méndez, Stephen R. Gleissman, David Goodman, and Jonathan A. Fox, 127–54. Cambridge: Massachusetts Institute of Technology Press, 2008.

Guhl, Andrés. "Coffee Production Intensification and Landscape Change in Colombia, 1970–2002." In *Land Change Science in the Tropics: Changing Agricultural Landscapes*, 93–116. Boston: Springer, 2008. http://dx.doi.org/10.1007/978-0-387-78864-7_6.

Haarer, Alec Ernest. *Modern Coffee Production*. London: Leonard Hill, 1962.

Hansford, C. G. "Diseases of Coffee." In *Agriculture in Uganda*, edited by J. D. Tothill, 380–85. Oxford: Oxford University Press, 1940.

Harwood, Jonathan. "The Green Revolution as a Process of Global Circulation: Plants, People and Practices." *Historia Agraria*, no. 75 (June 2018): 7–31. https://doi.org/10.26882/histagrar.075e01h.

———. "Has the Green Revolution Been a Cumulative Learning Process?" *Third World Quarterly* 34, no. 3 (April 2013): 397–404. https://doi.org/10.1080/01436597.2013.784599.

Hattox, Ralph. *Coffee and Coffeehouses: The Origins of a Social Beverage in the Medieval Near East*. Seattle: University of Washington Press, 1985.

Hausermann, Heidi, and Mónica P. Hernández. "Los sustentos del café, el uso de suelo y las políticas de re-regulación en el centro de Veracruz, México." *Journal of Latin American Geography* 14, no. 2 (July 2015): 7–27. https://doi.org/10.1353/lag.2015.0017.

Hays, J. N. *The Burdens of Disease: Epidemics and Human Response in Western History*. New Brunswick, NJ: Rutgers University Press, 2003.

Hefner, Robert W. *The Political Economy of Mountain Java: An Interpretive History*. Berkeley: University of California Press, 1990.

Henri Lecomte, Paul. *Le café: culture-manipulation, production*. Paris: G. Carré and C. Naud, 1899. http://archive.org/details/lecafcultureman00lecogoog.

Henríquez, Helio. "Se aplicará producto biológico en 44 mil hectáreas afectadas: Sagarpa." *La Jornada*, July 14, 2013. http://www.jornada.unam.mx/2013/07/14/estados/026n2est.

Herbert, Eugenia W. "Peradeniya and the Plantation Raj in Nineteenth-Century Ceylon." In *Eco-Cultural Networks and the British Empire: New Views on Environmental History*, edited by James Beattie, Edward D. Melillo, and Emily O'Gorman, 123–50. London: Bloomsbury Academic, 2015.

Hernández Paz, Mario, and ANACAFÉ. *Manual de caficultura Guatemala.* 3rd ed. Guatemala: ANACAFÉ, 1988.

Hiern, W. P. "X. On the African Species of the Genus *Coffea*, Linn." *Transactions of the Linnean Society of London*, 2nd ser., *Botany* 1, no. 4 (1876): 169–76.

Hill, Mervyn F. *Planters' Progress: The Story of Coffee in Kenya.* Nairobi: Coffee Board of Kenya, 1956.

Hodge, Joseph. *Triumph of the Expert: Agrarian Doctrines of Development and the Legacies of British Colonialism.* Athens: Ohio University Press, 2007.

Hoffmann, James. *The World Atlas of Coffee: From Beans to Brewing; Coffees Explored, Explained and Enjoyed.* Richmond Hill, Ontario: Firefly Books, 2016.

Hooker, J. D. "The Royal Gardens, Kew." *Gardeners' Chronicle*, no. 8 (October 1877): 141–42.

Hruska, Allan J. "Apoyo de FAO en el manejo de enfermedades en cultivos de Centroamérica." In *Manejo agroecológico de la roya del café*, edited by FAO, 3–5. Panama: FAO, 2015. http://www.fao.org/3/a-i5137s.pdf.

Huitema, Waling Karst. *De bevolkingskoffiecultuur op Sumatra: Met een inleiding tot hare geschiedenis op Java en Sumatra.* Wageningen, Neth.: Veenman, 1935. http://library.wur.nl/WebQuery/wurpubs/525451.

Hull, Edmond C. P. *Coffee Planting in Southern India and Ceylon.* London: E. and F. N. Spon, 1877.

"Hybrid Coffee in Mysore." *Bulletin of Miscellaneous Information* (Royal Gardens, Kew), 3rd ser., no. 133/134 (February 1898): 30.

"Hybrid Coffee in the Straits: Freedom of Coorg Coffee from Leaf Disease." *Tropical Agriculturist*, no. 19 (August 1899): 126.

IBC. *Cultura do café no Brasil: Manual de recomendações.* 5th ed. Rio de Janeiro: IBC, 1985.

ICAFÉ. *Informe de Comisión de Café Robusta.* Costa Rica: ICAFÉ, August 2016. http://www.icafe.cr/informe-de-comision-de-cafe-robusta/.

———. *Manual de recomendaciones para el cultivo del café.* 6th ed. San José, Costa Rica: ICAFÉ, 1989.

IICA. *Reunión técnica sobre las royas del cafeto.* San José, Costa Rica: IICA, 1970.

Iliffe, John. *A Modern History of Tanganyika.* African Studies 25. Cambridge: Cambridge University Press, 1979.

"Imposible erradicar totalmente la roya." *La nación*, January 10, 1977.

India, Office of the Agricultural Marketing Adviser. *Report on the Marketing of Coffee in India and Burma.* Agricultural Marketing in India 21. New

Delhi: Government of India Press, 1940. http://archive.org/details/in.ernet .dli.2015.33539.

"Instalan cerca de 200 hectáreas con café de alta calidad y resistente a la roya." *La república*, June 22, 2017. http://larepublica.pe/economia/888620-instalan -cerca-de-200-hectareas-con-cafe-de-alta-calidad-y-resistente-la-roya.

"Intensifican control sobre roya del café y el moho azul." *La nación*, November 25 1986.

Inter-American Development Bank. "IDB Partners with IFC, Exportadora Atlantic and Starbucks to Help Nicaraguan Farmers Combat Coffee Rust Disease." News release, June 24, 2015. http://www.iadb.org/en/news/news -releases/2015-06-24/nicaraguan-farmers-defeat-coffee-blight,11190 .html.

International Coffee Organization. *ICO Annual Review, 2013–14.* London: International Coffee Organization, 2014. http://www.ico.org/documents /cy2014-15/annual-review-2013-14-electronic-e.pdf.

———. "ICO Composite and Group Indicator Prices (Annual Monthly Averages)." International Coffee Organization, Accessed August 1, 2017. http:// www.ico.org/historical/1990%20onwards/Excel/3a%20-%20Prices%20 paid%20to%20growers.xlsx.

———. "Total Production by All Exporting Countries." Historical Data on the Coffee Trade, Accessed August 1, 2017. http://www.ico.org/historical /1990%20onwards/PDF/1a-total-production.pdf.

———. *World Coffee Trade (1963–2013): A Review of the Markets, Challenges, and Opportunities Facing the Sector.* London: International Coffee Organization, 2014. http://www.ico.org/news/icc-111-5-r1e-world-coffee -outlook.pdf.

International Institute of Agriculture, and Walter Bally. *Coffee in 1931 and 1932: Economic and Technical Aspects.* Rome: Printing Office of the Chamber of the Deputies, 1934. http://archive.org/details/in.ernet.dli.2015.205476.

Jamieson, Ross W. "The Essence of Commodification: Caffeine Dependencies in the Early Modern World." *Journal of Social History* 35, no. 2 (Winter 2001): 269–94. https://doi.org/10.2307/3790189.

Jiménez, Michael F. "'From Plantation to Cup': Coffee and Capitalism in the United States, 1830–1930." In *Coffee, Society, and Power in Latin America*, edited by William Roseberry, Lowell Gudmundson, and Mario Samper K., 38–64. Baltimore: Johns Hopkins University Press, 1995.

Jones, P. A. "Information on the Work of Coffee Research Institutions: The Coffee Research Station, Kenya." *Coffee: Coffee and Cacao Technical Services* 4, no. 12 (March 1962): 5–15.

Jussieu, Antoine de. "Histoire du café." *Histoire de l'académie royale des sciences* (1713): 291–99.

Kenya, Department of Agriculture. *Report of Proceedings of Coffee Conference Held in Nairobi, June, 1927.* Nairobi: Government Printer, 1927.

Kew Guild. "Thomas Douglas Maitland." *Journal of the Kew Guild* 7, no. 59 (1954): 176–77.

Kieran, J. A. "The Origins of Commercial Arabica Coffee Production in East Africa." *African Historical Studies* 2, no. 1 (1969): 51–68.

Koehler, Jeff. *Where the Wild Coffee Grows: The Untold Story of Coffee from the Cloud Forests of Ethiopia to Your Cup.* New York: Bloomsbury USA, 2017.

Krug, C., and R. A. De Poerck. *World Coffee Survey.* Rome: FAO, 1968.

Kumar, Deepak. *Science and the Raj, 1857–1905.* Delhi: Oxford University Press, 2006.

Kumar, Prakash, Timothy Lorek, Tore C. Olsson, Nicole Sackley, Sigrid Schmalzer, and Gabriela Soto Laveaga. "Roundtable: New Narratives of the Green Revolution." *Agricultural History* 91, no. 3 (2017): 397–422. https://doi.org/10.3098/ah.2017.091.3.397.

Kumari Drapkin, Julia. "Central American Coffee Plague behind Recent Wave of Immigrants to Metro New Orleans, Elsewhere." *NOLA.com*, August 21, 2014. http://www.nola.com/environment/index.ssf/2014/08/coffee_rust_fungus_pushes_chil.html.

Kushalappa, Ajjamada C. "Biology and Epidemiology." In *Coffee Rust: Epidemiology, Resistance, and Management*, edited by Albertus B. Eskes and Ajjamada C. Kushalappa, 16–76. Boca Raton: CRC, 1989.

Kushalappa, Ajjamada C., and Albertus B. Eskes. "Advances in Coffee Rust Research." *Annual Review of Phytopathology* 27, no. 1 (1989): 503–31.

"La roya en México." *La nación*, May 8, 1984.

"La 'roya' llegó a Nicaragua por correo." *La prensa libre*, January 22, 1977.

Laborie, P. J. *The Coffee Planter of Saint Domingo.* London: T. Cadell and W. Davies, 1798.

Lains e Silva, Hélder. *Timor e a cultura do café.* Lisbon: Ministério do Ultramar, Junta de Investigações do Ultramar, 1956.

Large, Ernest. *The Advance of the Fungi.* London: J. Cape, 1940.

"Leaf Disease in Netherlands India." *Tropical Agriculturist*, no. 5 (September 1885): 198.

"'Le cayó la roya' a Colombia afirma *Wall Street Journal*." Colombia.com. Last modified December 21, 2011. https://www.colombia.com/actualidad/economia/sdi/27709/le-cayo-la-roya-a-colombia-afirma-wall-street-journal.

Leechman, A. "The Story of *Hemileia vastatrix*: 'Ceylon Leaf Disease' and Its Lessons." In *Coffee Growing: With Special Reference to East Africa*, edited by John Holt McDonald, 7–22. London: East Africa, 1930.

Legarda, Benito J. *After the Galleons: Foreign Trade, Economic Change and Entrepreneurship in the Nineteenth Century Philippines*. Madison: Center for Southeast Asian Studies, University of Wisconsin-Madison, 1999.

Leplae, Edmond. *Les plantations de café au Congo belge: Leur histoire (1881–1935) leur importance actuelle*. Brussels: G. van Campenhout, 1936.

Lewis, W. J., J. C. van Lenteren, Sharad C. Phatak, and J. H. Tumlinson. "A Total System Approach to Sustainable Pest Management." *Proceedings of the National Academy of Sciences* 94, no. 23 (November 1997): 12243–48. https://doi.org/10.1073/pnas.94.23.12243.

"Liberian Coffee and Tea in Java." *Tropical Agriculturist*, no. 1 (July 1881): 159–60.

"List of Staffs of the Royal Botanic Gardens, Kew, and of Botanical Departments, Establishments and Officers at Home, and in India and the Colonies, in Correspondence with Kew." *Bulletin of Miscellaneous Information* (Royal Botanic Gardens, Kew) 1913, no. 2 (1913): 80–93.

Llano, A. "The Orange Coffee Rust in Nicaragua." *Plant Disease Reporter* 61, no. 12 (1977): 999–1002.

Lock, Charles G. Warnford. *Coffee: Its Culture and Commerce in All Countries*. London : E. and F. N. Spon, 1888.

"Los cafeteros continúan trabajando por una 'Colombia sin Roya.'" Eje21, April 2011. http://www.eje21.com.co/2011/04/los-cafeteros-continan-trabajando -por-una-colombia-sin-roya/.

Maat, Harro. "Agricultural Sciences in Colonial Indonesia." *Historia scientiarum* 16, no. 3 (2007): 244–63.

———. *Science Cultivating Practice: A History of Agricultural Science in the Netherlands and Its Colonies, 1863–1986*. Dordrecht: Springer Netherlands, 2001.

Marcus, George E. "Ethnography in/of the World System: The Emergence of Multi-Sited Ethnography." *Annual Review of Anthropology*, no. 24 (October 1995): 95–117. https://doi.org/10.1146/annurev.an.24.100195.000523.

Margolis, Maxine. "Natural Disaster and Socioeconomic Change: Post-frost Adjustments in Paraná, Brazil." *Disasters* 4, no. 2 (June 1980): 231–35. https://doi.org/10.1111/j.1467-7717.1980.tb00276.x.

Marshall, D. R., and A. J. Pryor. "Multiline Varieties and Disease Control. II. The 'Dirty Crop' Approach with Components Carrying Two or More Genes for Resistance." *Euphytica* 28, no. 1 (February 1979): 145–59. https://doi.org/10.1007/BF00029185.

Martinez, J. A., Deniza A. Palazzo, Missae Karazawa, Marcos Vilela M. Monteiro, and Nelson R. N. Reu. "Presença de esporos de *Hemileia vastatrix* Berk e Br agente causal da ferrugem do cafeeiro, em diferentes altitudes nas principais áreas cafeeiras dos Estados de São Paulo e Paraná (Brasil)." *O biológico* 41, no. 3 (1975): 77–88.

Masefield, Geoffrey Bussell. *Short History of Agriculture in the British Colonies.* Westport, CT: Greenwood Press, 1978.

Massee, George. "Miles Joseph Berkeley, 1803–1889." In *Makers of British Botany: A Collection of Biographies by Living Botanists,* edited by Francis Wall Oliver, 225–32. Cambridge: Cambridge University Press, 1913.

Maurin, Olivier, Aaron P. Davis, Michael Chester, Esther F. Mvungi, Yasmina Jaufeerally-Fakim, and Michael F. Fay. "Towards a Phylogeny for *Coffea* (Rubiaceae): Identifying Well-Supported Lineages Based on Nuclear and Plastid DNA Sequences." *Annals of Botany* 100, no. 7 (December 2007): 1565–83.

Mayne, W. W. "Control of Coffee Leaf Disease in Southern India." *World Crops* 23, no. 4 (1971): 206–7.

———. "The Experiences of a Coffee Biologist in the Jungles of Mysore." *Indo-British Review* 19, no. 2 (1991): 95–109.

———. "Physiological Specialisation of *Hemileia vastatrix* B. and Br." *Nature* 129, no. 3257 (April 1932): 510. https://doi.org/10.1038/129510a0.

———. "Seasonal Periodicity of Coffee Leaf Disease." *Bulletin of the Mysore Coffee Experiment Station,* no. 4 (1930): 1–16.

———. "Seasonal Periodicity of Coffee Leaf Disease Second Report." *Bulletin of the Mysore Coffee Experiment Station,* no. 6 (1931): 1–22.

Mayne, W. W., M. J. Narasimhan, and K. H. Sreenivasan. "Spraying of Coffee in South India." *Bulletin of the Mysore Coffee Experiment Station,* no. 9 (1933): 1–69.

McCallan, S. E. A. "History of Fungicides." In *Agricultural and Industrial Applications, Environmental Interactions: An Advanced Treatise,* edited by Dewayne Torgeson, 1–37. New York: Academic Press, 1967.

McCann, James. *Maize and Grace: Africa's Encounter with a New World Crop, 1500–2000.* Cambridge, MA: Harvard University Press, 2005.

McCants, Anne E. C. "Poor Consumers as Global Consumers: The Diffusion of Tea and Coffee Drinking in the Eighteenth Century." *Economic History Review* 61, no. S1 (2008): 172–200. https://doi.org/10.1111/j.1468-0289.2008.00429.x.

McCook, Stuart. "The Ecology of Taste: Robusta Coffee and the Limits of the Specialty Revolution." In *Coffee: A Comprehensive Guide to the Bean, the Beverage, and the Industry*, edited by Robert W Thurston, Jonathan Morris, and Shawn Steiman, 248–61. Lanham, MD.: Rowman and Littlefield, 2013.

———. "Ephemeral Plantations: The Rise and Fall of Liberian Coffee, 1870–1900." In *Comparing Apples, Oranges, and Cotton: Environmental Histories of the Global Plantation*, edited by Frank Uekötter, 85–112. Frankfurt am Main: Campus Verlag, 2014.

———. "Las epidemias liberales: Agricultura, ambiente y globalización en Ecuador (1790–1930)." In *Estudios sobre historia y ambiente en América*, edited by Bernardo García Martínez and María del Rosario Prieto, 2:223–46. Mexico, DF: Instituto Panamericano de Geografía e Historia, 2002.

———. "La roya del café en Costa Rica: Epidemias, innovación, y ambiente, 1980–1995." *Revista de historia* (Costa Rica), no. 59–60 (2009): 99–117.

———. " 'Squares of Tropic Summer': The Wardian Case, Victorian Horticulture, and the Logistics of Global Plant Transfers, 1770–1910." In *Global Scientific Practice in an Age of Revolutions, 1750–1850*, edited by Patrick Manning and Daniel Rood, 199–215. Pittsburgh: University of Pittsburgh Press, 2016.

———. *States of Nature: Science, Agriculture, and Environment in the Spanish Caribbean, 1760–1940*. Austin: University of Texas Press, 2002.

McCook, Stuart, and John Vandermeer. "The Big Rust and the Red Queen: Long-Term Perspectives on Coffee Rust Research." *Phytopathology* 105, no. 9 (2015): 1164–73.

McDonald, John Holt. *Coffee Growing: With Special Reference to East Africa*. London: East Africa, 1930.

Meiffren, M. *Les maladies du caféier en Côte d'Ivoire*. Bingerville, Ivory Coast: Centre de Recherches Agronomiques de Bingerville, 1957.

Menchú, J. Francisco. "Algunos datos sobre la 'roya del café.'" *Revista cafetalera*, no. 97 (April 1970): 13–17.

Messing, Russell H. "The Coffee Berry Borer (*Hypothenemus hampei*) Invades Hawaii: Preliminary Investigations on Trap Response and Alternate Hosts." *Insects* 3, no. 3 (July 2012): 640–52. https://doi.org/10.3390/insects3030640.

Meyer, Frederick, L. M. Fernie, R. L. Narasimhaswamy, L. C. Monaco, and D. J. Greathead. *FAO Coffee Mission to Ethiopia, 1964–1965*. Rome: FAO, 1968.

Meyer, Frederick G. "Notes on Wild *Coffea arabica* from Southwestern Ethiopia, with Some Historical Considerations." *Economic Botany* 19, no. 2 (April 1965): 136–51. https://doi.org/10.1007/BF02862825.

Mills, Lennox. *Ceylon under British Rule, 1795–1932*. London: Frank Cass, 1964.

Ministerio de Agricultura y Ganadería, *Manual del caficultor: Combate de la roya del cafeto*. Costa Rica: Ministerio de Agricultura y Ganadería, 1985.

"Misc. Rept. Ceylon Coffee Diseases, 1871–1887," n.d. Royal Botanic Gardens, Kew.

"Miscellaneous Notes." *Bulletin of Miscellaneous Information* (Royal Botanic Gardens, Kew) 1913, no. 2 (1913): 90–98.

Monaco, Lourival Carmo. "Consequences of the Introduction of Coffee Rust into Brazil." *Annals of the New York Academy of Sciences* 287, no. 1 (February 1977): 57–71. https://doi.org/10.1111/j.1749-6632.1977.tb34231.x.

Monselise, S. P., and E. E. Goldschmidt. "Alternate Bearing in Fruit Trees." *Horticultural Reviews*, no. 4 (1982): 128–73. https://doi.org/10.1002/9781118060773.ch5.

Moraes, S. A. de. *A ferrugem do cafeeiro: Importância, condições predisponentes, evolução e situação no Brasil*. Circular 119. Campinas: IAC, 1983.

Moreno R., L. G., and G. Alvarado A. *La variedad Colombia: Veinte años de adopción y comportamiento frente a nuevas razas de la roya del cafeto*. Chinchiná, Colombia: CENICAFÉ, 2000. http://biblioteca.cenicafe.org/handle/10778/592.

Moreno Ruiz, Luis Germán. "Obtención de variedades de café con resistencia durable a enfermedades, usando la diversidad genética como estrategia de mejoramiento." *Revista de la Academia Colombiana de Ciencias Exactas, Físicas y Naturales* (Bogota) 28, no. 107 (2004): 187–200.

———. "TABI: Variedad de café de porte alto con resistencia a la roya." *Avances técnicos CENICAFÉ*, no. 300 (June 2002). http://www.cenicafe.org/es/publications/avt0300.pdf.

Morris, Daniel, ed. *The Campaign of 1879 against Coffee Leaf Disease (Hemileia vastatrix) by the Coffee Planters of Ceylon*. Colombo: Ceylon Observer Press, 1879.

———. "Coffee-Leaf Disease of Ceylon and Southern India." *Nature*, no. 20 (October 1879): 557–59.

———. *Notes on Liberian Coffee, Its History and Cultivation*. Kingston, Jamaica: Government Printing Establishment, 1881.

———. "Note on the Structure and Habit of *Hemileia vastatrix*, the Coffee-Leaf Disease of Ceylon and Southern India." *Journal of the Linnean Society (Botany)*, no. 17 (1880): 512–17.

Morris, Jonathan. *Coffee: A Global History*. London: Reaktion Books, 2019.

"Mr. Storck's Remedy for Coffee Leaf Disease Nearly Identical with That of Mr. Schrottky." *Tropical Agriculturist*, no. 1 (April 1882): 910–12.

Muller, R. A. "La rouille du caféier *Hemileia vastatrix* sur le continent américain." *Café, cacao, thé* 15, no. 1 (1971): 24–30.

Mundt, C. C. "Use of Multiline Cultivars and Cultivar Mixtures for Disease Management." *Annual Review of Phytopathology* 40, no. 1 (September 2002): 381–410. https://doi.org/10.1146/annurev.phyto.40.011402.113723.

Munro, J. Forbes. *Maritime Enterprise and Empire: Sir William Mackinnon and His Business Network, 1823–93.* Woodbridge, UK: Boydell Press, 2003.

Murphy, Denis. *Plant Breeding and Biotechnology: Societal Context and the Future of Agriculture.* Cambridge: Cambridge University Press, 2007.

Muthiah, S. *A Planting Century: The First Hundred Years of the United Planters' Association of Southern India, 1893–1993.* New Delhi: Affiliated East-West Press, 1993.

Mysore State, Department of Agriculture. *Progress Report of Work Done on the Coffee Experiment Station, Balehonnur, for the Period 1932 to 1936.* Mysore: Government Press, 1939.

Nagarajan, S., and D. V. Singh. "Long-Distance Dispersion of Rust Pathogens." *Annual Review of Phytopathology* 28, no. 1 (1990): 139–53. https://doi.org/10.1146/annurev.py.28.090190.001035.

"'Nakanaad Coffee'; and Crop Prospects." *Tropical Agriculturist*, no. 1 (October 1881): 329.

Naranjo, Carlos, Mario Samper K., and Paul Sfez. *Entre la tradición y el cambio: Evolución tecnológica de la caficultura costarricense.* San José, Costa Rica: Escuela de Historia, Universidad Nacional, 2000.

Nares, Peter. "Colombia: Exporters Content, Growers Unhappy." *Tea and Coffee Trade Journal* 162, no. 9 (September 1990): 60–62.

———. "Will Colombia Be Able to Produce High Quality Milds 10 Years from Now?" *Tea and Coffee Trade Journal* 160, no. 5 (May 1988): 16–19.

Neill, Deborah Joy. *Networks in Tropical Medicine: Internationalism, Colonialism, and the Rise of a Medical Specialty, 1890–1930.* Stanford: Stanford University Press, 2012.

"New Rust-Resistant Hybrid Centroamericano Scores 90+ at Nicaragua CoE." *Daily Coffee News by Roast Magazine* (blog), May 24, 2017. https://dailycoffeenews.com/2017/05/24/new-rust-resistant-hybrid-centroamericano-scores-90-at-nicaragua-coe/.

Newton, Adrian, Scott Johnson, and Peter Gregory. "Implications of Climate Change for Diseases, Crop Yields and Food Security." *Euphytica* 179, no. 1 (2011): 3–18. https://doi.org/10.1007/s10681-011-0359-4.

"Nicaragua no puede todavía con la roya." *Excelsior* (San José, Costa Rica), January 18, 1977.

Nietner, J. *The Coffee Tree and Its Enemies: Being Observations on the Natural History of the Enemies of the Coffee Tree in Ceylon.* 2nd ed. Colombo: Ceylon Observer Press, 1880.

"No hemos tirado la toalla contra la roya." *La prensa libre,* January 22, 1977.

"No Reward for a Remedy for Leaf-Disease." *Tropical Agriculturist,* no. 2 (1882): 8–9.

Nutter, F. W., P. S. Teng, and M. H. Royer. "Terms and Concepts for Yield, Crop Loss, and Disease Thresholds." *Plant Disease* 77, no. 2 (February 1993): 211–16.

OIRSA. "Informe de la misión OIRSA de observación y estudio de la roya del cafeto en Brasil." *Revista cafetalera,* no. 108 (November 1971): 17–28.

Olmstead, Alan L., and Paul W. Rhode. "The Red Queen and the Hard Reds: Productivity Growth in American Wheat, 1800–1940." *Journal of Economic History* 62, no. 4 (December 2002): 929–66. https://doi.org/10.1017/S0022050702001602.

Orozco Miranda, Edin F. "Roya del cafeto, manejo integrado y perspectivas de la caficultura en Guatemala." In *Manejo agroecológico de la roya del café,* edited by FAO, 26–34. Panama: FAO, 2015. http://www.fao.org/3/a-i5137s.pdf.

Orton, W. A. "Plant Diseases in 1903." In *Yearbook of the United States Department of Agriculture, 1903,* 550–55. Washington, DC: Government Printing Office, 1904.

Otero, Guillermo R. "An Effort to Control and Possibly Eradicate Coffee Rust in Nicaragua." In *Coffee Rust in the Americas,* edited by Robert H. Fulton, 93–104. St. Paul: American Phytopathological Society, 1984.

Ovalle-Rivera, Oriana, Peter Läderach, Christian Bunn, Michael Obersteiner, and Götz Schroth. "Projected Shifts in *Coffea arabica* Suitability among Major Global Producing Regions Due to Climate Change." *PLoS ONE* 10, no. 4 (April 2015): e0124155. https://doi.org/10.1371/journal.pone.0124155.

"Paro cafetero en Colombia une a rivales políticos." BBC Mundo, February 26, 2013. http://www.bbc.com/mundo/noticias/2013/02/130225_paro_colombia_cafe_uribistas_izquierda_msd.

Parr, William Fillingham. "How a Planter Is Treated in Fiji." *Tropical Agriculturist,* no. 2 (August 1882): 139–42.

Pauly, Philip J. "The Beauty and Menace of the Japanese Cherry Trees: Conflicting Visions of American Ecological Independence." *Isis* 87, no. 1 (March 1996): 51–73.

"Peligro de que llegue la roya es iminente." *La nación,* January 21, 1977.

Penagos Dardón, Hugo. "Amenaza de la Roya del Cafeto en Guatemala (3)." *Revista cafetalera*, no. 163 (March 1977): 33–53.

Pendergrast, Mark. *Uncommon Grounds: The History of Coffee and How It Transformed Our World*. New York: Basic Books, 1999.

Phoofolo, Pule. "Epidemics and Revolutions: The Rinderpest Epidemic in Late Nineteenth-Century Southern Africa." *Past and Present*, no. 138 (1993): 112–43.

Picado Umaña, Wilson, Rafael Ledezma Díaz, and Roberto Granados Porras. "Territorio de coyotes, agroecosistemas y cambio tecnológico en una región cafetalera de Costa Rica." *Revista de historia* (Costa Rica), no. 59–60 (2009): 119–65.

Planter. "Indian Experiences: The Coffee Leaf Disease." *Tropical Agriculturist*, no. 7 (September 1887): 199–200.

"Planting Position and Prospects of Travancore." *Tropical Agriculturist*, no. 2 (December 1882): 526–27.

Ploetz, Randy C. "Diseases of Tropical Perennial Crops: Challenging Problems in Diverse Environments." *Plant Disease* 91, no. 6 (June 2007): 644–63. https://doi.org/10.1094/PDIS-91-6-0644.

Ploetz, Randy C., Gert H. J. Kema, and Li-Jun Ma. "Impact of Diseases on Export and Smallholder Production of Banana." *Annual Review of Phytopathology* 53, no. 1 (2015): 269–88. https://doi.org/10.1146/annurev-phyto-080614-120305.

"¿Por qué el programa PSF es clave para recuperar la producción cafetera?" *Al Grano*, March 2012. https://www.federaciondecafeteros.org/algrano-fnc-es/index.php/comments/por_que_el_programa_permanencia_sostenibilidad_y_futuro_es_clave_para_recup.

Price, James H. "Berkeley, Miles Joseph (1803–1889)." In *Oxford Dictionary of National Biography*. Oxford: Oxford University Press, 2004. http://www.oxforddnb.com/view/article/2220.

PROMECAFÉ. *Coffee Crisis in Mesoamerica*. PROMECAFÉ, June 2013. http://promecafe.org/portal/documents/Publicaciones/coffee%20rust%20in%20central%20america.pdf.

———. *Plan de acción con medidas inmediatas 2013: Programa integrado de combate a la roya del café y recuperacion de la capacidad productiva en Centroamérica*. PROMECAFÉ, March 2013. http://www.ico.org/clr/promecafe-medidas.pdf.

———. *Sétima reunión del Consejo Asesor del Programa Cooperativo para la Protección y Modernización de la Caficultura, "PROMECAFÉ."* San José, Costa Rica: IICA, 1983.

"Protección al cultivo del café." *Excelsior*, June 30, 1977.

Raoul, E., and E. Darolles. *Culture du caféier*. Paris: A. Challamel, 1894.

Rayner, R. W. "Rust Disease of Coffee 2: Spread of the Disease." *World Crops* 12, no. 6 (June 1960): 222–24.

———. "Rust Disease of Coffee 3: Resistance." *World Crops* 12, no. 7 (July 1960): 261–64.

———. "Rust Disease of Coffee 4: Control by Fungicide." *World Crops* 12, no. 8 (August 1960): 309–12.

Razafindramamba, Razafindrambahy. "Biologie de la rouille du caféier." *Revue de mycologie*. 23, no. 2 (1958): 177–200.

Reuters. "Starbucks Buys First Coffee Farm, Will Research Devastating Leaf Rust." Reuters, March 19, 2013. https://www.reuters.com/article /us-starbucks-coffee-costarica/starbucks-buys-first-coffee-farm-will -research-devastating-leaf-rust-idUSBRE92I14A20130319.

Rice, Robert A. "A Place Unbecoming: The Coffee Farm of Northern Latin America." *Geographical Review* 89, no. 4 (October 1999): 554–70.

———. "Transforming Agriculture: The Case of Coffee Leaf Rust and Coffee Renovation in Southern Nicaragua." PhD thesis, University of California, Berkeley, 1990.

Richter, G. *Manual of Coorg: A Gazeteer of the Natural Features of the Country and the Social and Political Condition of Its Inhabitants*. Mangalore: Basler Mission, 1870.

Ridley, H. N. "Dr. Burck's Method of Treatment of the Coffee-Leaf Disease in Java." *Agricultural Bulletin of the Malay Peninsula*, no. 1 (1891): 2–17.

Risbec, J. "Le café en Nouvelle-Calédonie (1)." *L'agronomie coloniale*, no. 154 (October 1930): 97–104.

Rist, Gilbert. *The History of Development: From Western Origins to Global Faith*. 4th ed. London: Zed Books, 2014.

Rivillas Osorio, Carlos A. "Acciones emprendidas por Colombia en el manejo de la roya del cafeto." In *Manejo agroecológico de la roya del café*, edited by FAO, 11–16. Panama: FAO, 2015. http://www.fao.org/3/a-i5137s.pdf.

Rivillas Osorio, Carlos A., César A. Giraldo Serna, Marco A. Cristancho Ardila, and Alvaro L. Gaitán Bustamante. *La roya del cafeto en Colombia: Impacto, manejo y costos del control*. Boletín técnico. Cinchina: CENICAFÉ, 2011.

Rodrigues, C. J., Jr. "Prof. Branquinho D'Oliveira: Esboço de sua vida científica." *Garcia de orta: Serie de estudos agronomicos* 9, no. 1–2 (1982): 5–12.

———. "Professor Branquinho D'Oliveira: A Portuguese Leader in Plant Pathology." *Annual Review of Phytopathology* 30, no. 1 (1992): 39–45.

Rodrigues, C. J., Jr., A. J. Bettencourt, and L. Rijo. "Races of the Pathogen and Resistance to Coffee Rust." *Annual Review of Phytopathology*, no. 13 (September 1975): 49–70.

Rodrigues, C. J., Jr., and A. B. Eskes. "Resistance to Coffee Leaf Rust and Coffee Berry Disease." In *Coffee: Growing, Processing, Sustainable Production: A Guidebook for Growers, Processors, Traders and Researchers*, edited by Jean Nicolas Wintgens, 551–64. Weinheim, Germany: Wiley-VCH, 2004.

Rodrigues, C. J., Jr., M. M. Gonçalves, V. M. P. Varzea, C. E. de Produção, and T. Agrícolas. "Importância do Hibrido de Timor para o territorio e para o melhoramento da cafeicultura mundial." *Revista de ciências agrarias*, no. 27 (2004): 203–16.

Rosenberg, Charles E. *The Cholera Years*. Chicago: University of Chicago Press, 1987.

Rowe, J. *The World's Coffee: A Study of the Economics and Politics of the Coffee Industries of Certain Countries and of the International Problem*. London: H. M. Stationery Office, 1963.

"Roya del café no se desplaza hacia C.R." *La prensa libre*, July 2, 1980.

"Roya del café no será una calamidad nacional." *La prensa libre*, December 1, 1976.

"Roya devora esperanzas de pequeños productores de café." *La prensa libre*. February 10, 2013. https://www.prensalibre.com/noticias/comunitario/DESOLADOS_0_863313683.html.

Rozier, François. *Cours complet d'agriculture théorique, pratique, économique et de médecine rurale et vétérinaire*. Vol. 2. Paris, 1782.

Rutherford, Mike A. "Current Knowledge of Coffee Wilt Disease, a Major Constraint to Coffee Production in Africa." *Phytopathology* 96, no. 6 (June 2006): 663–66. https://doi.org/10.1094/PHYTO-96-0663.

Sabonadière, William. *The Coffee-Planter of Ceylon*. 2nd ed. London: E. and F.N. Spon, 1870.

Sadebeck, Richard. *Die wichtigeren Nutzpflanzen und deren Erzeugnisse aus den deutschen Colonien: Ein mit Erläuterungen versehenes Verzeichniss der Colonial-Abtheilung des Hamburgischen Botanischen Museums*. Hamburg: Gräfe and Sillem, 1897.

Samper, Mario, and Radin Fernando. "Appendix: Historical Statistics of Coffee Production and Trade from 1700 to 1960." In *The Global Coffee Economy in Africa, Asia and Latin America, 1500–1989*, edited by W. Clarence-Smith and Steven Topik, 411–62. Cambridge: Cambridge University Press, 2003.

Samper K., Mario. "Modelos vs. prácticas: Acercamiento inicial a la cuestión tecnológica en algunos manuales sobre caficultura, 1774–1895." *Revista de historia* (Costa Rica), no. 30 (1994): 11–40.

———. "Trayectoria y viabilidad de las caficulturas centroamericanas." In *Desafíos de la caficultura en Centroamérica*, edited by Benoît Bertrand and Bruno Rapidel, 1–68. San José, Costa Rica: Agroamerica, 1999.

Samper K., Mario, and Steven Topik. *Crisis y transformaciones del mundo del café: Dinámicas locales y estrategias nacionales en un periodo de adversidad e incertidumbre*. Bogota: Pontificia Universidad Javeriana, 2012.

Sánchez Víquez, Aquileo. "Cafetaleros temen avance de la roya." *La República*. August 14, 1992.

Saraiva, Tiago. "Fascist Labscapes: Geneticists, Wheat, and the Landscapes of Fascism in Italy and Portugal." *Historical Studies in the Natural Sciences* 40, no. 4 (November 2010): 457–98. https://doi.org/10.1525/hsns.2010.40.4.457.

Sargos, F. "Une plantation dans le Kuilou (Congo Français)." *Revue des cultures coloniales* 3, no. 4 (May 1899): 291–93.

Sarria, Cristian Martinez. "Campaña de prevención contra la roya en la frontera Colombo-Venezolana." *Revista Cafetera de Colombia* 29, no. 174 (1980): 9–16.

Schaefer, Charles G. H. "Coffee Unobserved: Consumption and Commoditization of Coffee in Ethiopia before the Eighteenth Century." In *Le commerce du café avant l'ère des plantations coloniales: Espaces, réseaux, sociétés (XV'-XIX'siècle)*, edited by Michel Tuchscherer, 361–70. Cairo: Institut Français d'Archéologie Orientale, 2001.

Schafer, J. F., A. P. Roelfs, and W. R. Bushnell. "Contribution of Early Scientists to Knowledge of Cereal Rusts." In *The Cereal Rusts: Origins, Specificity, Structure, and Physiology*, edited by William Bushnell, 1:4–38. Orlando: Academic Press, 1984.

Schieber, E. "Economic Impact of Coffee Rust in Latin America." *Annual Review of Phytopathology*, no. 10 (September 1972): 491–510.

———. "Observaciones comparativas sobre la roya del cafeto en Brasil y Kenia, Africa." *Revista cafetalera*, no. 99 (June 1970): 34–38.

———. "Present Status of Coffee Rust in South America." *Annual Review of Phytopathology*, no. 13 (September 1975): 375–82. https://doi.org/doi:10.1146/annurev.py.13.090175.002111.

Schieber, E., and G. Zentmyer. "Coffee Rust in the Western Hemisphere." *Plant Disease* 68, no. 2 (1984): 89–93.

———. "Distribution and Spread of Coffee Rust in Latin America." In *Coffee Rust in the Americas*, edited by Robert H. Fulton, 1–14. St. Paul: American Phytopathological Society, 1984.

Scholthof, Karen-Beth G. "The Disease Triangle: Pathogens, the Environment and Society." *Nature Reviews Microbiology* 5, no. 2 (February 2007): 152–56. https://doi.org/10.1038/nrmicro1596.

Schumann, Gail L., and Cleora J. D'Arcy. *Hungry Planet: Stories of Plant Diseases*. St. Paul: American Phytopathological Society, 2012.

Schuppener, H., J. Harr, and A. Sequeira. "First Occurrence of the Coffee Leaf Rust *Hemileia vastatrix* in Nicaragua, 1976, and Its Control." *Café, cacao, thé* 21, no. 2 (1977): 197–202.

Shepherd, Christopher. *Development and Environmental Politics Unmasked: Authority, Participation and Equity in East Timor*. New York: Routledge, 2014.

Sheridan, Michael. "Leaf Rust Fallout: 'Negative Coping Strategies' and Food Insecurity." *Daily Coffee News by Roast Magazine* (blog), February 17, 2014. http://dailycoffeenews.com/2014/02/17/leaf-rust-fallout-negative-coping-strategies-and-food-insecurity/.

———. "A Simple Question: Castillo or Caturra?" *CRS Coffeelands* (blog), April 9, 2015. http://coffeelands.crs.org/2015/04/a-simple-question-castillo-or-caturra/.

Shriver, Jefferson, Jimmy Largaespada, and Martha Estela Gutiérrez. *Sustainable Good Agriculture Practices Manual: To Improve Yields of Organic Coffee and Control Coffee Rust*. Nicaragua: CAFÉNICA, 2015. http://coffeelands.crs.org/wp-content/uploads/2017/05/Good-Agriculture-Practices-Manual-English-Final.pdf.

Sick, Deborah. "Coping with Crisis: Costa Rican Households and the International Coffee Market." *Ethnology* 36, no. 3 (Summer 1997): 255–75.

Silva, Maria do Mar de Mello Gago da. "Robusta Empire: Coffee, Scientists and the Making of Colonial Angola (1898–1961)." PhD thesis, Universidade de Lisboa, 2018. http://hdl.handle.net/10451/32678.

Simmonds, P. L. *Tropical Agriculture: A Treatise on the Culture, Preparation, Commerce and Consumption of the Principal Products of the Vegetable Kingdom*. 3rd ed. London: E. and F. N. Spon, 1889.

Simpson, S. "Report on Coffee Leaf Disease (*Hemileia vastatrix*) in Uganda," February 10, 1913. Uganda: Coffee Diseases. Library and Archives, Royal Botanic Gardens, Kew.

Singh, Ravi P., David P. Hodson, Julio Huerta-Espino, Yue Jin, Sridhar Bhavani, Peter Njau, Sybil Herrera-Foessel, Pawan K. Singh, Sukhwinder Singh, and Velu Govindan. "The Emergence of Ug99 Races of the Stem Rust Fungus Is a Threat to World Wheat Production." *Annual Review of Phytopathology* 49, no. 1 (2011): 465–81. https://doi.org/10.1146/annurev-phyto-072910 -095423.

Small, W. "Coffee Cultivation in Uganda." *Tropical Agriculturist*, no. 44 (January 1915): 52–53.

Smith, Harley M., and Alon Samach. "Constraints to Obtaining Consistent Annual Yields in Perennial Tree Crops. I: Heavy Fruit Load Dominates over Vegetative Growth." *Plant Science*, no. 207 (2013): 158–67. https://doi .org/10.1016/j.plantsci.2013.02.014.

Soluri, John. "Accounting for Taste: Export Bananas, Mass Markets, and Panama Disease." *Environmental History* 7, no. 3 (2002): 386–410.

———. *Banana Cultures: Agriculture, Consumption, and Environmental Change in Honduras and the United States.* Austin: University of Texas Press, 2005.

———. "Something Fishy: Chile's Blue Revolution, Commodity Diseases, and the Problem of Sustainability." *Latin American Research Review* 46, no. 4 (November 2011): 55–81. https://doi.org/10.1353/lar.2011.0042.

Soto, Gabriela. "Manejo de la roya por los productores orgánicos de Costa Rica." In *Manejo agroecológico de la roya del café*, edited by FAO, 64–66. Panama: FAO, 2015. http://www.fao.org/3/a-i5137s.pdf.

Sovani, N. V. *The International Position of India's Raw Materials.* New Delhi: Indian Council of World Affairs, 1948.

Sprott, F. H. *Coffee Planting in Kenya Colony.* Nairobi: East African Standard, 1930.

Starbucks Coffee Company. "Growing the Future of Coffee One Tree at a Time." 1912 Pike, March 4, 2016. https://1912pike.com/growing-the-future-of-coffee -one-tree-at-a-time-a/.

"Starbucks donará 360 mil plantas de café a productores de Chiapas." *El financiero*, September 28, 2015. http://www.elfinanciero.com.mx/empresas /starbucks-donara-360-mil-plantas-a-productores-de-chiapas.html.

"Starbucks' 'One Tree for Every Bag' Sustainable Coffee Partnership." Conservation International. Accessed October 3, 2017. http://www.conservation .org/stories/Pages/Starbucks-One-Tree-Conservation-International.aspx.

Steiman, Shawn. "Coffee Berry Borer in Hawai'i: What Can We Expect?" October 18, 2010. http://www.roaste.com/CoffeeBlogs/shawn/Coffee-Berry -Borer-Hawai'i-what-can-we-expect.

Storck, James C. P. "Cure for Leaf Disease in Fiji." *Tropical Agriculturist*, no. 1 (July 1881): 126–27.

Storey, William. *Science and Power in Colonial Mauritius*. Rochester, NY: University of Rochester Press, 1997.

Sweet Maria's. "Costa Rica: Can a Coffee Be Too Perfect?" *Tiny Joy* (blog), July 2003. https://legacy.sweetmarias.com/library/jun-jul-2003-costa-rica -can-a-coffee-be-too-perfect-on-the-flip-side-just-one-more-inscrutable -detail/.

Sylvain, Pierre G. "Ethiopian Coffee: Its Significance to World Coffee Problems." *Economic Botany* 12, no. 2 (1958): 111–39. https://doi.org/10.2307/4287976.

———. "Le café du Yémen." *Agronomie Tropicale* 11, no. 1 (1956): 62–73.

Talbot, G. A. "Mr. Marshall Ward's Report on Leaf-Disease." *Tropical Agriculturist*, no. 1 (1882): 626–27.

Talbot, John. *Grounds for Agreement: The Political Economy of the Coffee Commodity Chain*. Lanham, MD: Rowman and Littlefield, 2004.

Tancredi, D. "Global Networks of Excellence: Vehicles Fostering Therapeutic Innovation." *Clinical Pharmacology and Therapeutics* 93, no. 1 (January 2013): 17–19. https://doi.org/10.1038/clpt.2012.205.

Thiselton-Dyer, William. "The Coffee-Leaf Disease of Ceylon." *Quarterly Journal of Microscopical Science*, n.s., 20 (1880): 119–29.

———. "No Reward for a Remedy for Leaf-Disease." *Tropical Agriculturist*, no. 2 (1882): 8–9.

Thomas, A. S. "Robusta Coffee." In *Agriculture in Uganda*, edited by J. D. Tothill, 289–312. Oxford: Oxford University Press, 1940.

Thrall, P. H., and J. J. Burdon. "Evolution of Gene-for-Gene Systems in Metapopulations: The Effect of Spatial Scale of Host and Pathogen Dispersal." *Plant Pathology* 51, no. 2 (April 2002): 169–84. https://doi.org/10.1046 /j.1365-3059.2002.00683.x.

Thrupp, Lori Ann. "Pesticides and Policies: Approaches to Pest-Control Dilemmas in Nicaragua and Costa Rica." *Latin American Perspectives* 15, no. 4 (1988): 37–70.

Thurber, Francis. *Coffee: From Plantation to Cup; A Brief History of Coffee Production and Consumption*. 14th ed. New York: American Grocer Publ. Association, 1887.

Thwaites, G. H. K. "The Ceylon Coffee Fungus." *Gardeners' Chronicle*, no. 24 (June 6, 1874): 725–26.

Thwaites, G. H. K., and J. D. Hooker. *Enumeratio Plantarum Zeylaniae: An Enumeration of Ceylon Plants, with Descriptions of the New and Little Known*

Genera and Species, Observations on Their Habitats, Uses, Native Names [. . .]. London: Dulau, 1864.

Topik, Steven. "The Integration of the World Coffee Market." In *The Global Coffee Economy in Africa, Asia and Latin America, 1500–1989*, edited by W. G. Clarence-Smith and Steven Topik, 21–49. Cambridge: Cambridge University Press, 2003.

———. *The Political Economy of the Brazilian State, 1889–1930*. Austin: University of Texas, 1987.

Topik, Steven, John M. Talbot, and Mario Samper. "Introduction: Globalization, Neoliberalism, and the Latin American Coffee Societies." *Latin American Perspectives* 37, no. 2 (2010): 5–20.

Topik, Steven, and Allen Wells. "Commodity Chains in a Global Economy." In *A World Connecting, 1870–1945*, edited by Emily S. Rosenberg, 593–812. Cambridge, MA: Belknap Press of Harvard University Press, 2012.

Tothill, J. D. *Agriculture in Uganda*. Oxford: Oxford University Press, 1940.

Tourte, Rene. *Histoire de la recherche agricole en Afrique tropicale francophone*. Rome: FAO, 2005.

Tuchscherer, Michel. "Coffee in the Red Sea Area from the Sixteenth to the Nineteenth Century." In *The Global Coffee Economy in Africa, Asia and Latin America, 1500–1989*, edited by W. G. Clarence-Smith and Steven Topik, 50–55. Cambridge: Cambridge University Press, 2003.

———. "Commerce et production du café en mer Rouge au XVIe siècle." In *Le commerce du café avant l'ère des plantations coloniales: Espaces, réseaux, sociétés (XV*ᵉ*-XIX*ᵉ*siècle)*, edited by Michel Tuchscherer, 69–89. Cairo: Institut Français d'Archéologie Orientale, 2001.

Turing Mackenzie, W. "Leaf Disease and Coffee." *Tropical Agriculturist*, no. 9 (April 1890): 705.

Uekötter, Frank. "The Magic of One: Reflections on the Pathologies of Monoculture." *RCC Perspectives* 2011, no. 2 (2011). https://doi.org/10.5282/rcc/5584.

Uganda Coffee Development Authority, and Coffee Quality Institute. "Fine Robusta Coffee Standards and Protocols." Fine Robusta. Accessed June 13, 2017. https://finerobusta.coffee/.

Ukers, William H. *All About Coffee*. New York: Tea and Coffee Trade Journal, 1922.

———. *All About Coffee*. 2nd ed. New York: Tea and Coffee Trade Journal, 1935.

Um, Nancy. *The Merchant Houses of Mocha: Trade and Architecture in an Indian Ocean Port*. Seattle: University of Washington Press, 2009.

USDA Foreign Agricultural Service. "2011 Coffee Annual: Colombia." GAIN Report. Washington, DC: USDA, 2011. https://gain.fas.usda.gov

/Recent%20GAIN%20Publications/Coffee%20Annual_Bogota_Colombia
_5-24-2011.pdf.

———. "2012 Coffee Semi-Annual: Colombia." GAIN Report. Washington, DC: USDA, 2012. https://gain.fas.usda.gov/Recent%20GAIN%20Publications /Coffee%20Semi-annual_Bogota_Colombia_11-29-2012.pdf.

———. "2013 Coffee Annual: Colombia." GAIN Report. Washington, DC: USDA, 2013. http://gain.fas.usda.gov/Recent%20GAIN%20Publications /Coffee%20Annual_Bogota_Colombia_5-7-2013.pdf.

———. "2013 Coffee Semi-Annual: Colombia." GAIN Report. Washington, DC: USDA, 2013. http://gain.fas.usda.gov/Recent%20GAIN%20Publications /Coffee%20Semi-annual_Bogota_Colombia_11-15-2013.pdf.

———. "2015 Coffee Annual: El Salvador." GAIN Report. Washington, DC: USDA, 2015. https://gain.fas.usda.gov/Recent%20GAIN%20Publications /Coffee%20Annual_San%20Salvador_El%20Salvador_4-28-2015.pdf.

———. "2016 Coffee Annual: Peru." GAIN Report. Washington, DC: USDA, 2015. https://gain.fas.usda.gov/Recent%20GAIN%20Publications/Coffee %20Annual_Lima_Peru_5-25-2016.pdf.

———. "2017 Coffee Annual: Colombia." GAIN Report. Washington, DC: USDA, 2017. http://gain.fas.usda.gov/Recent%20GAIN%20Publications /Coffee%20Annual_Bogota_Colombia_5-15-2017.pdf.

———. "2017 Coffee Annual: Guatemala." GAIN Report. Washington, DC: USDA, 2017. https://gain.fas.usda.gov/Recent%20GAIN%20Publications /Coffee%20Annual_Guatemala%20City_Guatemala_5-15-2017.pdf

———. "2017 Coffee Annual: Mexico." GAIN Report. Washington, DC: USDA, 2017. https://gain.fas.usda.gov/Recent%20GAIN%20Publications /Coffee%20Annual_Mexico%20City_Mexico_5-25-2017.pdf

———. "Coffee: World Markets and Trade." Washington, DC: Foreign Agricultural Service, June 2017. http://usda.mannlib.cornell.edu/usda/fas /tropprod//2010s/2017/tropprod-06-16-2017.pdf.

———. "PS&D (Production, Supply, and Distribution)." PSD Online, June 16, 2017. https://apps.fas.usda.gov/psdonline/app/index.html#/app/advQuery.

———. "Situation Update: Coffee Rust in Mexico." GAIN Report. Washington, DC: USDA, 2013. https://gain.fas.usda.gov/Recent%20GAIN %20Publications/Situation%20Update--Coffee%20Rust%20in%20Mexico _Mexico_Mexico_2-27-2013.pdf.

Valenzuela Samper, Germán. "La temible roya del cafeto." *Revista cafetera de Colombia* 20, no. 149 (1971): 3–7.

Vanden Driesen, I. H. "Coffee Cultivation in Ceylon (2)." *Ceylon Historical Journal*, no. 3 (1953): 156–72.

Vandermeer, John, Doug Jackson, and Ivette Perfecto. "Qualitative Dynamics of the Coffee Rust Epidemic: Educating Intuition with Theoretical Ecology." *BioScience* 64, no. 3 (March 2014): 210–18. https://doi.org/10.1093/biosci/bit034.

Vandermeer, John, I. Perfecto, and H. Liere. "Evidence for Hyperparasitism of Coffee Rust (*Hemileia vastatrix*) by the Entomogenous Fungus, *Lecanicillium lecanii*, through a Complex Ecological Web." *Plant Pathology* 58, no. 4 (August 2009): 636–41. https://doi.org/10.1111/j.1365-3059.2009.02067.x.

Vandermeer, John, and Pejman Rohani. "The Interaction of Regional and Local in the Dynamics of the Coffee Rust Disease." arXiv:1407.8247 [q-Bio], July 30, 2014. http://arxiv.org/abs/1407.8247.

Van der Plank, J. E. *Principles of Plant Infection*. New York: Academic Press, 1975.

Van Hall, C. J. J. "Robusta and Some Allied Coffee Species." *Agricultural Bulletin of the Federated Malay States* 1, no. 7 (February 1913): 251–59.

"Varieties of Liberian Coffee." *Tropical Agriculturist*, no. 2 (August 1882): 153–54.

Varisco, Daniel Martin. "Agriculture in Al-Hamdānī's Yemen: A Survey from Early Islamic Geographical Texts." *Journal of the Economic and Social History of the Orient* 52, no. 3 (June 2009): 382–412. https://doi.org/10.1163/156852009X458205.

———. "Indigenous Plant Protection Methods in Yemen." *GeoJournal* 37, no. 1 (September 1995): 27–38. https://doi.org/10.1007/BF00814882.

Vega M., Leví. "Países centroamericanos forman bloque para control de la roya." *La nación*, August 2, 1979.

———. "Temen que roya puede estar en Valle Central." *La nación*, January 16, 1984.

———. "La vulnerable zona norte abrió su paso a la roya." *La nación*. December 18, 1983.

———. "Roya no ha detenido auge en la producción de café." *La nación*, November 11, 1986, sec. Suplemento Agropecuario.

Velasquez, Kelly. "A Berlusconi le cayó la roya." *El tiempo*, November 27, 1994. https://www.eltiempo.com/archivo/documento/MAM-254705.

Vergne, A. "Les plantations de café et de cacao de la maison Ancel-Seitz." *Revue des cultures coloniales* 1, no. 2 (July 1897): 66–69.

Vetter, Jeremy. "Introduction." In *Knowing Global Environments: New Historical Perspectives on the Field Sciences*, edited by Jeremy Vetter, 1–16. New Brunswick, NJ: Rutgers University Press, 2011.

Viehover, Arno, and H. A. Lepper. "Robusta Coffee." *Journal of the Association of Official Agricultural Chemists* 5, no. 2 (November 1921): 274–88.

Virginio Filho, Elías de Melo, and Carlos Astorga Domian. *Prevención y control de la roya del café: Manual de buenas prácticas para técnicos y facilitadores.* Manual técnico 131. Turrialba, Costa Rica: CATIE, 2015. http://hdl.handle.net/11554/8186.

Vossen, Herbert van der. "The Cup Quality of Disease-Resistant Cultivars of Arabica Coffee (*Coffea arabica*)." *Experimental Agriculture* 45, no. 3 (2009): 323–32. https://doi.org/10.1017/S0014479709007595.

Vossen, Herbert van der, Benoît Bertrand, and André Charrier. "Next Generation Variety Development for Sustainable Production of Arabica Coffee (*Coffea arabica* L.): A Review." *Euphytica* 204, no. 2 (July 2015): 243–56. https://doi.org/10.1007/s10681-015-1398-z.

Waller, J. M. "Coffee Rust: Epidemiology and Control." *Crop Protection* 1, no. 4 (1982): 385–404.

Waller, J. M., M. Bigger, and R. J. Hillocks. *Coffee Pests, Diseases and Their Management.* Wallingford, UK: CABI, 2007.

War Department, Office of the Secretary, ed. "Coffee in the Philippines." In *Eighth Annual Report of the Philippine Commission to the Secretary of War, 1907*, Appendix:901–31. Washington, DC: Government Printing Office, 1907.

Ward, Harry Marshall. *Coffee Leaf Disease: Second Report.* Reprint. Government of Ceylon Sessional Paper 50. Colombo, 1880.

———. *Coffee Leaf Disease: Third Report.* Proceedings of the Ceylon Planters Association. Colombo, 1882.

Watson, Andrew. *Agricultural Innovation in the Early Islamic World: The Diffusion of Crops and Farming Techniques, 700–1100.* Cambridge: Cambridge University Press, 1983.

Watt, George. *Dictionary of the Economic Products of India.* Vol. 2, *Cabbage to Cyperus.* Calcutta: Superintendent of Government Printing, India, 1889.

Webb, James L. A. *Tropical Pioneers: Human Agency and Ecological Change in the Highlands of Sri Lanka, 1800–1900.* Athens: Ohio University Press, 2002.

Weiss, Brad. *Sacred Trees, Bitter Harvests: Globalizing Coffee in Northwest Tanzania.* Portsmouth, NH: Heinemann, 2003.

Wellman, Frederick L. *Coffee: Botany, Cultivation and Utilization.* London: Leonard Hill, 1961.

———. *Hemileia vastatrix.* San Salvador: FEDCAME, 1957.

———. "Rust of Coffee in Brazil." *Plant Disease Reporter*, no. 54 (1970): 355.

———. *Tropical American Plant Disease: Neotropical Phytopathology Problems.* Metuchen, NJ: Scarecrow Press, 1972.

Wellman, F. L., and W. H. Cowgill. "Report of the 1952 Coffee Rust Survey Mission to Europe, Africa, Asia, and Hawaii." Foreign Agricultural Circulars. Washington, DC: Office of Foreign Agricultural Relations, USDA, 1952.

Wellman, F. L., and E. Echandi. "The Coffee Rust Situation in Latin America in 1980." *Phytopathology* 71, no. 9 (1981): 968–71.

Wenzlhuemer, Roland. *From Coffee to Tea Cultivation in Ceylon, 1880–1900: An Economic and Social History.* Leiden: Brill, 2008.

Wester, P. J. "Coffee in the Philippines." *Philippine Agricultural Review*, no. 8 (1915): 39–46.

———. "Notes on Coffee in Java." *Philippine Agricultural Review*, no. 9 (1916): 120–32.

Wickizer, V. D. *Coffee, Tea, and Cocoa: An Economic and Political Analysis.* Stanford: Stanford University Press, 1951.

———. *The World Coffee Economy with Special Reference to Control Schemes.* Commodity Policy Studies 2. Stanford: Food Research Institute, Stanford University, 1943.

Williams, Michael. *Deforesting the Earth: From Prehistory to Global Crisis.* Chicago: University of Chicago Press, 2003.

Willis, John Christopher. *Agriculture in the Tropics: An Elementary Treatise.* 3rd ed. Cambridge: Cambridge University Press, 1922.

Windle, E. *Modern Coffee Planting.* London: J. Bale, Sons, and Danielsson, 1933.

Wintgens, Jean Nicolas. *Coffee: Growing, Processing, Sustainable Production; A Guidebook for Growers, Processors, Traders and Researchers.* Weinheim, Germany: Wiley-VCH, 2004.

———. "The Coffee Plant." In *Coffee: Growing, Processing, Sustainable Production: A Guidebook for Growers, Processors, Traders and Researchers*, edited by Jean Nicolas Wintgens, 3–24. Weinheim, Germany: Wiley-VCH, 2004.

World Coffee Research. "About." Accessed June 12, 2017. https://worldcoffee research.org/about/.

———. "Bourbon." Coffee Varieties of Mesoamerica and the Caribbean. Accessed November 7, 2017. https://varieties.worldcoffeeresearch.org /varieties/bourbon.

———. "Caturra." Coffee Varieties of Mesoamerica and the Caribbean. Accessed November 7, 2017. https://varieties.worldcoffeeresearch.org /varieties/caturra.

———. "Centroamericano." Coffee Varieties of Mesoamerica and the Caribbean. Accessed October 25, 2017. https://varieties.worldcoffeeresearch.org/centroamericano.

———. "Coffee Varieties of Mesoamerica and the Caribbean." Accessed August 11, 2017. https://varieties.worldcoffeeresearch.org.

World Coffee Research, and PROMECAFÉ. *First International Coffee Rust Summit*. Guatemala: World Coffee Research; PROMECAFÉ, 2013. http://pdf.usaid.gov/pdf_docs/pbaaa203.pdf.

Wrigley, C. C. "Aspects of Economic History." In *From 1905 to 1940*, edited by Andrew Roberts, 77–139. Vol. 7 of *The Cambridge History of Africa*. Cambridge: Cambridge University Press, 1986. http://dx.doi.org/10.1017/CHOL9780521225052.

Wrigley, Gordon. *Coffee*. New York: Wiley, 1988.

Zadoks, J. C. "On the Conceptual Basis of Crop Loss Assessment: The Threshold Theory." *Annual Review of Phytopathology* 23, no. 1 (1985): 455–73.

Zadoks, J. C., and F. van den Bosch. "On the Spread of Plant Disease: A Theory on Foci." *Annual Review of Phytopathology* 32, no. 1 (1994): 503–21. https://doi.org/10.1146/annurev.py.32.090194.002443.

Zadoks, Jan C., and Richard D. Schein. *Epidemiology and Plant Disease Management*. New York: Oxford University Press, 1979.

Zambolim, Laércio. "Current Status and Management of Coffee Leaf Rust in Brazil." *Tropical Plant Pathology* 41, no. 1 (2016): 1–8. https://doi.org/10.1007/s40858-016-0065-9.

Index

Africa: agricultural research in, 117–18, 120–22, 123–24, 129–32; arabica coffee in, 109, 111–12, 118, 122, 124; chemical controls in, 120–21, 132; coffee cultivation in, 109, 110–12, 118–19, 123, 127; coffee leaf rust and, 109–10, 112–18, 128–29; decolonization in, 136–37; diseases and pests in, 119–21; Great Lakes region of, 41, 98, 110, 115; International Coffee Agreement (ICA) and, 136; robusta coffee in, 121–23, 127–28, 131–32; smallholders in, 111, 127–28; technification in, 126, 129–32; wild coffees from, 110–11; World War I and, 118. *See also individual African countries*
agricultural modernization. *See* technification of coffee farming
agricultural research. *See* research institutions and scientists
allogamy, 82
ANACAFÉ, 141, 166, 185, 186
Andean countries, 155–57
Angola, 129, 138–39
Arabian Peninsula, 23–25
arabica coffee: in Africa, 109, 111–12, 118, 122, 124; biology and ecology of, 18–22; genetic diversity and vulnerability of, 19, 20; in India, 80; Liberian coffee vs., 48,

82–83; New World, introduction to, 27; rust-resistant, 79–81, 149; spread of, 26–27; washed, 84, 166. *See also* mild arabicas
arabusta hybrid, 137–38
Arnold, David, 40
Asia and the Pacific: Dutch East Indies; India; Java; Sumatra; chemical controls in, 73, 77–78; hybrid coffees in, 85–86, 93; Liberian coffee in, 84; robusta coffee in, 100–102, 104–5. *See also* Ceylon (Sri Lanka)
autogamy, 19–20, 135
Avelino, Jacques, 203, 205

Bangelan Coffee Experiment Station (Java), 75, 86, 97, 102
Belgian Congo: agricultural research in, 123, 131, 137; coffee production boom in, 123
Berkeley, Miles, 42–43, 47
Berlin West Africa Conference, 98, 109
biennial bearing, 5, 44–45, 59–60
Big Rust, 1–2, 15–16, 171–96; in Central and South America, 184–95; climate change and, 177, 183; in Colombia, 179–83; crop management and, 173–76; effects on people in American coffeelands, 177–79; organic coffee production and, 193–94; production losses due to, 171